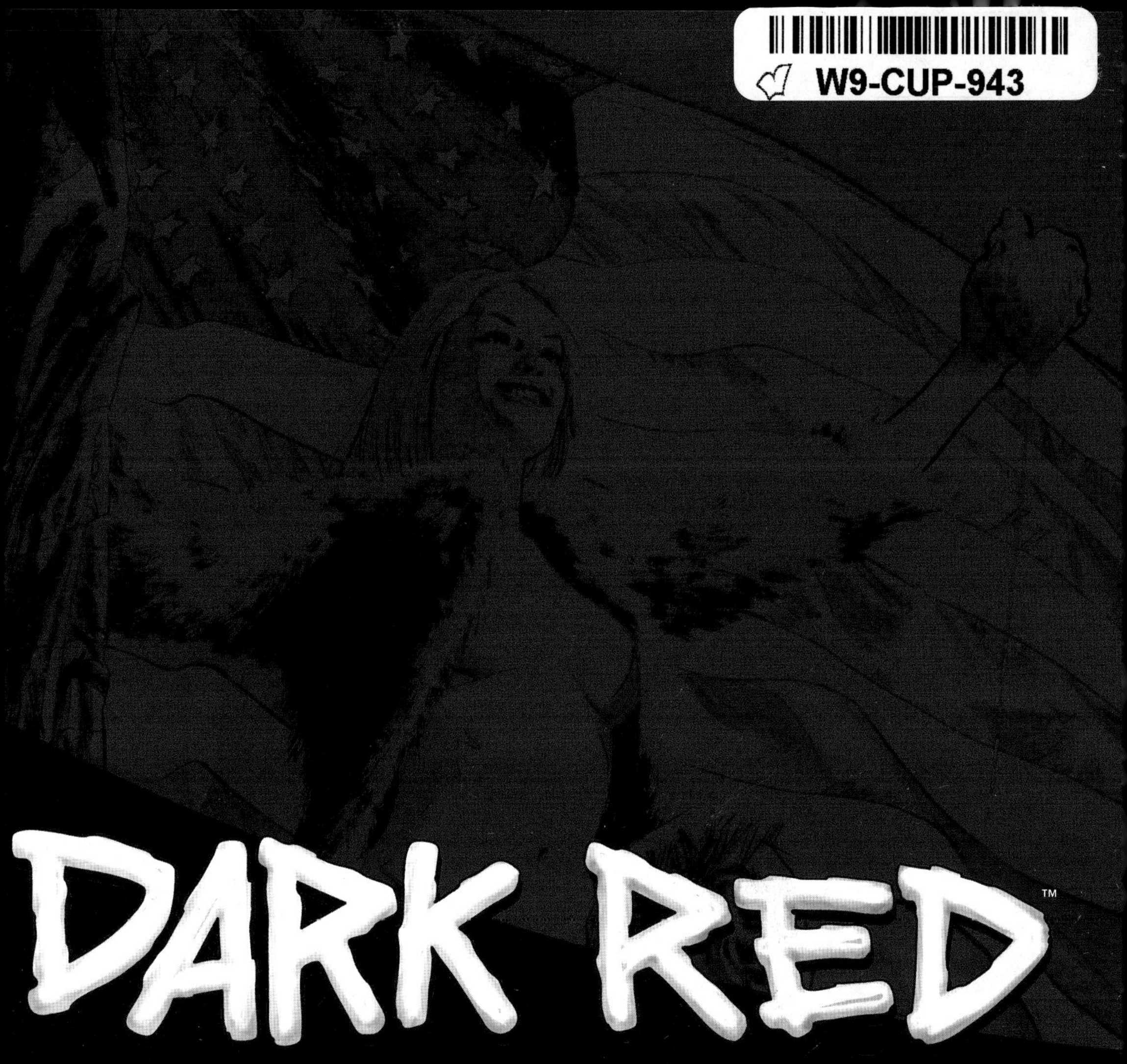

DARK RED™

VOLUME 1

THE FORGOTTEN MAN

TIM SEELEY

CORIN HOWELL

MARK ENGLERT

MARSHALL DILLON

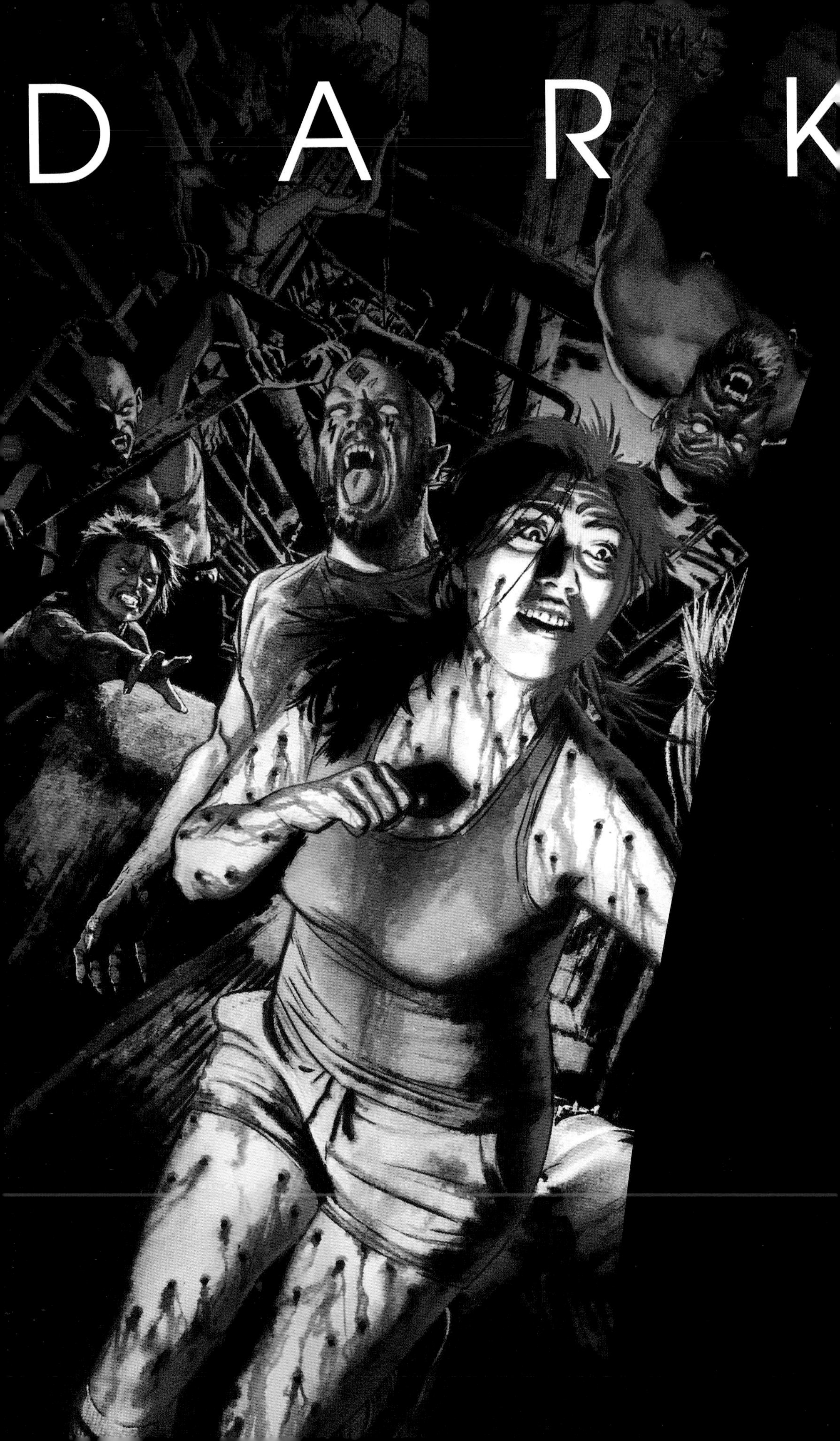
D A R K

RED™

VOLUME 1

THE FORGOTTEN MAN

TIM SEELEY co-creator & writer

CORIN HOWELL co-creator & artist

MARK ENGLERT colorist

MARSHALL DILLON letterer

AARON CAMPBELL front & original covers
JUAN DOE, JORDAN GUNDERSON, NAT JONES, RYAN KINCAID, BRIAN LEBLANC, SHANNON MAER, BILL MCKAY, TIM SEELEY w/ **MARK ENGLERT, LARRY STROMAN** and **ANNA ZHOU** variant covers

JARED K. FLETCHER logo designer

COREY BREEN book designer

MIKE MARTS editor

AFTERSHOCK™

MIKE MARTS - Editor-in-Chief • JOE PRUETT - Publisher/CCO • LEE KRAMER - President • JON KRAMER - Chief Executive Officer
STEVE ROTTERDAM - SVP, Sales & Marketing • DAN SHIRES - VP, Film & Television UK • CHRISTINA HARRINGTON - Managing Editor
MARC HAMMOND - Sr. Retail Sales Development Manager • RUTHANN THOMPSON - Sr. Retailer Relations Manager • BLAKE STOCKER - Director of Finance
AARON MARION - Publicist • LISA MOODY - Finance • RYAN CARROLL - Development Coordinator • STEPHAN NILSON - Publishing Operations
JAWAD QURESHI - Technology Advisor/Strategist • CHARLES PRITCHETT - Comics Production • COREY BREEN - Collections Production
TEDDY LEO - Editorial Assistant • STEPHANIE CASEBIER & SARAH PRUETT - Publishing Assistants

AfterShock Logo Design by COMICRAFT
Publicity: contact AARON MARION (aaron@publichausagency.com) & RYAN CROY (ryan@publichausagency.com) at PUBLICHAUS
Special thanks to: IRA KURGAN, MARINE KSADZHIKYAN & ANTONIA LIANOS

First Printing: September 2019. 10 9 8 7 6 5 4 3 2 1

AFTERSHOCKCOMICS.COM Follow us on social media

INTRODUCTION

The last few weeks have been kinda rough for me, honestly.

I hate to admit that, but it's true. I've been feeling overwhelmed with anxiety about the arrival of my first baby, and the fact that we just bought a house, and that I'm a freelancer with lousy insurance, and that it's been hard to get paid from various companies of late. I'm afraid I'll screw it all up, or I'll lose my jobs, or something will devastate my finances, or that I have the hanta virus, maybe, or that angry possums will eat my face in the night.

I'm afraid of the tenuous state my country is in at the moment, and how it seems to get more tenuous somehow by the day. I'm afraid politics is too broken to ever recover. I'm afraid of hate.

I dunno. I'm afraid, I guess. Just, *period*. More afraid of all of this than I am of monsters or demons or masked slashers or vampires.

And, of course, that's always the impetus behind my horror comics. Writing horror is a chance to flex my creative muscles and control my fear for just a few minutes, by deciding what happens to who and how bad it gets. And once the comic is published, I can hopefully extend that control to my reader who gets to decide when to turn the page, or maybe to never turn it.

Enjoying horror fiction is fighting back against fear by exercising the muscles that reign it in.

Being in the middle of this, feeling so afraid, makes me think of my Grandpa. My Grandfather, Vladislav "James" Legner, was born in 1923 to a poor immigrant farmer from Czechoslovakia. He had four brothers, all of whom worked on the rocky farm, eking out a living in the midst of a depression. My Grandpa fought in World War II, serving as a water truck driver, running back and forth to the front lines. He learned multiple languages and stayed on for an additional year after the war ended to help prisoners of war get back home.

He came back to the US, started a tile company, built houses, built his own house, got married, and had three kids. And as far as a I know, he did this all without any fear.

I mean, of course, he's human, and so he probably did feel fear...but he never showed it. He never dwelled in it. Never used it as an excuse for bad behavior or cruelty or intolerance. He just moved forward and got things done and is *still* doing it at 95 years old.

So, when I was considering writing a comic book series that acted as a metaphor for the plight of the rural American, and the temptation to become a bitter monster, I thought of my Grandpa...a man who has never succumbed to fear or bitterness.

I took my fictional vampire, Chip, and gave him some of my Grandpa's story, and some of his charm, and some of his wit, in the hopes that the reader might come to respect and love Chip as much as I love Jim "Vladislav" Legner. And yes, I know it's all kind of silly, and that in the end, this is still a story where condiments are used as weapons, and one of the leads is basically naked for 60 pages. I mean, I can get serious when I have to, but it's still me we're taking about.

I'm going to reread my own comic book, and escape for a while with Chip, a guy who isn't afraid, and hope maybe he helps me pull though these rough few weeks. I'm going to be thankful I've known my Grandpa as long as I have and hope my kid will be the kind of person he is.

TIM SEELEY
September 2019

1

THE FORGOTTEN MAN

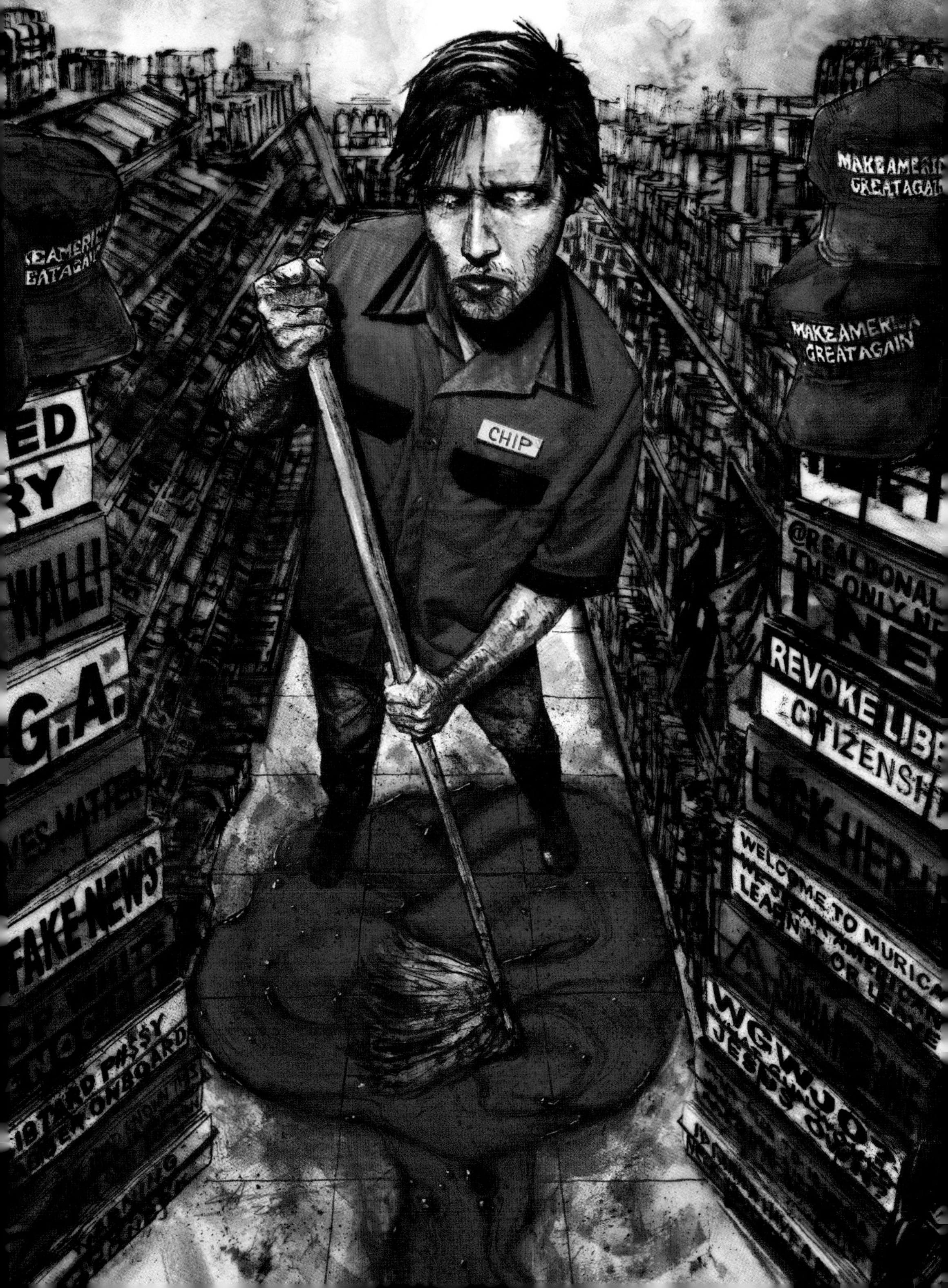
CHIP
MAKEAMERICA GREATAGAIN
FAKE NEWS
WELCOME TO MURICA

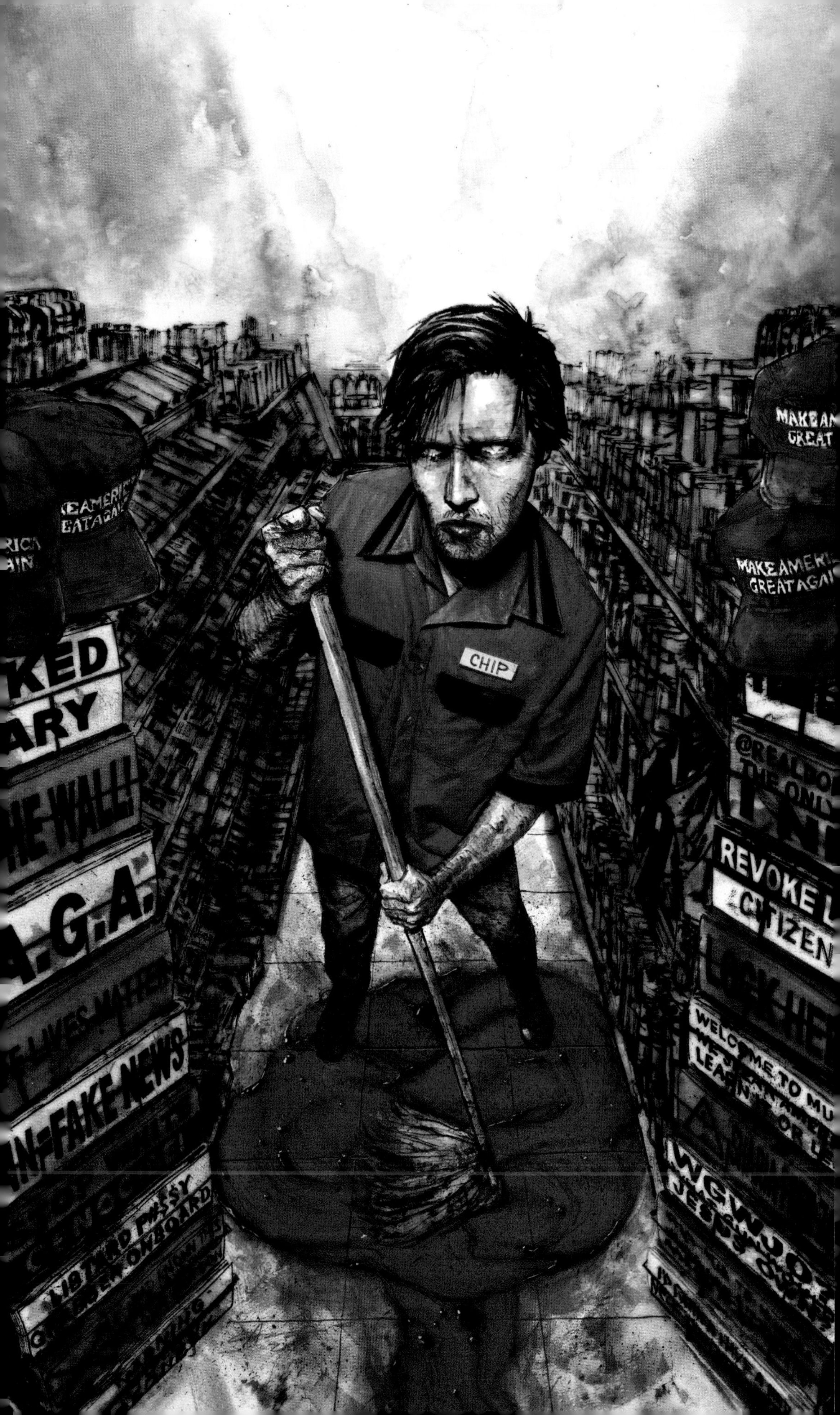
CHIP
KED
ARY
HE WALL!
A.G.A.
FAKE NEWS
MAKEAM
GREAT
MAKEAMERIC
GREATAGAI
REVOKE
CITIZEN

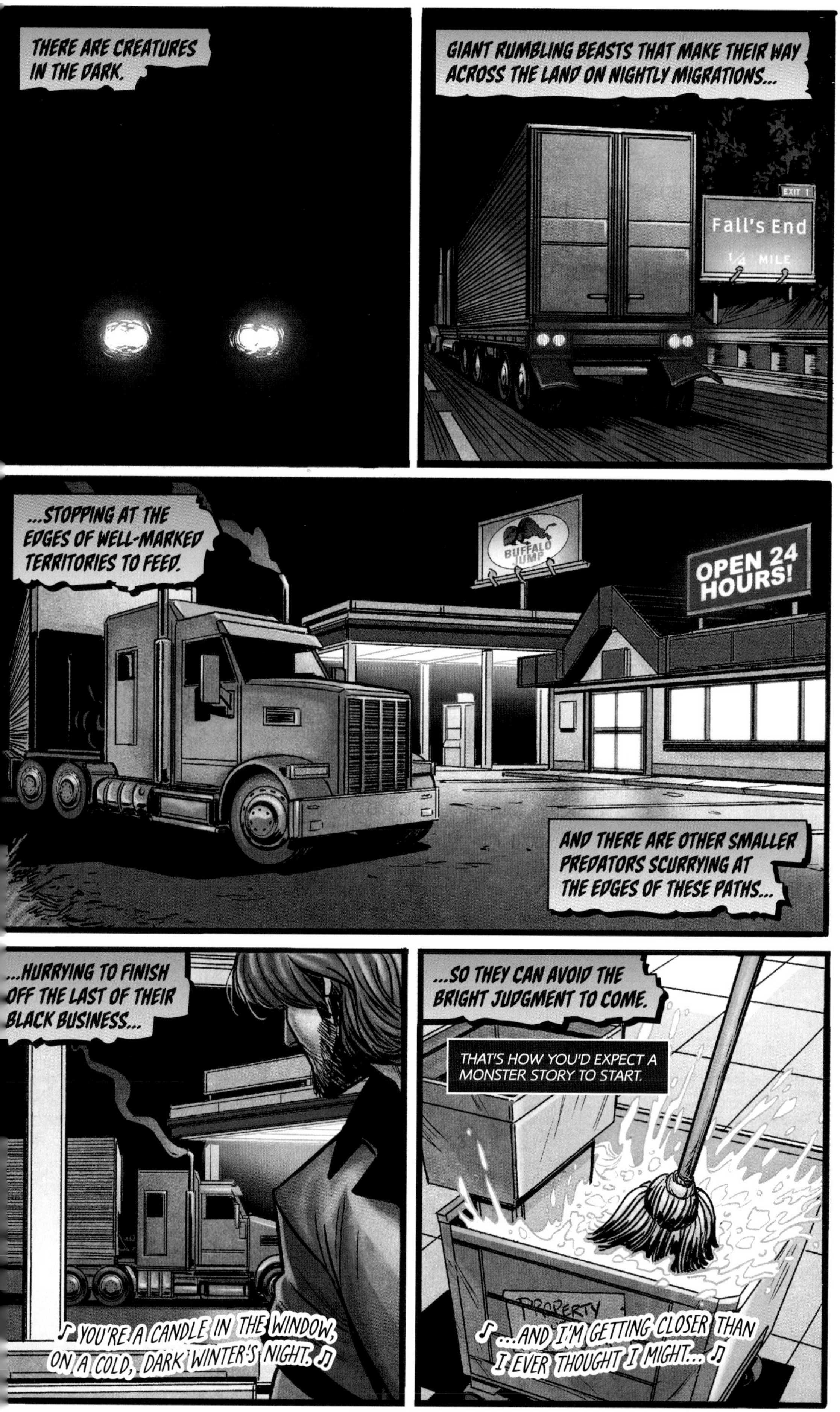
THERE ARE CREATURES IN THE DARK.
GIANT RUMBLING BEASTS THAT MAKE THEIR WAY ACROSS THE LAND ON NIGHTLY MIGRATIONS...
EXIT 1
Fall's End
1/4 MILE
...STOPPING AT THE EDGES OF WELL-MARKED TERRITORIES TO FEED.
BUFFALO JUMP
OPEN 24 HOURS!
AND THERE ARE OTHER SMALLER PREDATORS SCURRYING AT THE EDGES OF THESE PATHS...
...HURRYING TO FINISH OFF THE LAST OF THEIR BLACK BUSINESS...
♪ YOU'RE A CANDLE IN THE WINDOW, ON A COLD, DARK WINTER'S NIGHT. ♫
...SO THEY CAN AVOID THE BRIGHT JUDGMENT TO COME.
THAT'S HOW YOU'D EXPECT A MONSTER STORY TO START.
PROPERTY
♪ ...AND I'M GETTING CLOSER THAN I EVER THOUGHT I MIGHT... ♫

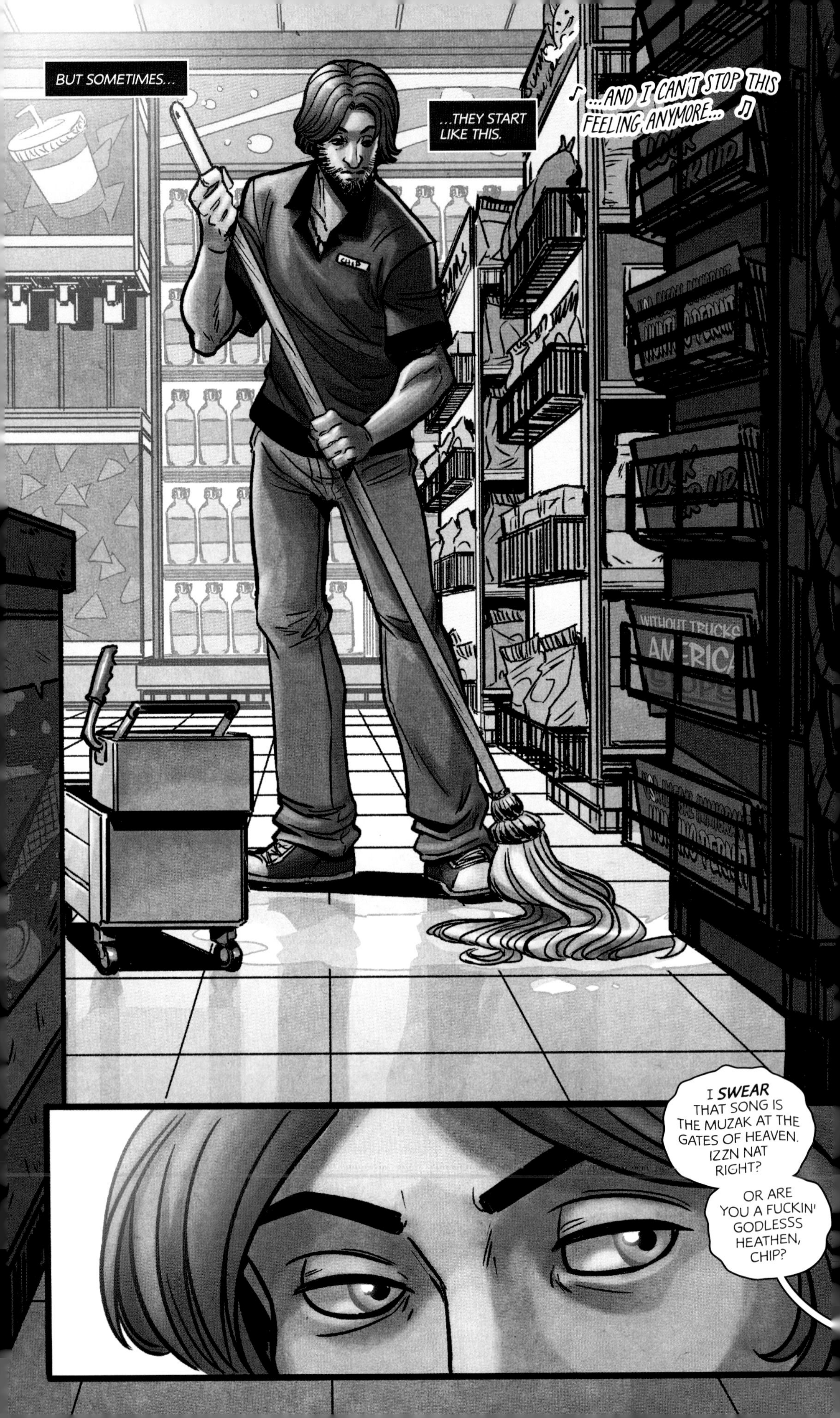
BUT SOMETIMES...
...THEY START LIKE THIS.
♪ ...AND I CAN'T STOP THIS FEELING ANYMORE... ♫
WITHOUT TRUCKS AMERICA
I SWEAR THAT SONG IS THE MUZAK AT THE GATES OF HEAVEN. IZZN NAT RIGHT?
OR ARE YOU A FUCKIN' GODLESSS HEATHEN, CHIP?

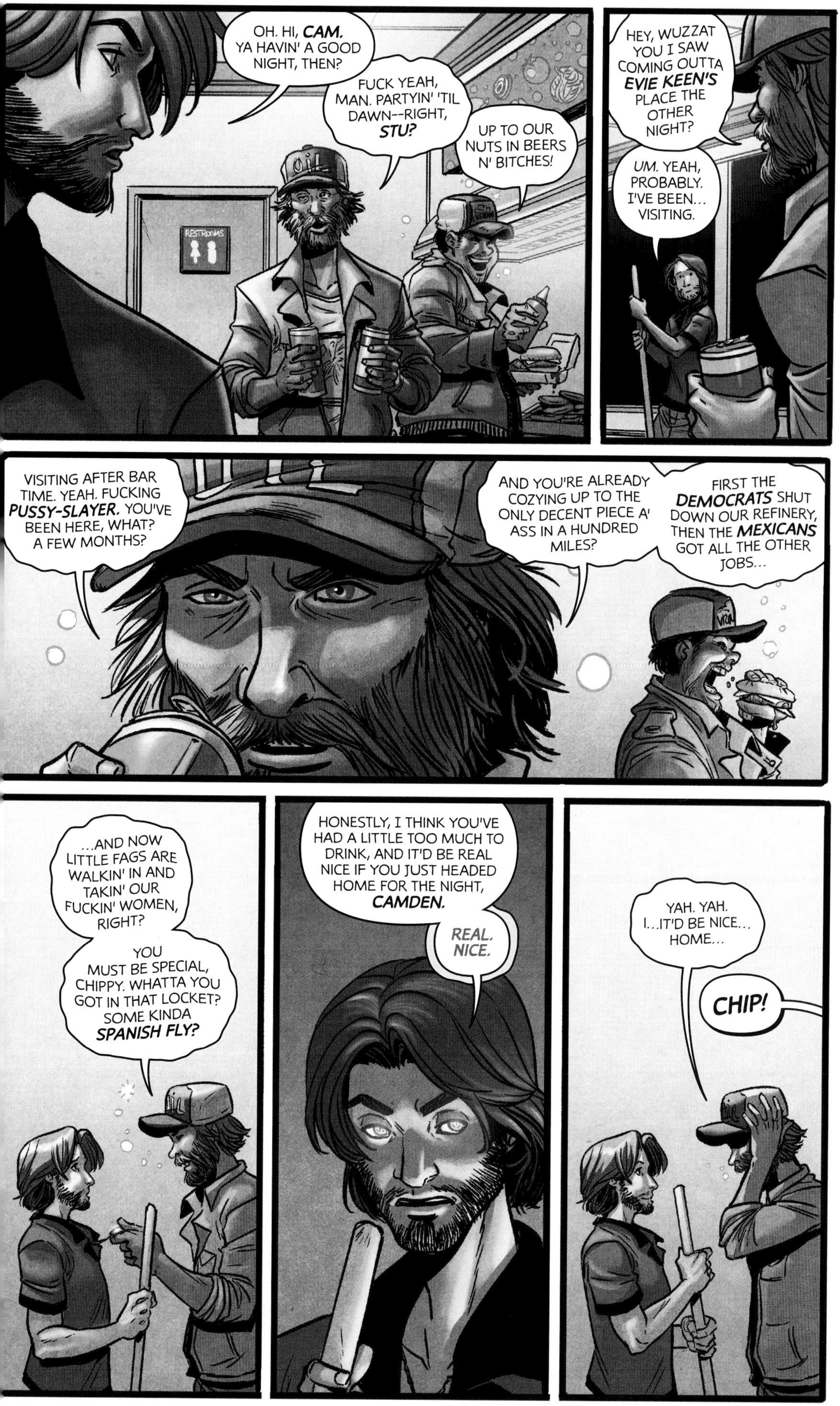
OH. HI, CAM. YA HAVIN' A GOOD NIGHT, THEN?
FUCK YEAH, MAN. PARTYIN' 'TIL DAWN--RIGHT, STU?
UP TO OUR NUTS IN BEERS N' BITCHES!
RESTROOMS
HEY, WUZZAT YOU I SAW COMING OUTTA EVIE KEEN'S PLACE THE OTHER NIGHT?
UM. YEAH, PROBABLY. I'VE BEEN... VISITING.
VISITING AFTER BAR TIME. YEAH. FUCKING PUSSY-SLAYER. YOU'VE BEEN HERE, WHAT? A FEW MONTHS?
AND YOU'RE ALREADY COZYING UP TO THE ONLY DECENT PIECE A' ASS IN A HUNDRED MILES?
FIRST THE DEMOCRATS SHUT DOWN OUR REFINERY, THEN THE MEXICANS GOT ALL THE OTHER JOBS...
...AND NOW LITTLE FAGS ARE WALKIN' IN AND TAKIN' OUR FUCKIN' WOMEN, RIGHT?
YOU MUST BE SPECIAL, CHIPPY. WHATTA YOU GOT IN THAT LOCKET? SOME KINDA SPANISH FLY?
HONESTLY, I THINK YOU'VE HAD A LITTLE TOO MUCH TO DRINK, AND IT'D BE REAL NICE IF YOU JUST HEADED HOME FOR THE NIGHT, CAMDEN.
REAL. NICE.
YAH. YAH. I...IT'D BE NICE... HOME...
CHIP!

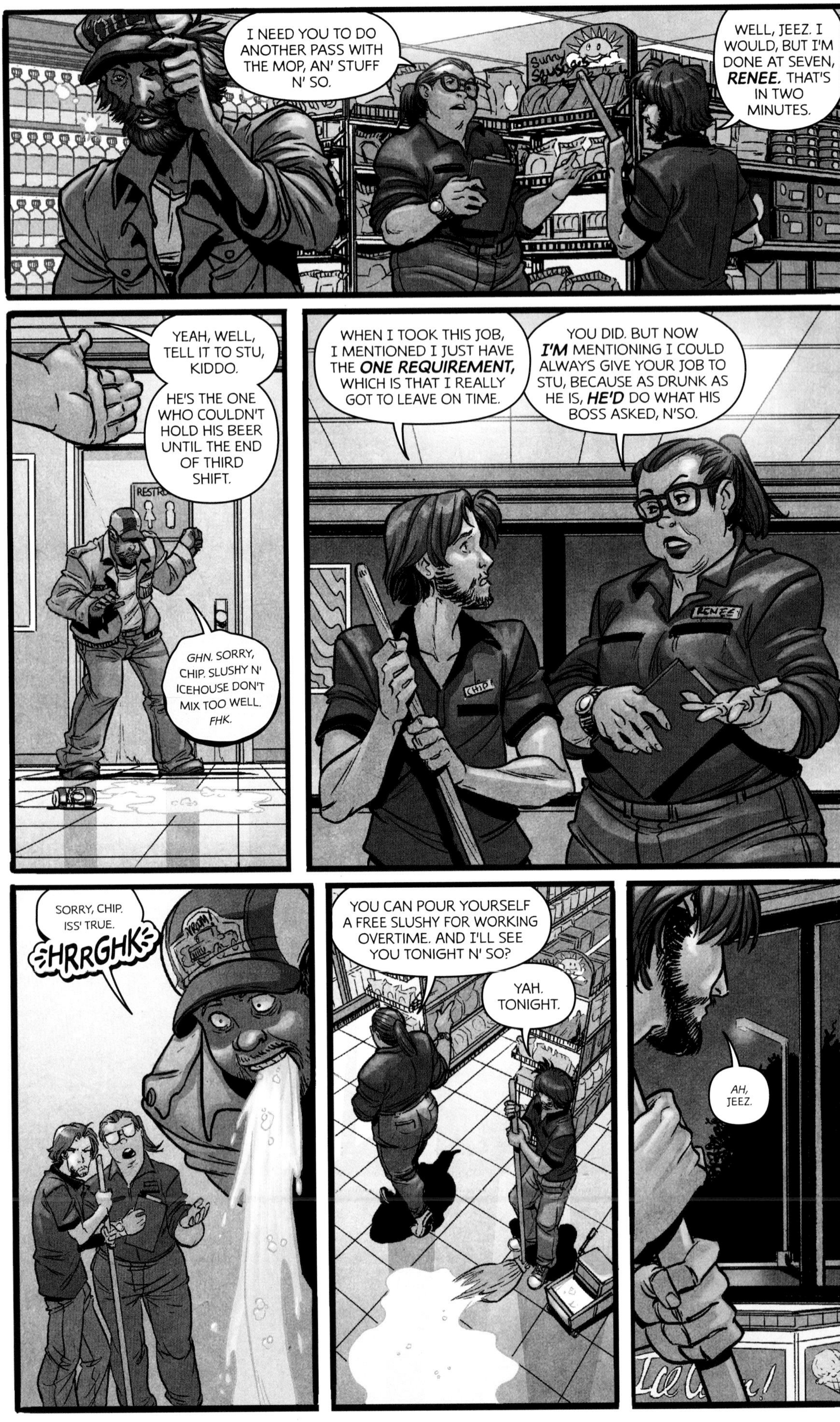
I NEED YOU TO DO ANOTHER PASS WITH THE MOP, AN' STUFF N' SO.
WELL, JEEZ. I WOULD, BUT I'M DONE AT SEVEN, *RENEE.* THAT'S IN TWO MINUTES.
YEAH, WELL, TELL IT TO STU, KIDDO.
HE'S THE ONE WHO COULDN'T HOLD HIS BEER UNTIL THE END OF THIRD SHIFT.
RESTRO
GHN. SORRY, CHIP. SLUSHY N' ICEHOUSE DON'T MIX TOO WELL. *FHK.*
WHEN I TOOK THIS JOB, I MENTIONED I JUST HAVE THE *ONE REQUIREMENT,* WHICH IS THAT I REALLY GOT TO LEAVE ON TIME.
YOU DID. BUT NOW *I'M* MENTIONING I COULD ALWAYS GIVE YOUR JOB TO STU, BECAUSE AS DRUNK AS HE IS, *HE'D* DO WHAT HIS BOSS ASKED, N'SO.
CHIP
RENEE
SORRY, CHIP. ISS' TRUE.
HRRGHK
YOU CAN POUR YOURSELF A FREE SLUSHY FOR WORKING OVERTIME. AND I'LL SEE YOU TONIGHT N' SO?
YAH. TONIGHT.
AH, JEEZ.

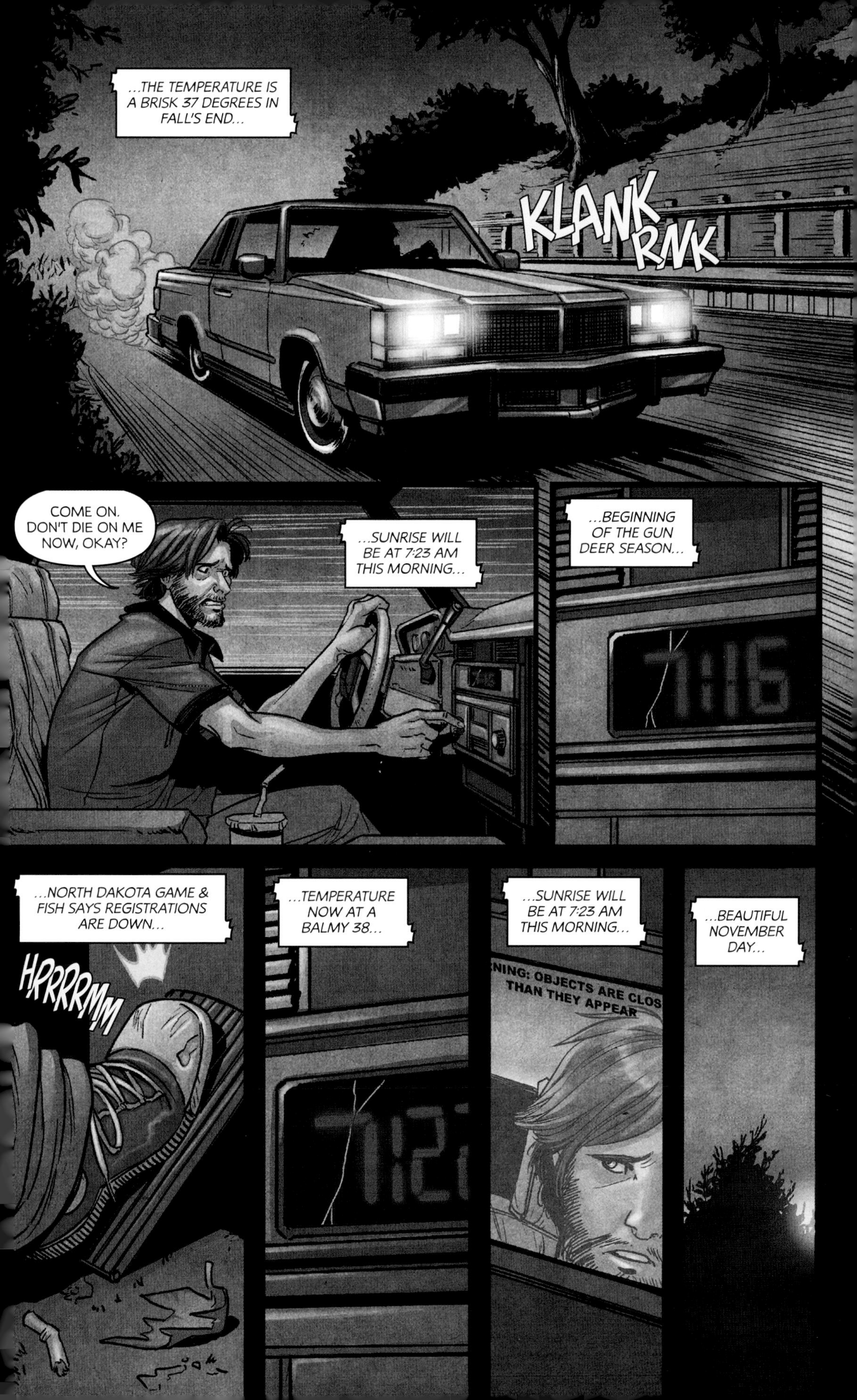
...THE TEMPERATURE IS A BRISK 37 DEGREES IN FALL'S END...
KLANK RNK
COME ON. DON'T DIE ON ME NOW, OKAY?
...SUNRISE WILL BE AT 7:23 AM THIS MORNING...
...BEGINNING OF THE GUN DEER SEASON...
7:16
...NORTH DAKOTA GAME & FISH SAYS REGISTRATIONS ARE DOWN...
HRRRRMM
...TEMPERATURE NOW AT A BALMY 38...
...SUNRISE WILL BE AT 7:23 AM THIS MORNING...
NING: OBJECTS ARE CLOS THAN THEY APPEAR
...BEAUTIFUL NOVEMBER DAY...

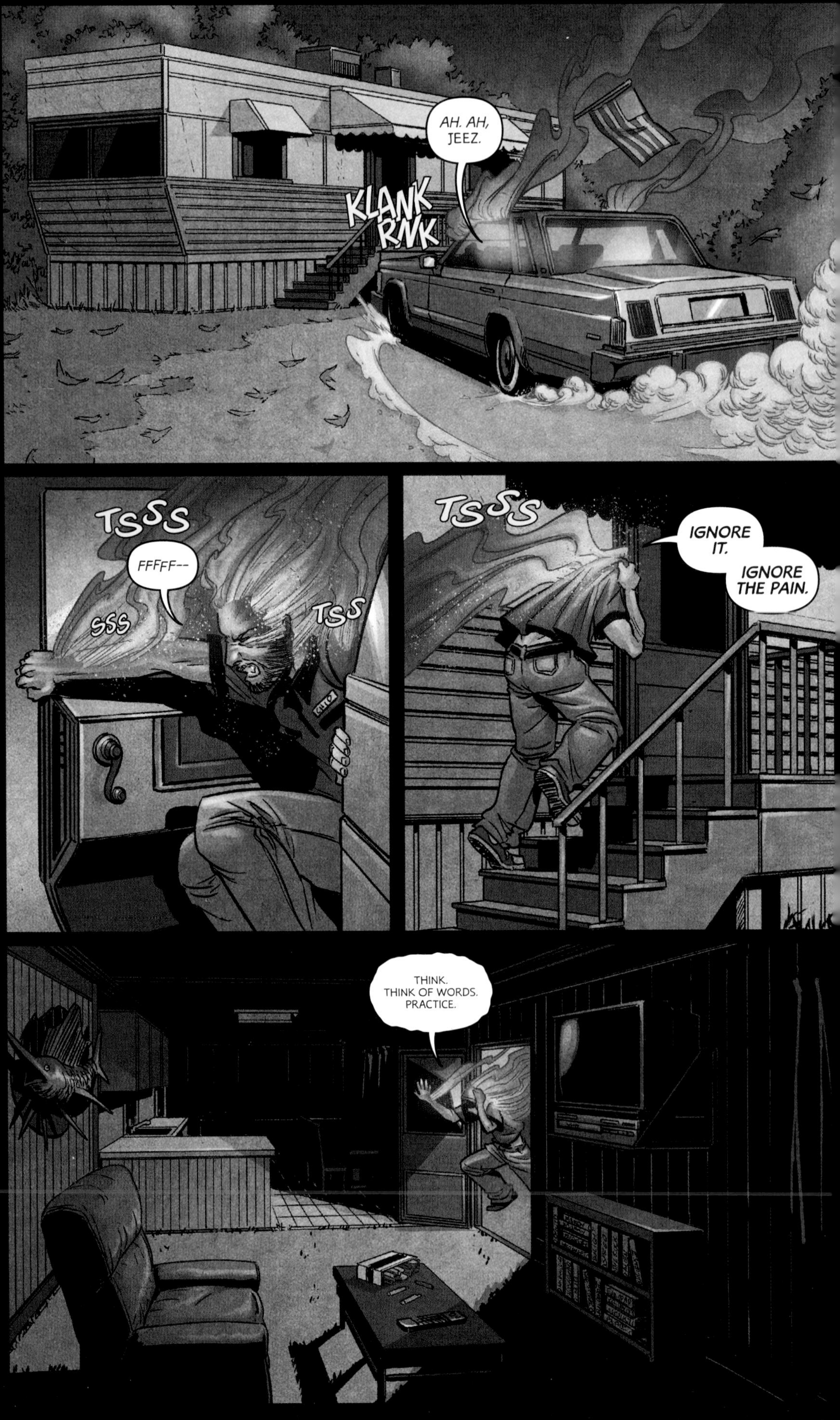
AH. AH, JEEZ.
KLANK RNK
TSSS
FFFFF--
SSS
TSS
TSSS
IGNORE IT.
IGNORE THE PAIN.
THINK. THINK OF WORDS. PRACTICE.

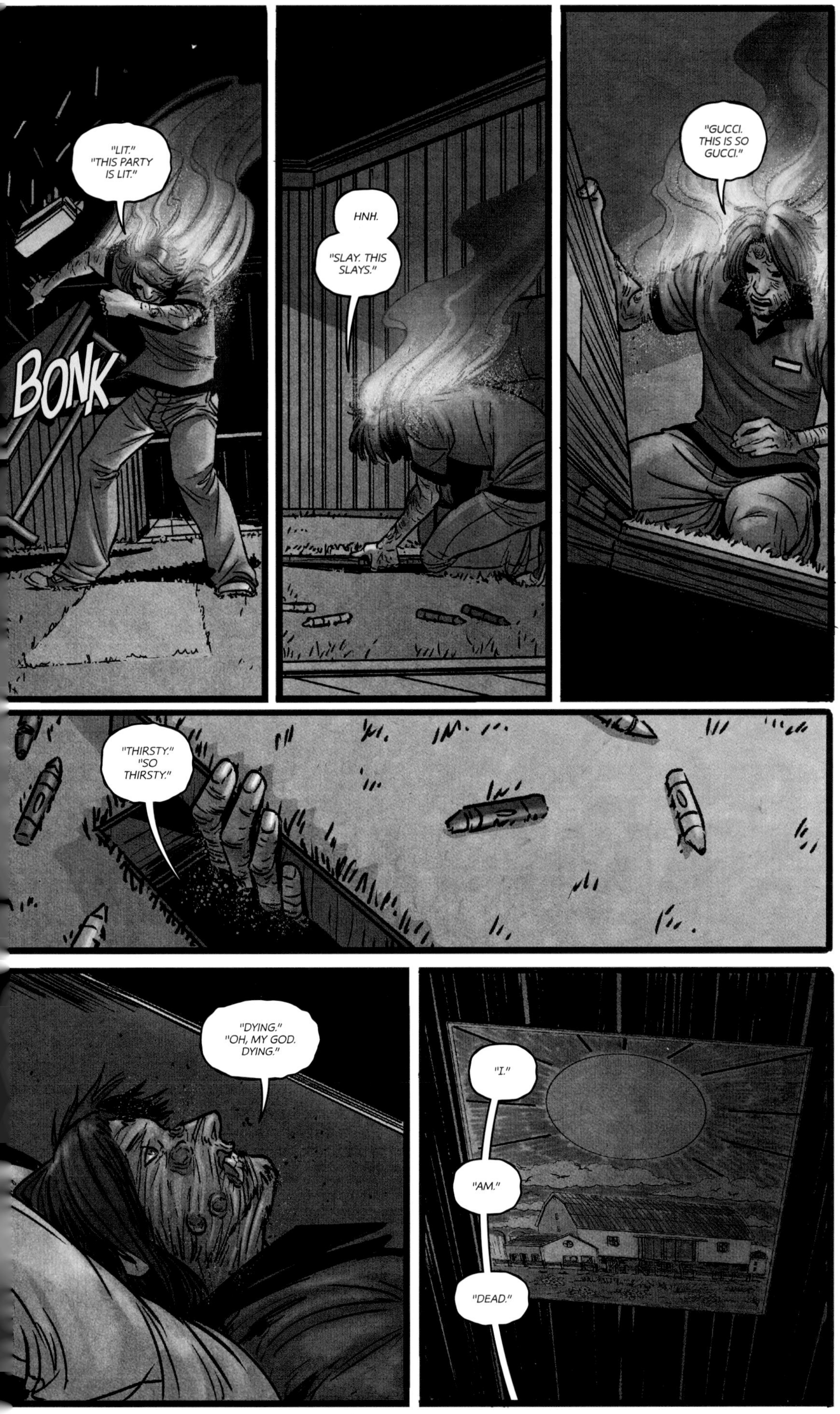
"LIT."
"THIS PARTY IS LIT."
BONK
HNH.
"SLAY. THIS SLAYS."
"GUCCI. THIS IS SO GUCCI."
"THIRSTY." "SO THIRSTY."
"DYING." "OH, MY GOD. DYING."
"I."
"AM."
"DEAD."

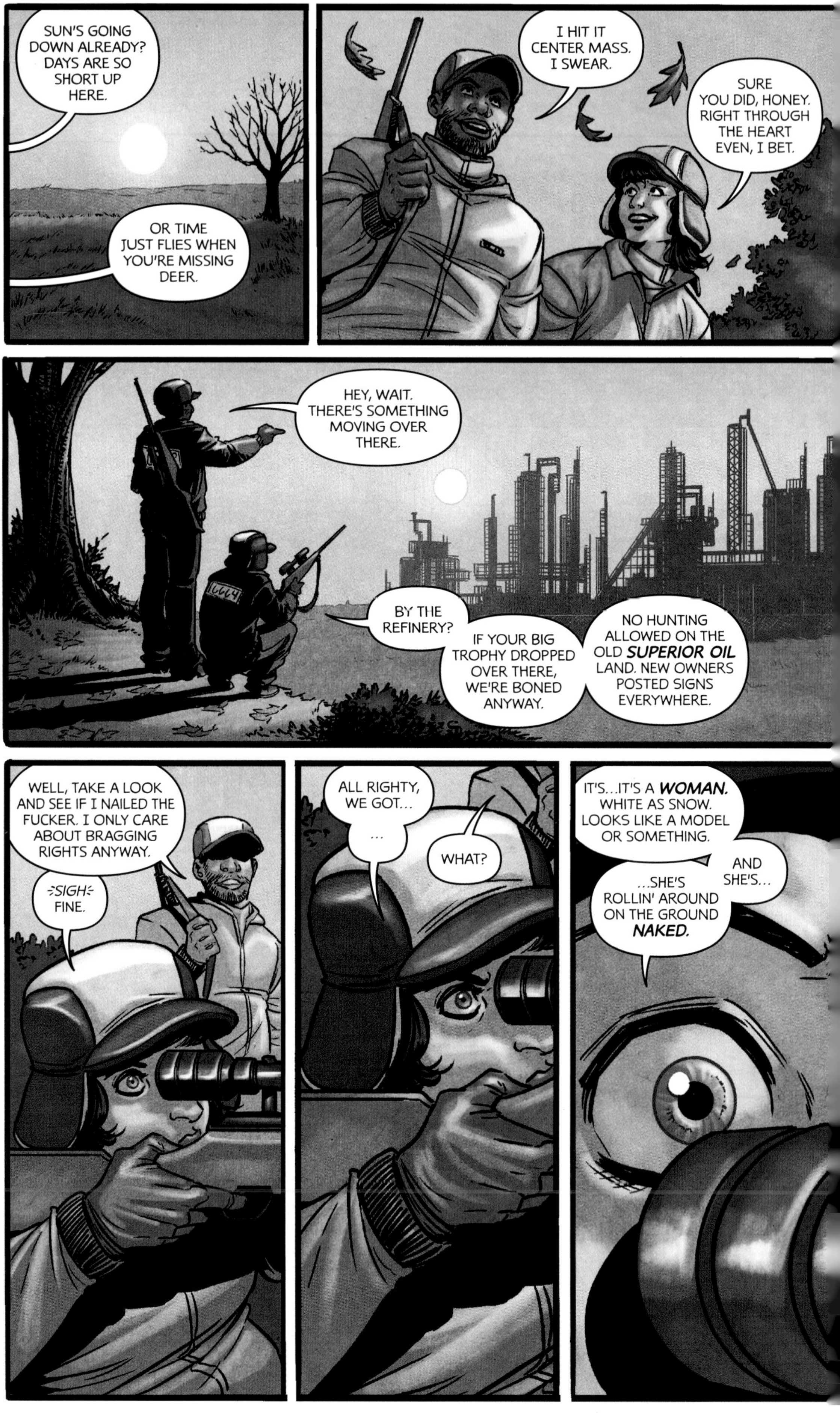
SUN'S GOING DOWN ALREADY? DAYS ARE SO SHORT UP HERE.
OR TIME JUST FLIES WHEN YOU'RE MISSING DEER.
I HIT IT CENTER MASS. I SWEAR.
SURE YOU DID, HONEY. RIGHT THROUGH THE HEART EVEN, I BET.
HEY, WAIT. THERE'S SOMETHING MOVING OVER THERE.
BY THE REFINERY?
IF YOUR BIG TROPHY DROPPED OVER THERE, WE'RE BONED ANYWAY.
NO HUNTING ALLOWED ON THE OLD SUPERIOR OIL LAND. NEW OWNERS POSTED SIGNS EVERYWHERE.
WELL, TAKE A LOOK AND SEE IF I NAILED THE FUCKER. I ONLY CARE ABOUT BRAGGING RIGHTS ANYWAY.
SIGH FINE.
ALL RIGHTY, WE GOT...
...
WHAT?
IT'S...IT'S A WOMAN. WHITE AS SNOW. LOOKS LIKE A MODEL OR SOMETHING.
AND SHE'S...
...SHE'S ROLLIN' AROUND ON THE GROUND NAKED.

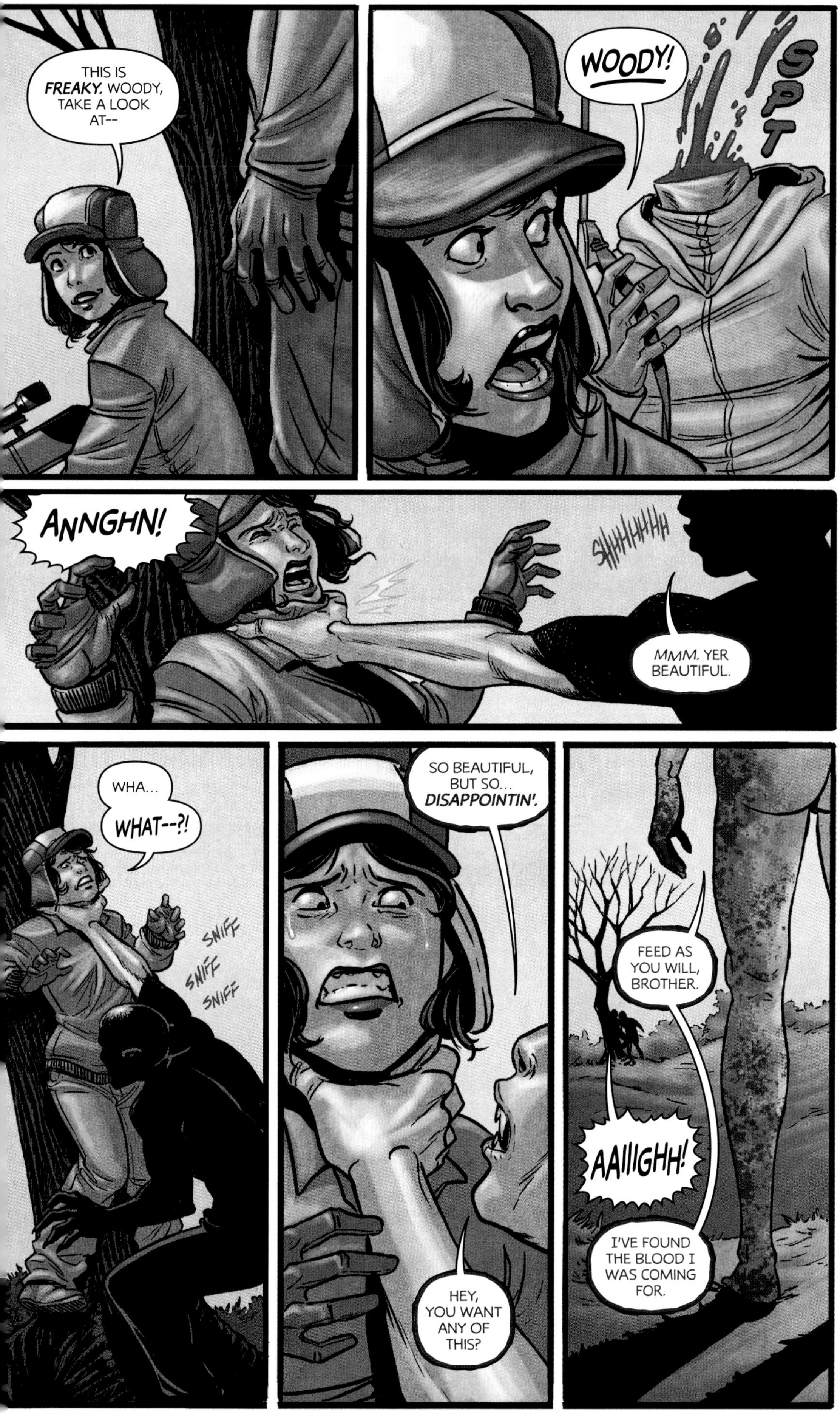
THIS IS FREAKY. WOODY, TAKE A LOOK AT--
WOODY!
SPT
ANNGHN!
SHHHHHHH
MMM. YER BEAUTIFUL.
WHA...
WHAT--?!
SNIFF
SNIFF
SNIFF
SO BEAUTIFUL, BUT SO... DISAPPOINTIN'.
HEY, YOU WANT ANY OF THIS?
FEED AS YOU WILL, BROTHER.
AAIIIGHH!
I'VE FOUND THE BLOOD I WAS COMING FOR.

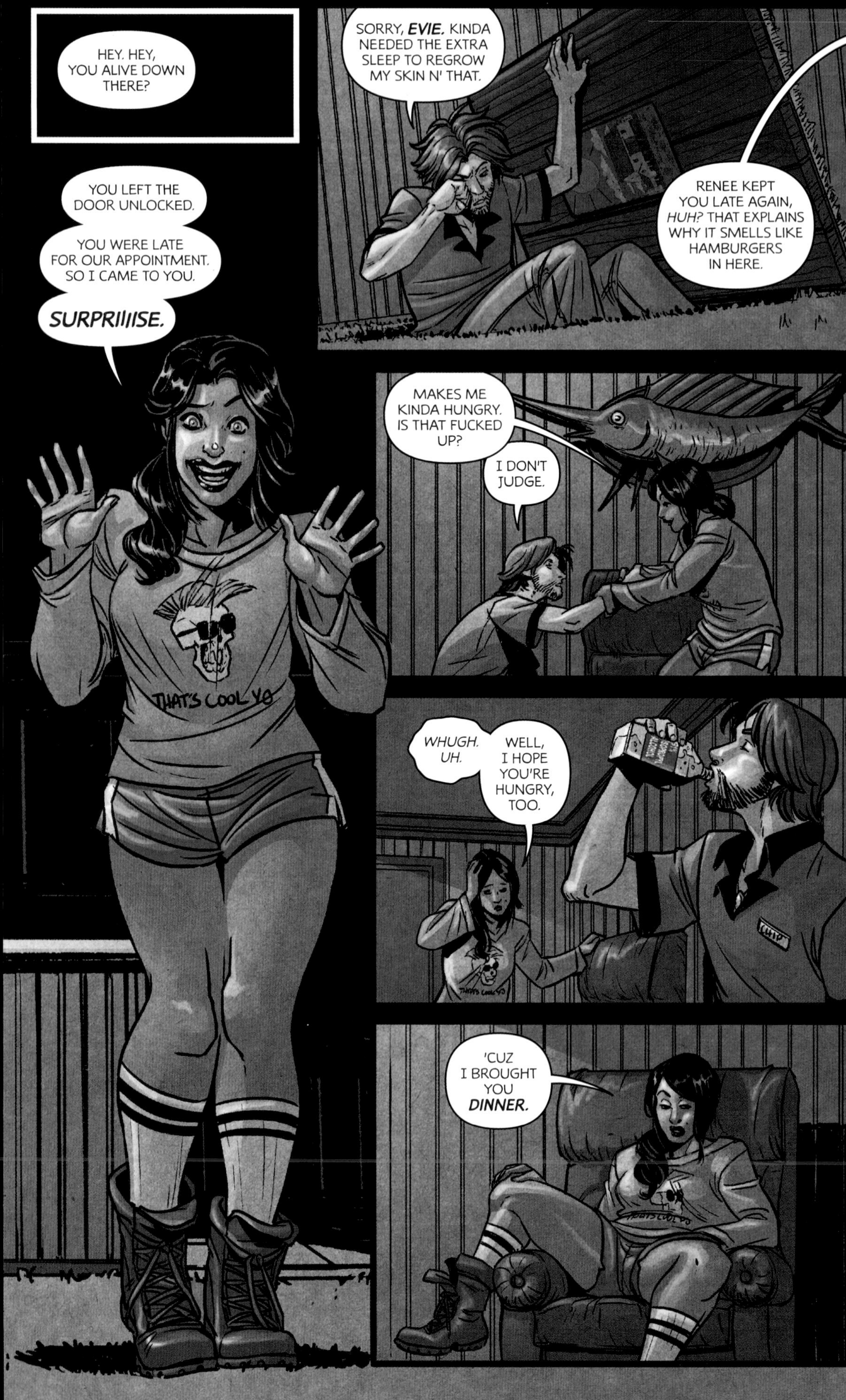
HEY. HEY, YOU ALIVE DOWN THERE?
SORRY, EVIE. KINDA NEEDED THE EXTRA SLEEP TO REGROW MY SKIN N' THAT.
RENEE KEPT YOU LATE AGAIN, HUH? THAT EXPLAINS WHY IT SMELLS LIKE HAMBURGERS IN HERE.
YOU LEFT THE DOOR UNLOCKED.
YOU WERE LATE FOR OUR APPOINTMENT. SO I CAME TO YOU.
SURPRIIIISE.
THAT'S COOL YO
MAKES ME KINDA HUNGRY. IS THAT FUCKED UP?
I DON'T JUDGE.
WHUGH. UH.
WELL, I HOPE YOU'RE HUNGRY, TOO.
'CUZ I BROUGHT YOU DINNER.

I...

...THAT'S A PLENTY *GUCCI*...UM... EFFICIENT...SPOT... BUT...UNLESS YOU REALLY...

÷COFF COFF÷

÷COFF÷

I'M KIDDING, CHIP. RELAX.

I MEAN, THE GUY I'M FUCKIN' DOESN'T PUT HIS FACE ANYWHERE CLOSE TO DOWN THERE, SO IT'S NOT LIKE ANYBODY'D SEE IT.

BUT YOU CAN DO MY ARMPIT OR BACK OF NECK. DEALER'S CHOICE.

WHUH.

I'VE GOT THE SPINS, SO GET TO IT, BOY, OR I'LL PUKE ON YOUR FLOOR.

OH. YAH. NO MORE PUKE, PLEASE.

HNG. LOOK AT US. A VAMPIRE AND A GIRL WHO MAKES TOO MUCH BLOOD.

CHK

WHAT A FUCKING PAIR.

SNK SNK SNK

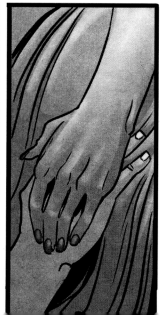

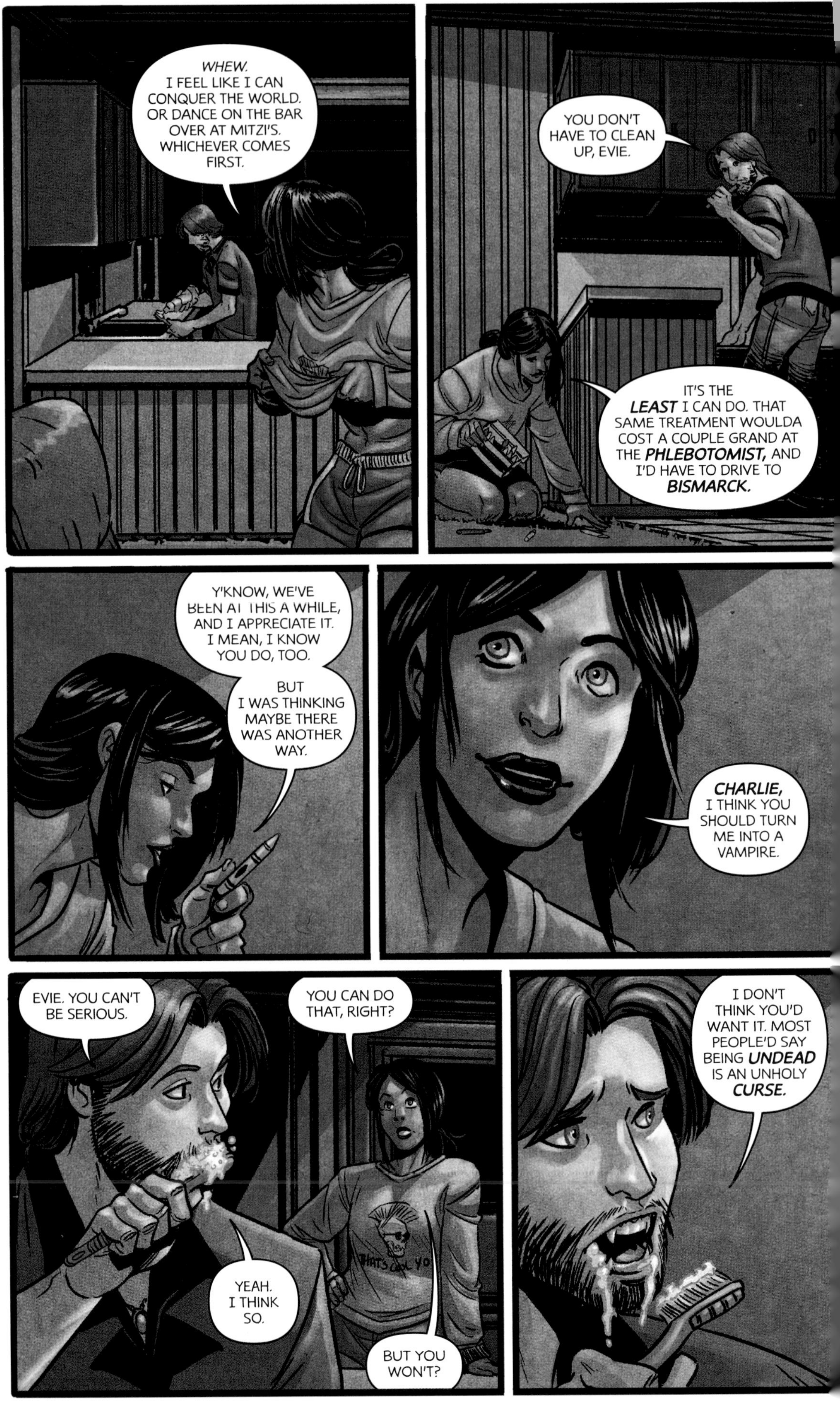
WHEW. I FEEL LIKE I CAN CONQUER THE WORLD. OR DANCE ON THE BAR OVER AT MITZI'S. WHICHEVER COMES FIRST.
YOU DON'T HAVE TO CLEAN UP, EVIE.
IT'S THE LEAST I CAN DO. THAT SAME TREATMENT WOULDA COST A COUPLE GRAND AT THE PHLEBOTOMIST, AND I'D HAVE TO DRIVE TO BISMARCK.
Y'KNOW, WE'VE BEEN AT THIS A WHILE, AND I APPRECIATE IT. I MEAN, I KNOW YOU DO, TOO.
BUT I WAS THINKING MAYBE THERE WAS ANOTHER WAY.
CHARLIE, I THINK YOU SHOULD TURN ME INTO A VAMPIRE.
EVIE. YOU CAN'T BE SERIOUS.
YOU CAN DO THAT, RIGHT?
YEAH. I THINK SO.
BUT YOU WON'T?
I DON'T THINK YOU'D WANT IT. MOST PEOPLE'D SAY BEING UNDEAD IS AN UNHOLY CURSE.

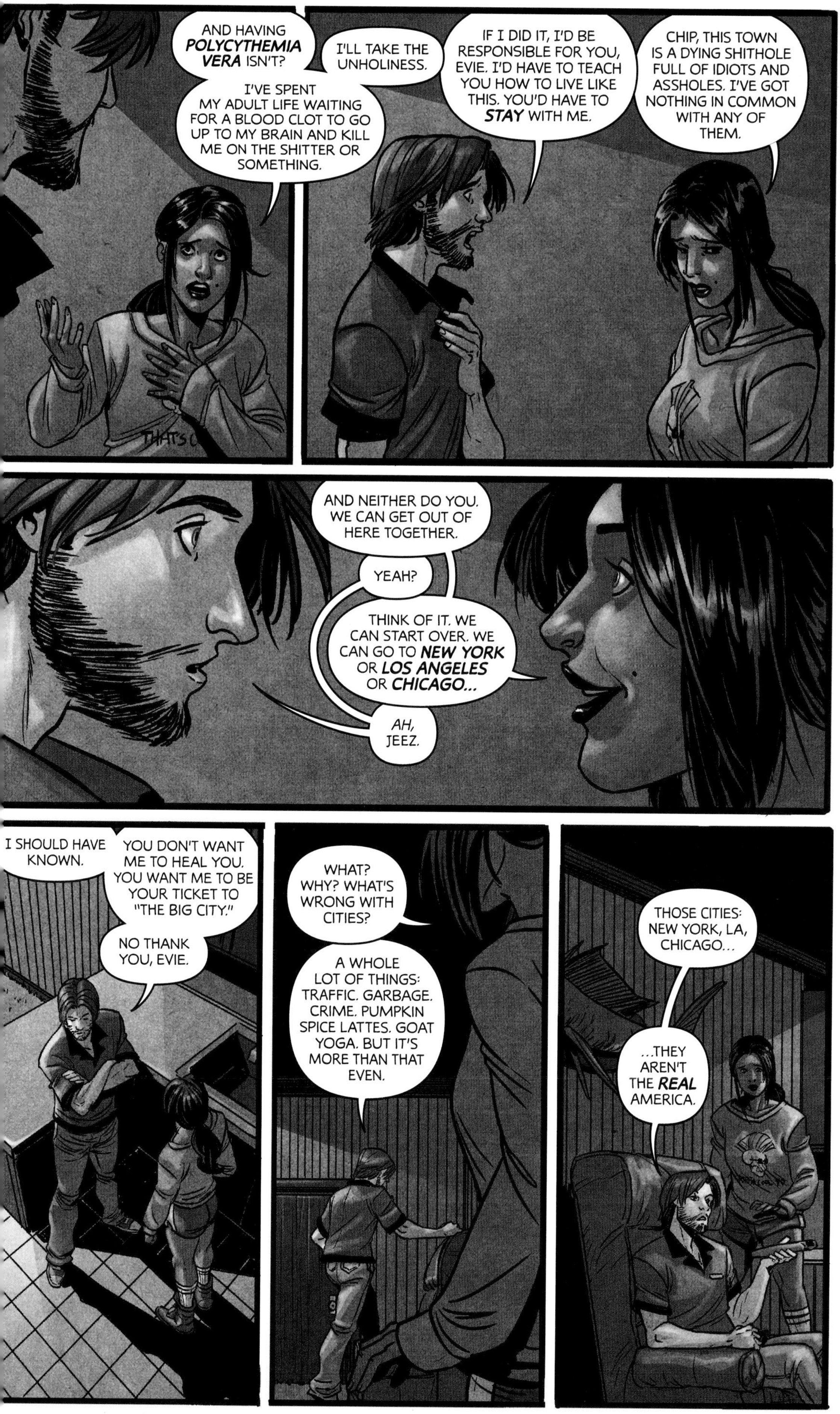
AND HAVING POLYCYTHEMIA VERA ISN'T?
I'LL TAKE THE UNHOLINESS.
I'VE SPENT MY ADULT LIFE WAITING FOR A BLOOD CLOT TO GO UP TO MY BRAIN AND KILL ME ON THE SHITTER OR SOMETHING.
IF I DID IT, I'D BE RESPONSIBLE FOR YOU, EVIE. I'D HAVE TO TEACH YOU HOW TO LIVE LIKE THIS. YOU'D HAVE TO STAY WITH ME.
CHIP, THIS TOWN IS A DYING SHITHOLE FULL OF IDIOTS AND ASSHOLES. I'VE GOT NOTHING IN COMMON WITH ANY OF THEM.
AND NEITHER DO YOU. WE CAN GET OUT OF HERE TOGETHER.
YEAH?
THINK OF IT. WE CAN START OVER. WE CAN GO TO NEW YORK OR LOS ANGELES OR CHICAGO...
AH, JEEZ.
I SHOULD HAVE KNOWN.
YOU DON'T WANT ME TO HEAL YOU. YOU WANT ME TO BE YOUR TICKET TO "THE BIG CITY."
NO THANK YOU, EVIE.
WHAT? WHY? WHAT'S WRONG WITH CITIES?
A WHOLE LOT OF THINGS: TRAFFIC. GARBAGE. CRIME. PUMPKIN SPICE LATTES. GOAT YOGA. BUT IT'S MORE THAN THAT EVEN.
THOSE CITIES: NEW YORK, LA, CHICAGO...
...THEY AREN'T THE REAL AMERICA.

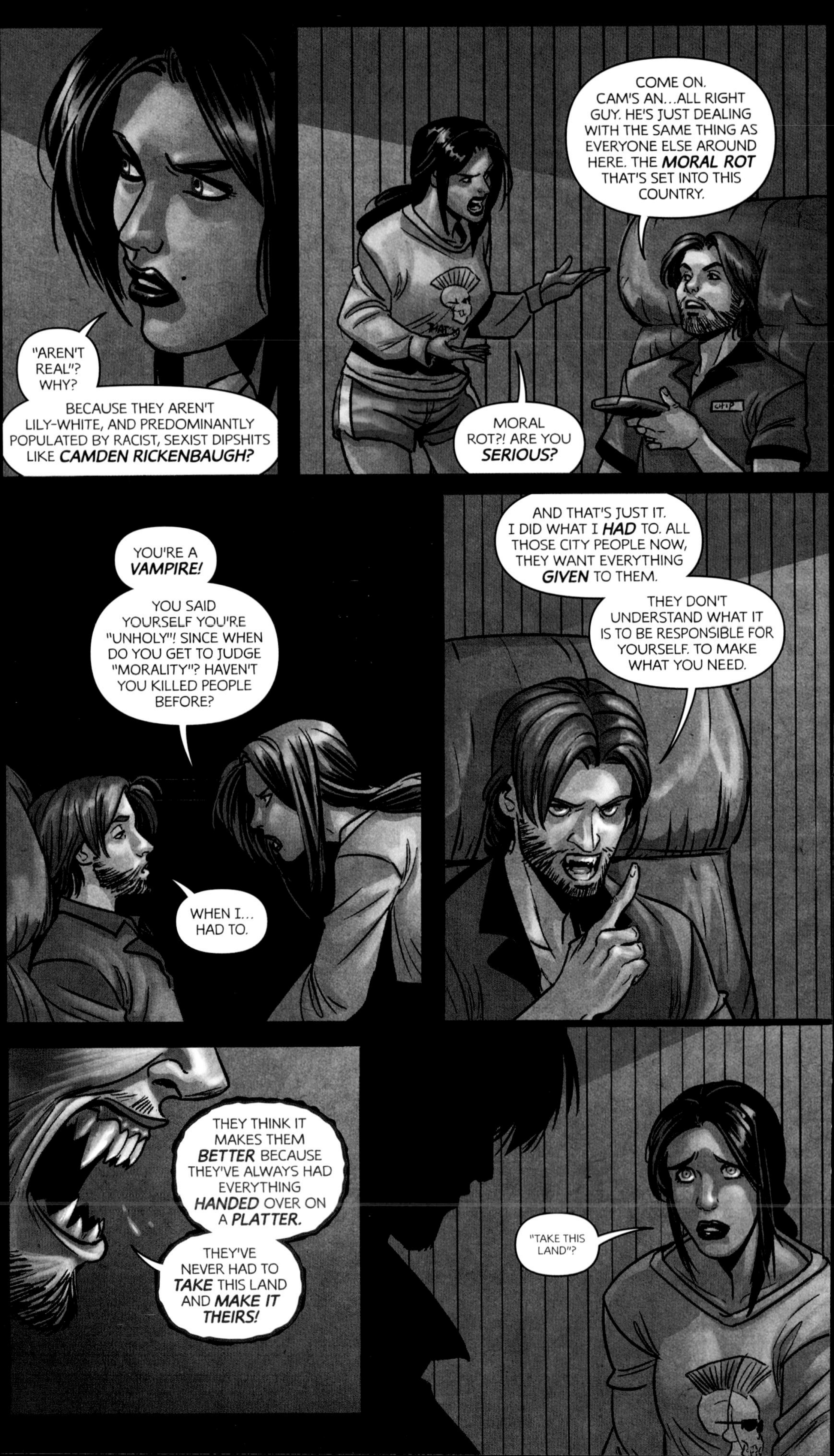
"AREN'T REAL"? WHY?
BECAUSE THEY AREN'T LILY-WHITE, AND PREDOMINANTLY POPULATED BY RACIST, SEXIST DIPSHITS LIKE CAMDEN RICKENBAUGH?
COME ON. CAM'S AN...ALL RIGHT GUY. HE'S JUST DEALING WITH THE SAME THING AS EVERYONE ELSE AROUND HERE. THE MORAL ROT THAT'S SET INTO THIS COUNTRY.
MORAL ROT?! ARE YOU SERIOUS?
YOU'RE A VAMPIRE!
YOU SAID YOURSELF YOU'RE "UNHOLY"! SINCE WHEN DO YOU GET TO JUDGE "MORALITY"? HAVEN'T YOU KILLED PEOPLE BEFORE?
WHEN I... HAD TO.
AND THAT'S JUST IT. I DID WHAT I HAD TO. ALL THOSE CITY PEOPLE NOW, THEY WANT EVERYTHING GIVEN TO THEM.
THEY DON'T UNDERSTAND WHAT IT IS TO BE RESPONSIBLE FOR YOURSELF. TO MAKE WHAT YOU NEED.
THEY THINK IT MAKES THEM BETTER BECAUSE THEY'VE ALWAYS HAD EVERYTHING HANDED OVER ON A PLATTER.
THEY'VE NEVER HAD TO TAKE THIS LAND AND MAKE IT THEIRS!
"TAKE THIS LAND"?

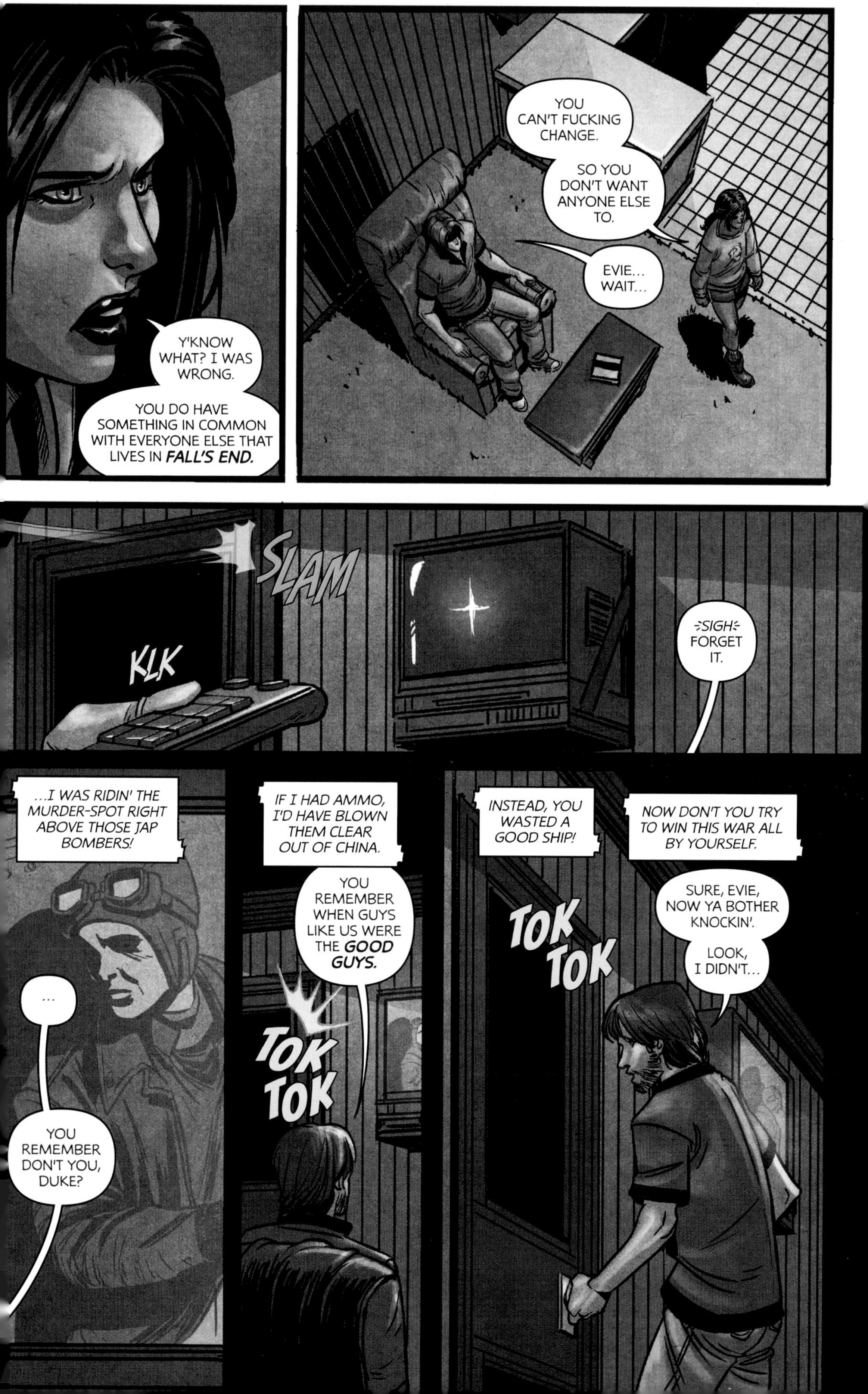

Y'KNOW WHAT? I WAS WRONG.
YOU DO HAVE SOMETHING IN COMMON WITH EVERYONE ELSE THAT LIVES IN ***FALL'S END.***
YOU CAN'T FUCKING CHANGE.
SO YOU DON'T WANT ANYONE ELSE TO.
EVIE... WAIT...
SLAM
KLK
~SIGH~ FORGET IT.
...I WAS RIDIN' THE MURDER-SPOT RIGHT ABOVE THOSE JAP BOMBERS!
...
YOU REMEMBER DON'T YOU, DUKE?
IF I HAD AMMO, I'D HAVE BLOWN THEM CLEAR OUT OF CHINA.
YOU REMEMBER WHEN GUYS LIKE US WERE THE ***GOOD GUYS.***
TOK TOK
INSTEAD, YOU WASTED A GOOD SHIP!
NOW DON'T YOU TRY TO WIN THIS WAR ALL BY YOURSELF.
TOK TOK
SURE, EVIE, NOW YA BOTHER KNOCKIN'.
LOOK, I DIDN'T...

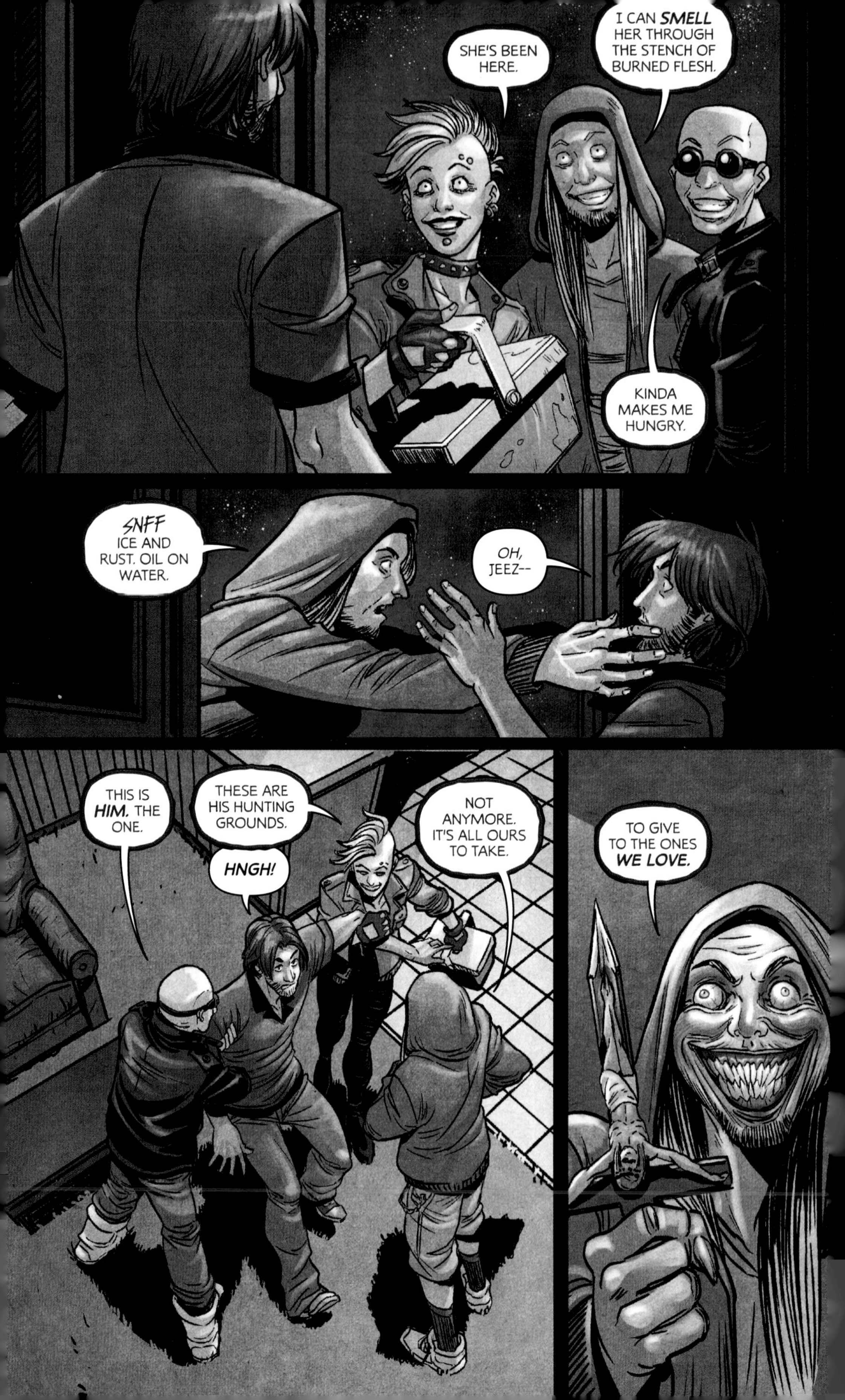
SHE'S BEEN HERE.
I CAN **SMELL** HER THROUGH THE STENCH OF BURNED FLESH.
KINDA MAKES ME HUNGRY.
SNFF ICE AND RUST. OIL ON WATER.
OH, JEEZ--
THIS IS **HIM.** THE ONE.
THESE ARE HIS HUNTING GROUNDS.
HNGH!
NOT ANYMORE. IT'S ALL OURS TO TAKE.
TO GIVE TO THE ONES **WE LOVE.**

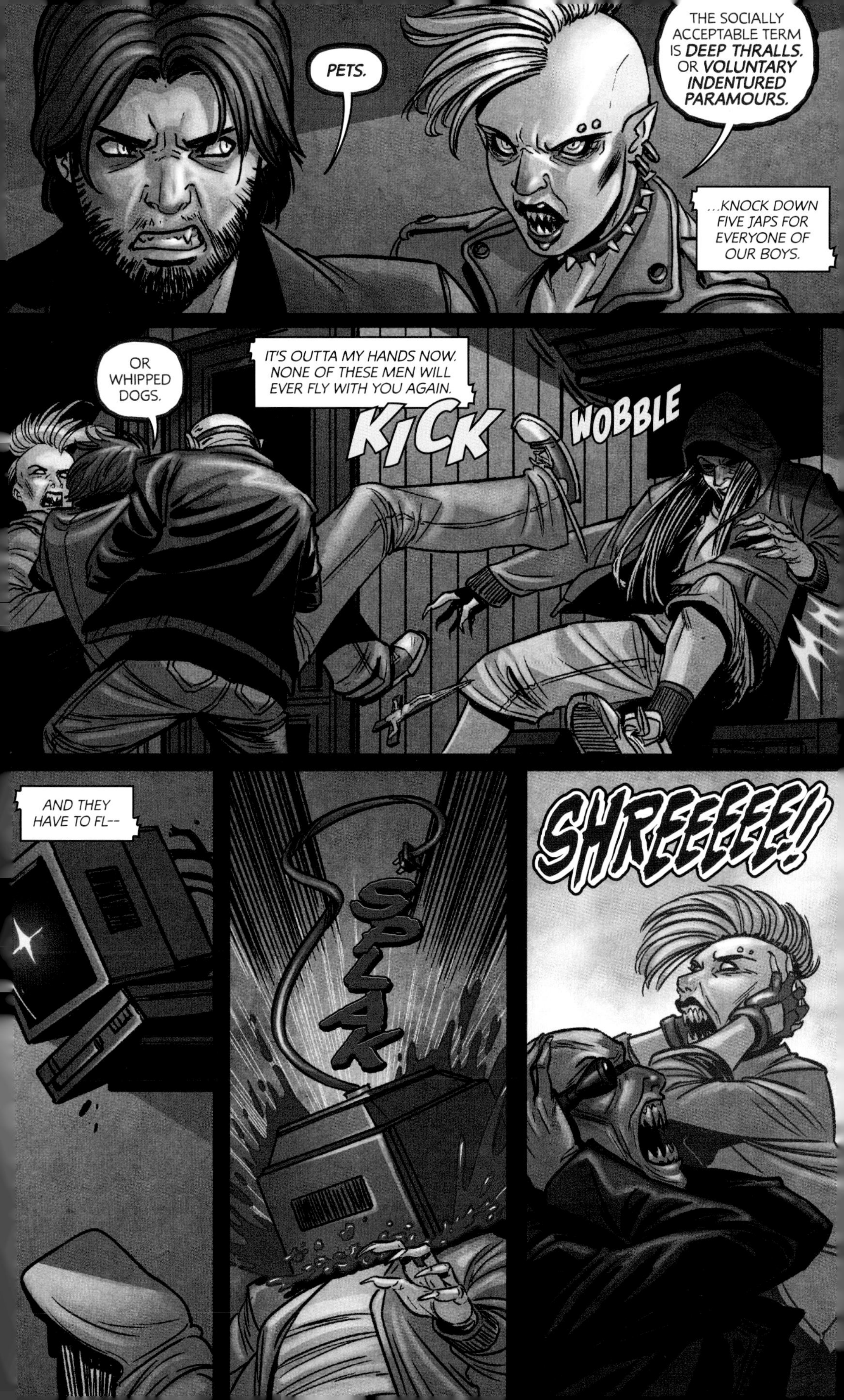
PETS.
THE SOCIALLY ACCEPTABLE TERM IS DEEP THRALLS. OR VOLUNTARY INDENTURED PARAMOURS.
...KNOCK DOWN FIVE JAPS FOR EVERYONE OF OUR BOYS.
OR WHIPPED DOGS.
IT'S OUTTA MY HANDS NOW. NONE OF THESE MEN WILL EVER FLY WITH YOU AGAIN.
KICK
WOBBLE
AND THEY HAVE TO FL--
SPLAK
SHREEEEEE!!

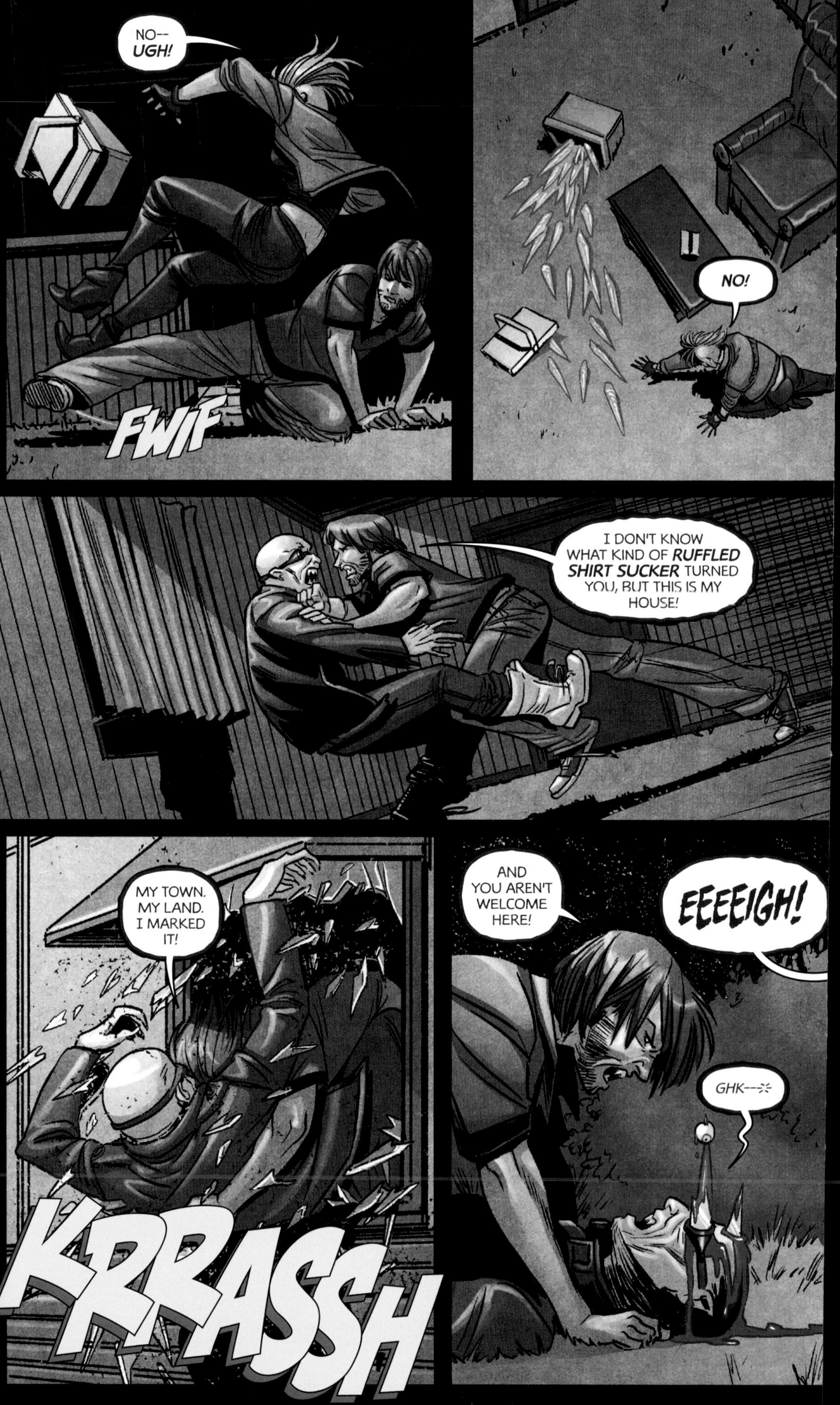
NO-- UGH!
FWIF
NO!
I DON'T KNOW WHAT KIND OF RUFFLED SHIRT SUCKER TURNED YOU, BUT THIS IS MY HOUSE!
MY TOWN. MY LAND. I MARKED IT!
KRRASSH
AND YOU AREN'T WELCOME HERE!
EEEEIGH!
GHK--

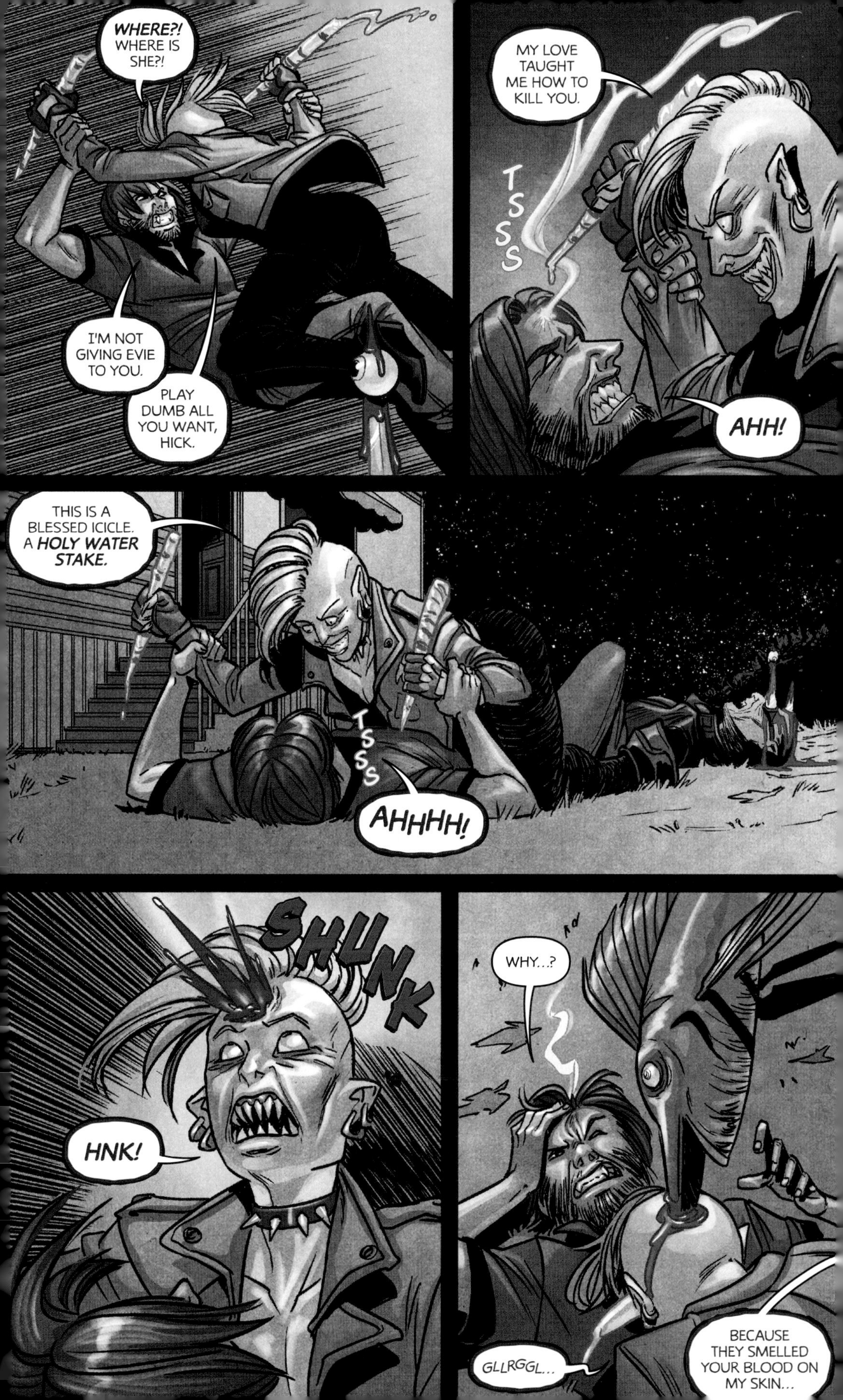
WHERE?! WHERE IS SHE?!
I'M NOT GIVING EVIE TO YOU.
PLAY DUMB ALL YOU WANT, HICK.
MY LOVE TAUGHT ME HOW TO KILL YOU.
TSSS
AHH!
THIS IS A BLESSED ICICLE. A HOLY WATER STAKE.
TSSS
AHHHH!
SHUNK
HNK!
WHY...?
GLLRGGL...
BECAUSE THEY SMELLED YOUR BLOOD ON MY SKIN...

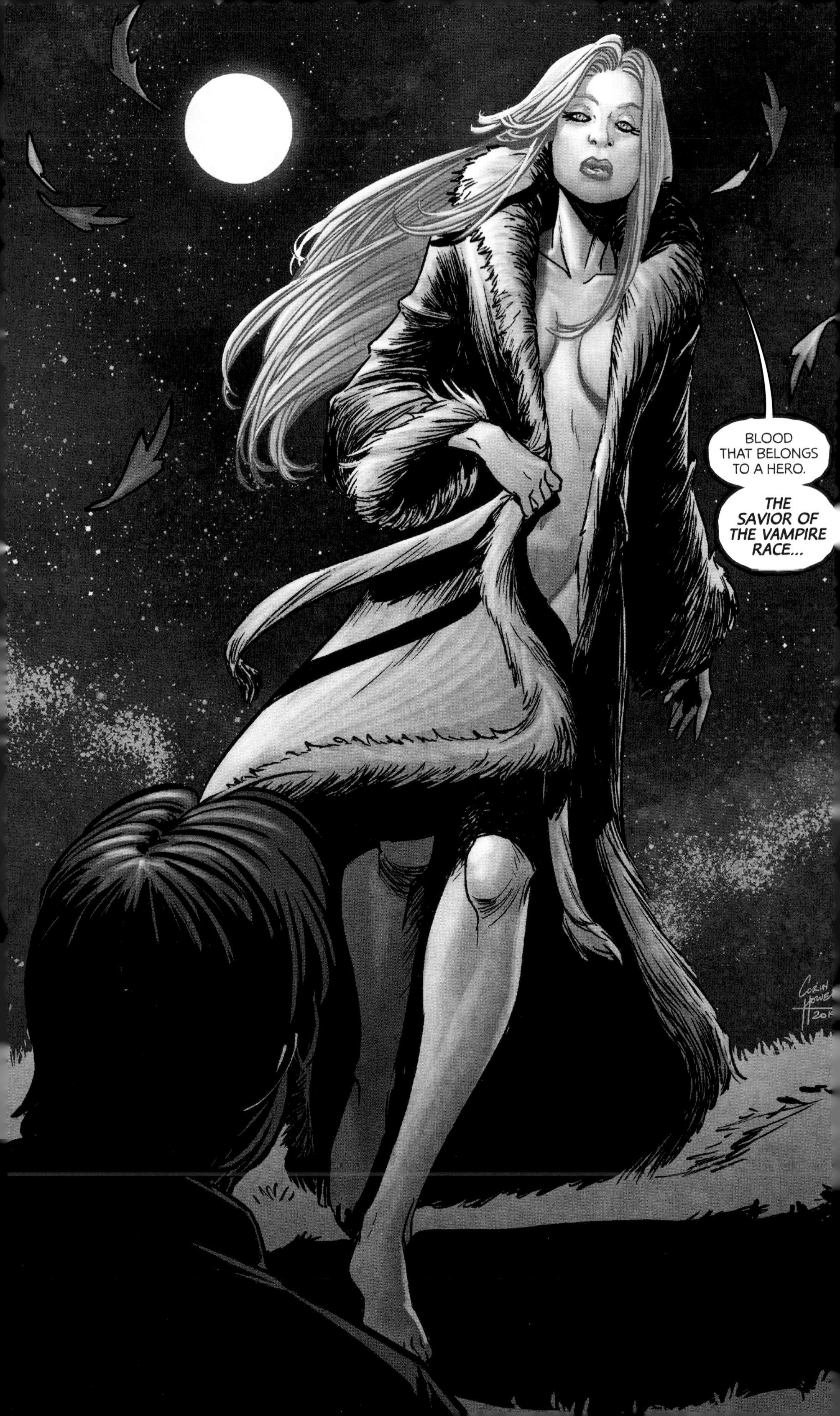
BLOOD THAT BELONGS TO A HERO.
THE SAVIOR OF THE VAMPIRE RACE...

2

FLYOVER STATES

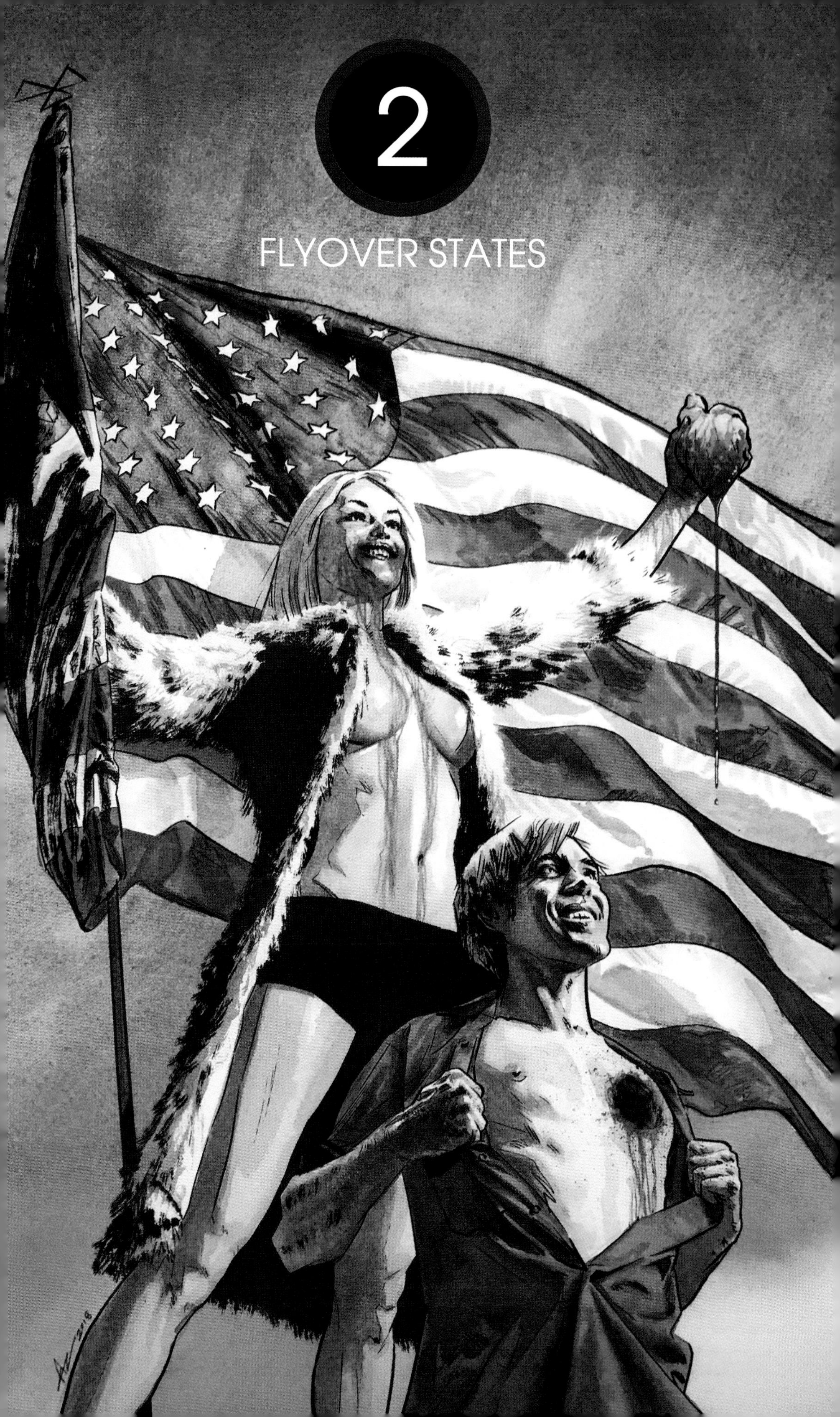

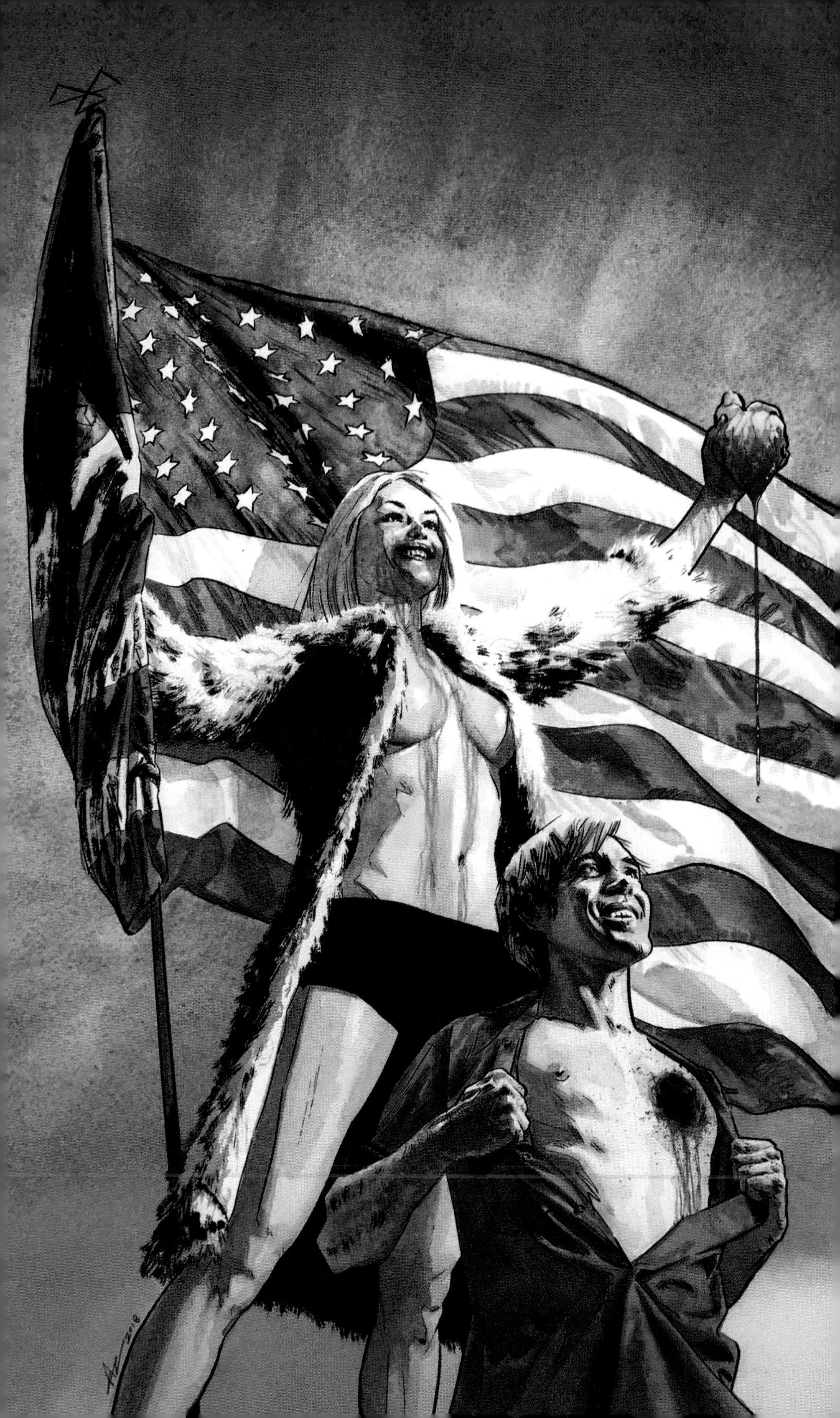

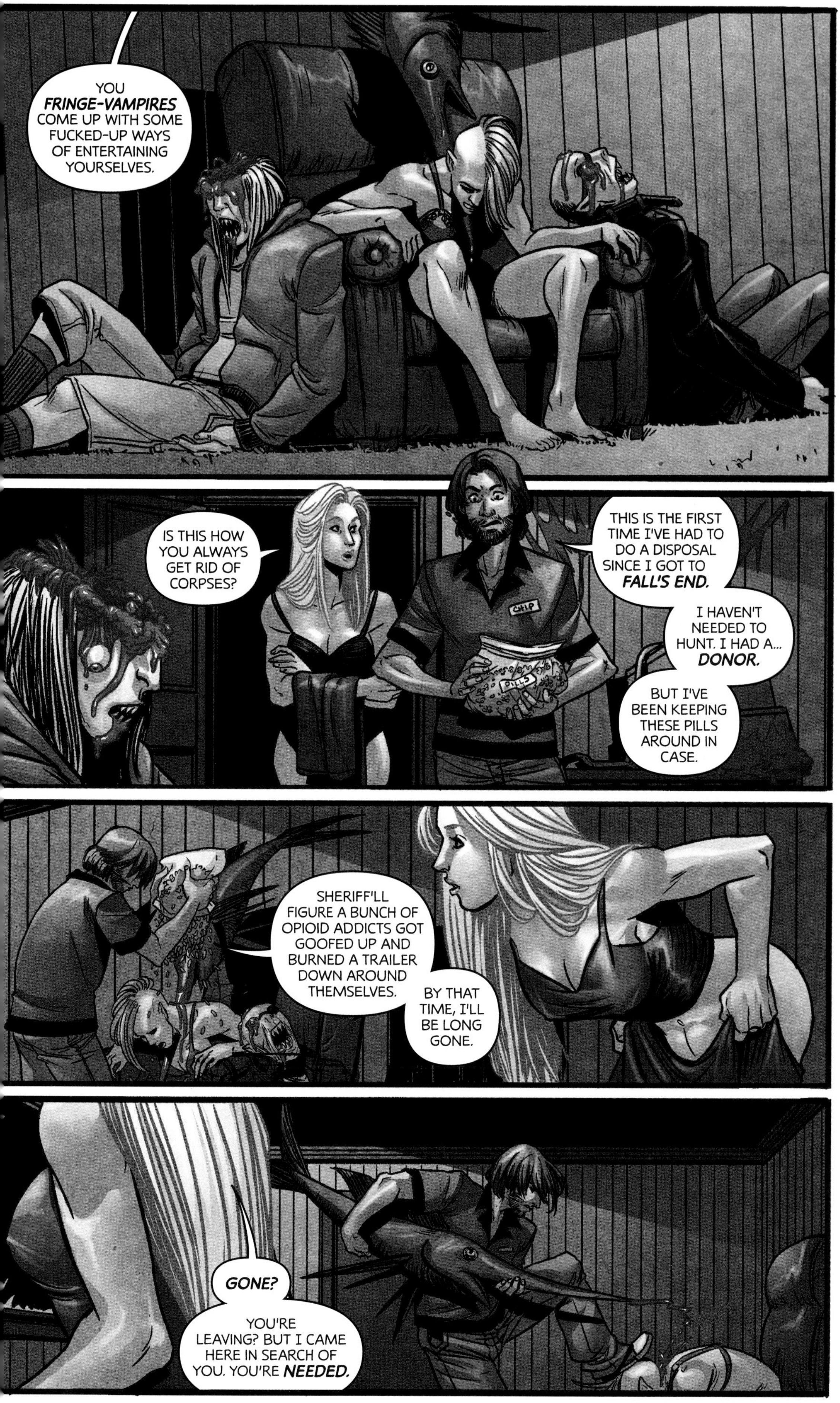
YOU **FRINGE-VAMPIRES** COME UP WITH SOME FUCKED-UP WAYS OF ENTERTAINING YOURSELVES.
IS THIS HOW YOU ALWAYS GET RID OF CORPSES?
THIS IS THE FIRST TIME I'VE HAD TO DO A DISPOSAL SINCE I GOT TO **FALL'S END.**
I HAVEN'T NEEDED TO HUNT. I HAD A... **DONOR.**
BUT I'VE BEEN KEEPING THESE PILLS AROUND IN CASE.
SHERIFF'LL FIGURE A BUNCH OF OPIOID ADDICTS GOT GOOFED UP AND BURNED A TRAILER DOWN AROUND THEMSELVES.
BY THAT TIME, I'LL BE LONG GONE.
GONE?
YOU'RE LEAVING? BUT I CAME HERE IN SEARCH OF YOU. YOU'RE **NEEDED.**

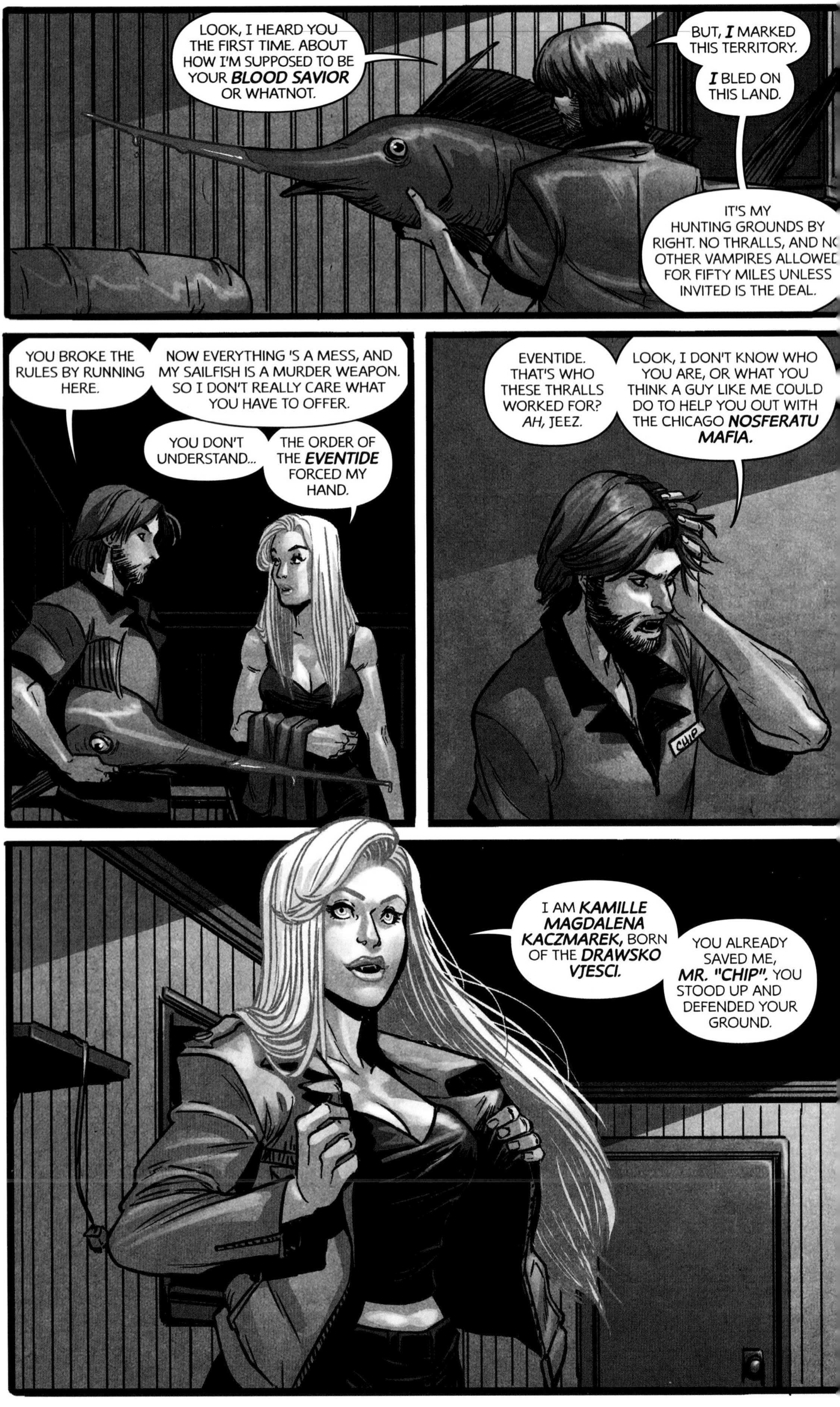
LOOK, I HEARD YOU THE FIRST TIME. ABOUT HOW I'M SUPPOSED TO BE YOUR BLOOD SAVIOR OR WHATNOT.
BUT, I MARKED THIS TERRITORY.
I BLED ON THIS LAND.
IT'S MY HUNTING GROUNDS BY RIGHT. NO THRALLS, AND NO OTHER VAMPIRES ALLOWED FOR FIFTY MILES UNLESS INVITED IS THE DEAL.
YOU BROKE THE RULES BY RUNNING HERE.
NOW EVERYTHING 'S A MESS, AND MY SAILFISH IS A MURDER WEAPON. SO I DON'T REALLY CARE WHAT YOU HAVE TO OFFER.
YOU DON'T UNDERSTAND...
THE ORDER OF THE EVENTIDE FORCED MY HAND.
EVENTIDE. THAT'S WHO THESE THRALLS WORKED FOR? AH, JEEZ.
LOOK, I DON'T KNOW WHO YOU ARE, OR WHAT YOU THINK A GUY LIKE ME COULD DO TO HELP YOU OUT WITH THE CHICAGO NOSFERATU MAFIA.
CHIP
I AM KAMILLE MAGDALENA KACZMAREK, BORN OF THE DRAWSKO VJESCI.
YOU ALREADY SAVED ME, MR. "CHIP". YOU STOOD UP AND DEFENDED YOUR GROUND.

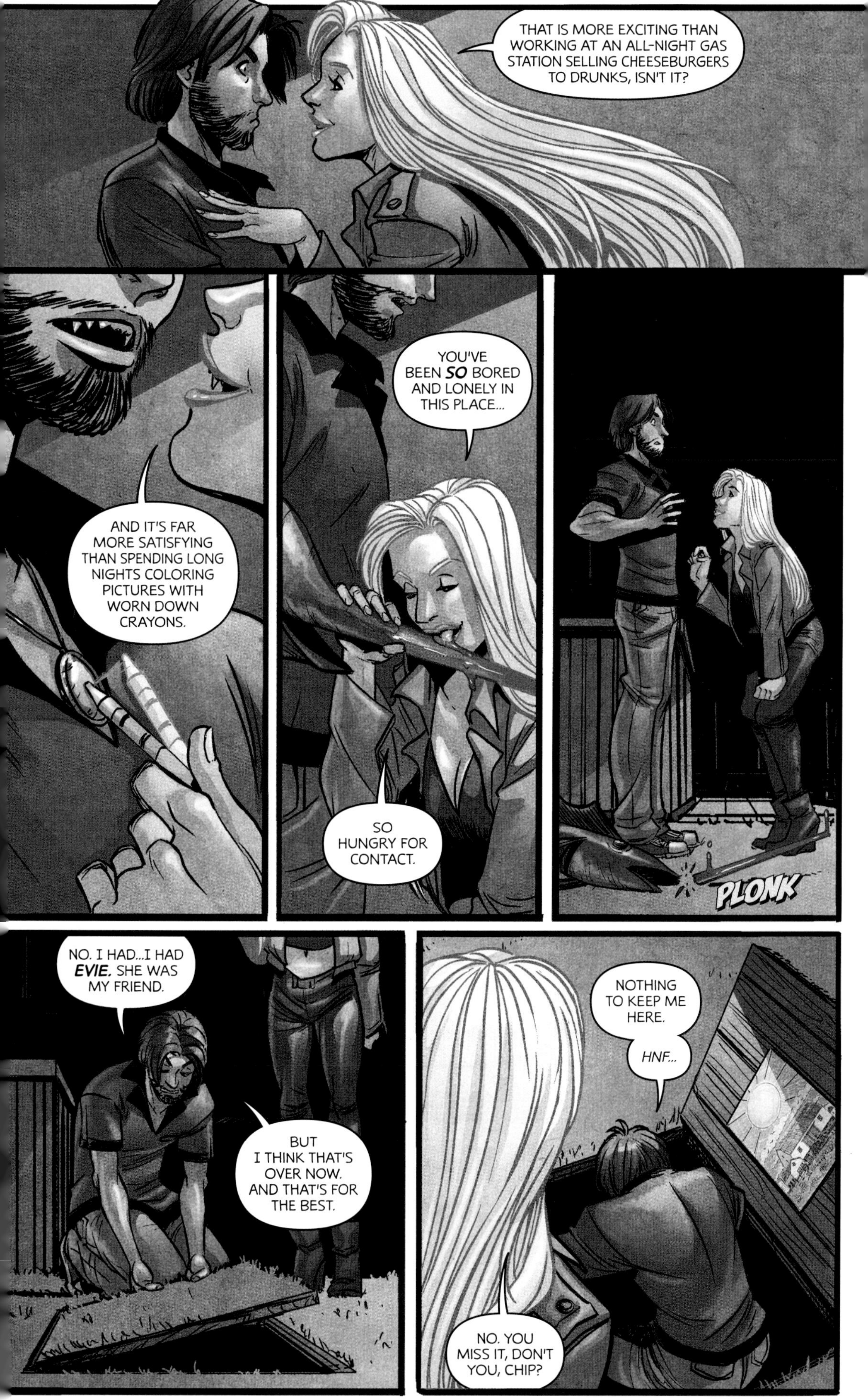
THAT IS MORE EXCITING THAN WORKING AT AN ALL-NIGHT GAS STATION SELLING CHEESEBURGERS TO DRUNKS, ISN'T IT?
AND IT'S FAR MORE SATISFYING THAN SPENDING LONG NIGHTS COLORING PICTURES WITH WORN DOWN CRAYONS.
YOU'VE BEEN ***SO*** BORED AND LONELY IN THIS PLACE...
SO HUNGRY FOR CONTACT.
PLONK
NO. I HAD...I HAD ***EVIE.*** SHE WAS MY FRIEND.
BUT I THINK THAT'S OVER NOW. AND THAT'S FOR THE BEST.
NOTHING TO KEEP ME HERE.
HNF...
NO. YOU MISS IT, DON'T YOU, CHIP?

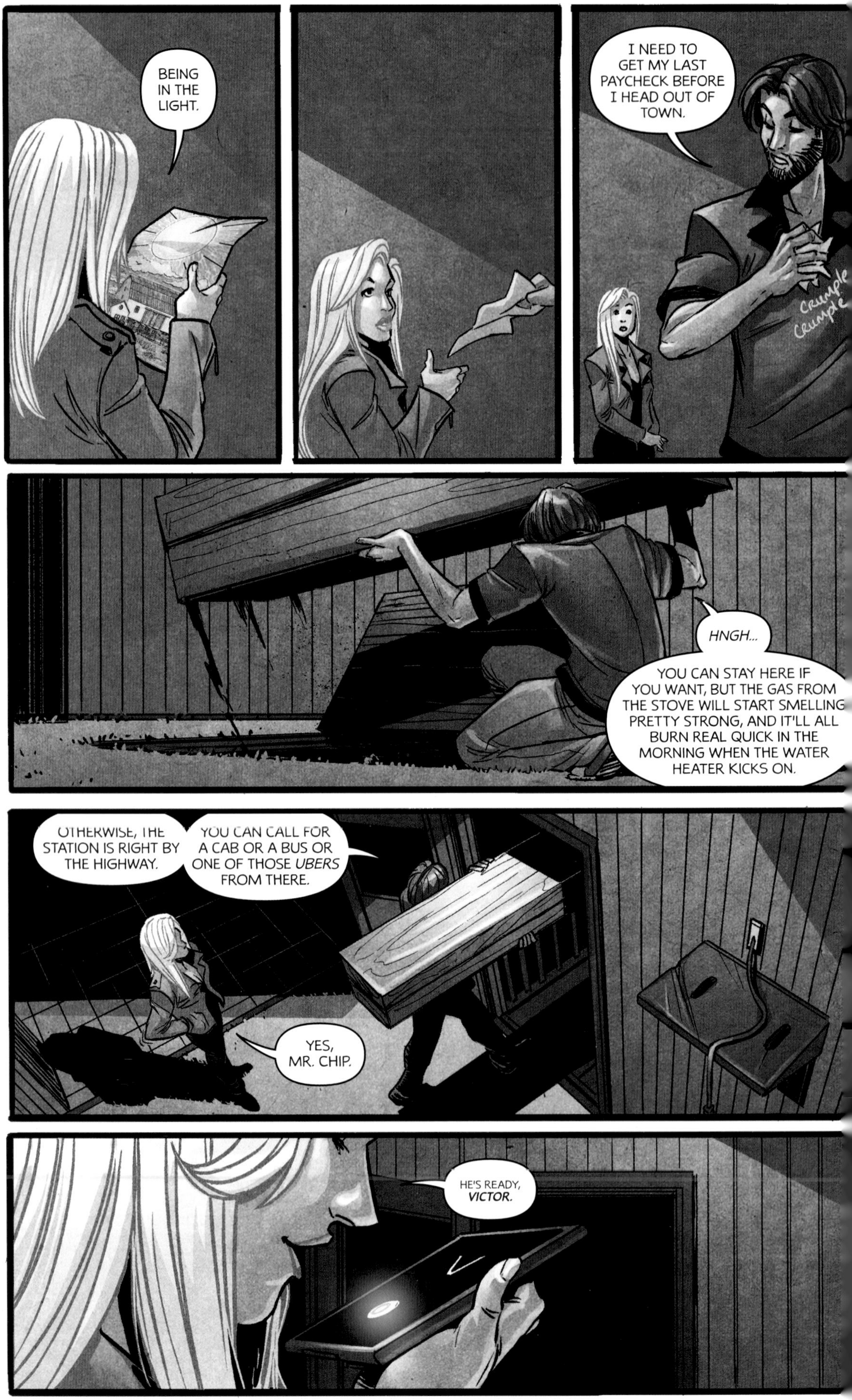
BEING IN THE LIGHT.
I NEED TO GET MY LAST PAYCHECK BEFORE I HEAD OUT OF TOWN.
Crumple Crumple
HNGH...
YOU CAN STAY HERE IF YOU WANT, BUT THE GAS FROM THE STOVE WILL START SMELLING PRETTY STRONG, AND IT'LL ALL BURN REAL QUICK IN THE MORNING WHEN THE WATER HEATER KICKS ON.
OTHERWISE, THE STATION IS RIGHT BY THE HIGHWAY.
YOU CAN CALL FOR A CAB OR A BUS OR ONE OF THOSE *UBERS* FROM THERE.
YES, MR. CHIP.
HE'S READY, ***VICTOR.***

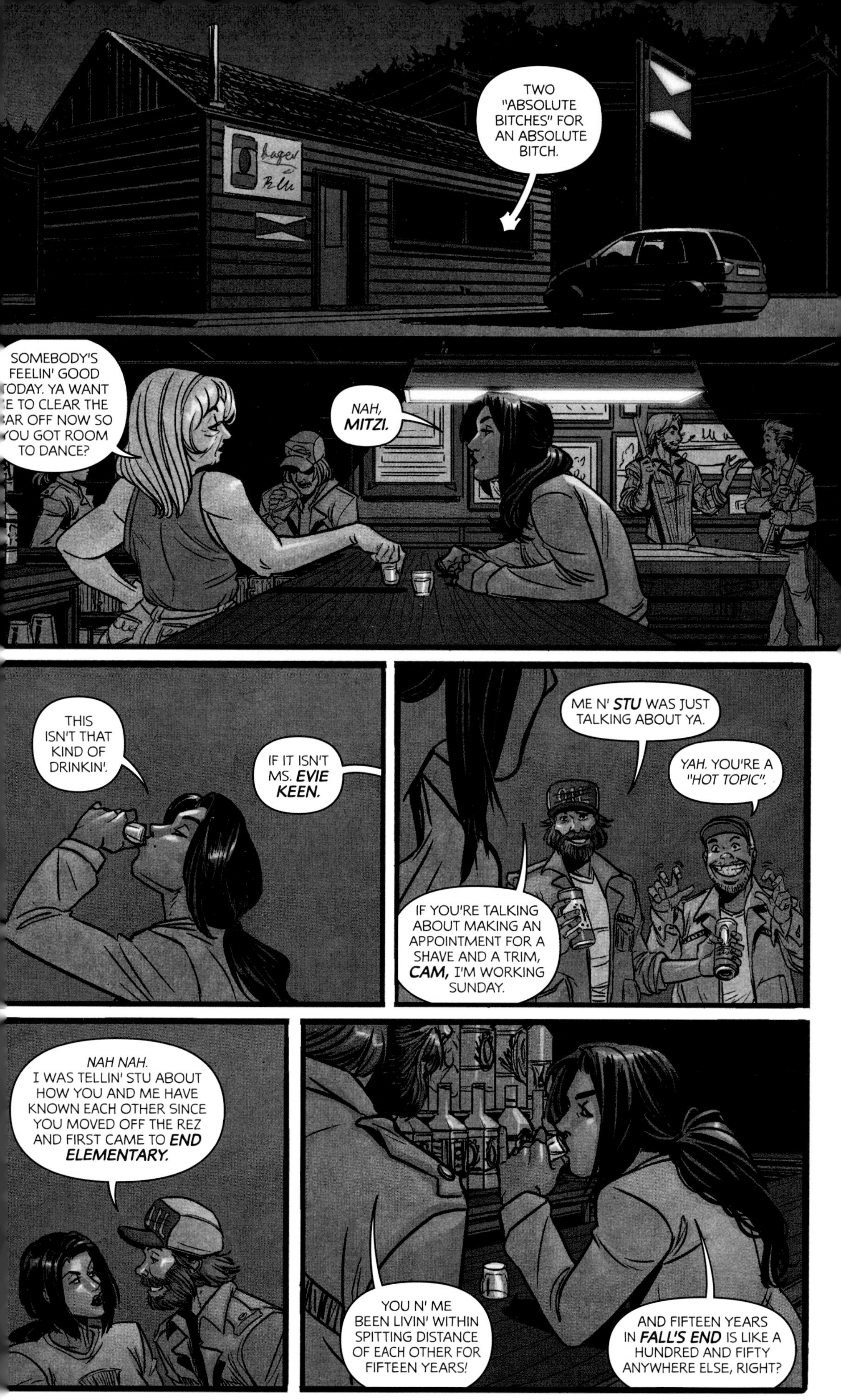
TWO "ABSOLUTE BITCHES" FOR AN ABSOLUTE BITCH.
SOMEBODY'S FEELIN' GOOD TODAY. YA WANT ME TO CLEAR THE BAR OFF NOW SO YOU GOT ROOM TO DANCE?
NAH, MITZI.
THIS ISN'T THAT KIND OF DRINKIN'.
IF IT ISN'T MS. EVIE KEEN.
ME N' STU WAS JUST TALKING ABOUT YA.
YAH. YOU'RE A "HOT TOPIC".
IF YOU'RE TALKING ABOUT MAKING AN APPOINTMENT FOR A SHAVE AND A TRIM, CAM, I'M WORKING SUNDAY.
NAH NAH. I WAS TELLIN' STU ABOUT HOW YOU AND ME HAVE KNOWN EACH OTHER SINCE YOU MOVED OFF THE REZ AND FIRST CAME TO END ELEMENTARY.
YOU N' ME BEEN LIVIN' WITHIN SPITTING DISTANCE OF EACH OTHER FOR FIFTEEN YEARS!
AND FIFTEEN YEARS IN FALL'S END IS LIKE A HUNDRED AND FIFTY ANYWHERE ELSE, RIGHT?

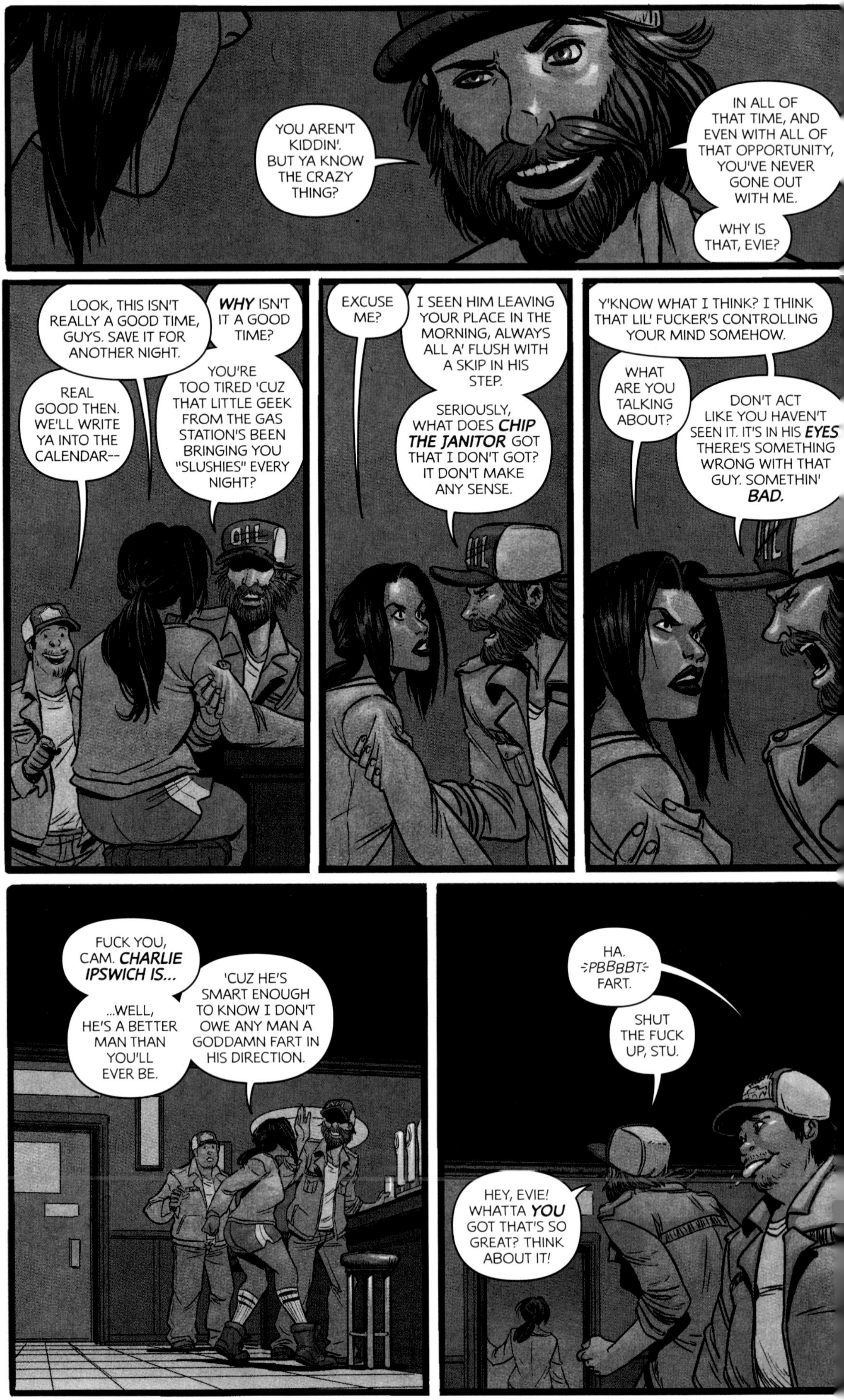
YOU AREN'T KIDDIN'. BUT YA KNOW THE CRAZY THING?
IN ALL OF THAT TIME, AND EVEN WITH ALL OF THAT OPPORTUNITY, YOU'VE NEVER GONE OUT WITH ME.
WHY IS THAT, EVIE?
LOOK, THIS ISN'T REALLY A GOOD TIME, GUYS. SAVE IT FOR ANOTHER NIGHT.
WHY ISN'T IT A GOOD TIME?
REAL GOOD THEN. WE'LL WRITE YA INTO THE CALENDAR--
YOU'RE TOO TIRED 'CUZ THAT LITTLE GEEK FROM THE GAS STATION'S BEEN BRINGING YOU "SLUSHIES" EVERY NIGHT?
EXCUSE ME?
I SEEN HIM LEAVING YOUR PLACE IN THE MORNING, ALWAYS ALL A' FLUSH WITH A SKIP IN HIS STEP.
SERIOUSLY, WHAT DOES CHIP THE JANITOR GOT THAT I DON'T GOT? IT DON'T MAKE ANY SENSE.
Y'KNOW WHAT I THINK? I THINK THAT LIL' FUCKER'S CONTROLLING YOUR MIND SOMEHOW.
WHAT ARE YOU TALKING ABOUT?
DON'T ACT LIKE YOU HAVEN'T SEEN IT. IT'S IN HIS EYES. THERE'S SOMETHING WRONG WITH THAT GUY. SOMETHIN' BAD.
FUCK YOU, CAM. CHARLIE IPSWICH IS...
...WELL, HE'S A BETTER MAN THAN YOU'LL EVER BE.
'CUZ HE'S SMART ENOUGH TO KNOW I DON'T OWE ANY MAN A GODDAMN FART IN HIS DIRECTION.
HA. PBBBBT FART.
SHUT THE FUCK UP, STU.
HEY, EVIE! WHATTA YOU GOT THAT'S SO GREAT? THINK ABOUT IT!

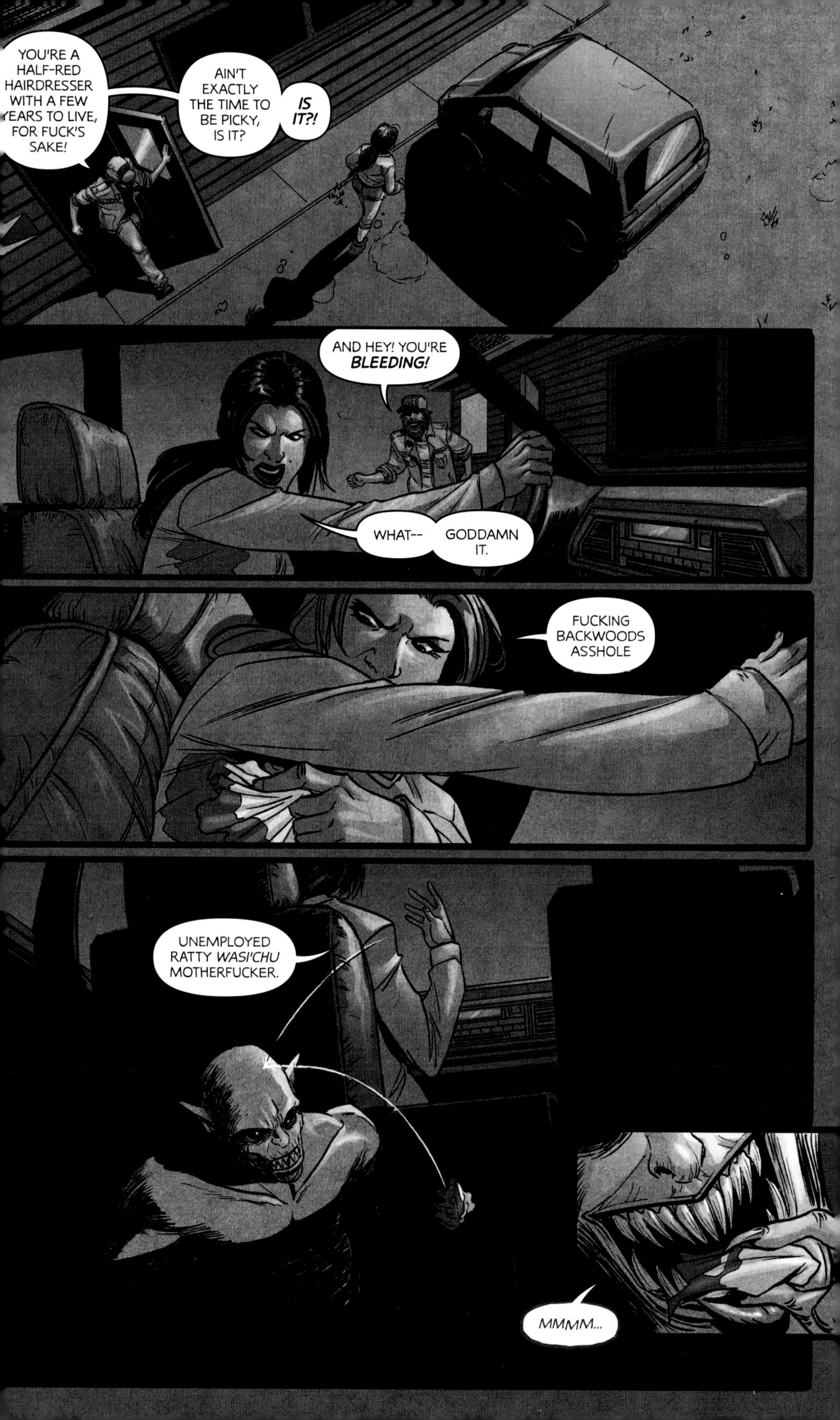

YOU'RE A HALF-RED HAIRDRESSER WITH A FEW YEARS TO LIVE, FOR FUCK'S SAKE!
AIN'T EXACTLY THE TIME TO BE PICKY, IS IT?
IS IT?!
AND HEY! YOU'RE ***BLEEDING!***
WHAT--
GODDAMN IT.
FUCKING BACKWOODS ASSHOLE
UNEMPLOYED RATTY *WASI'CHU* MOTHERFUCKER.
MMMM...

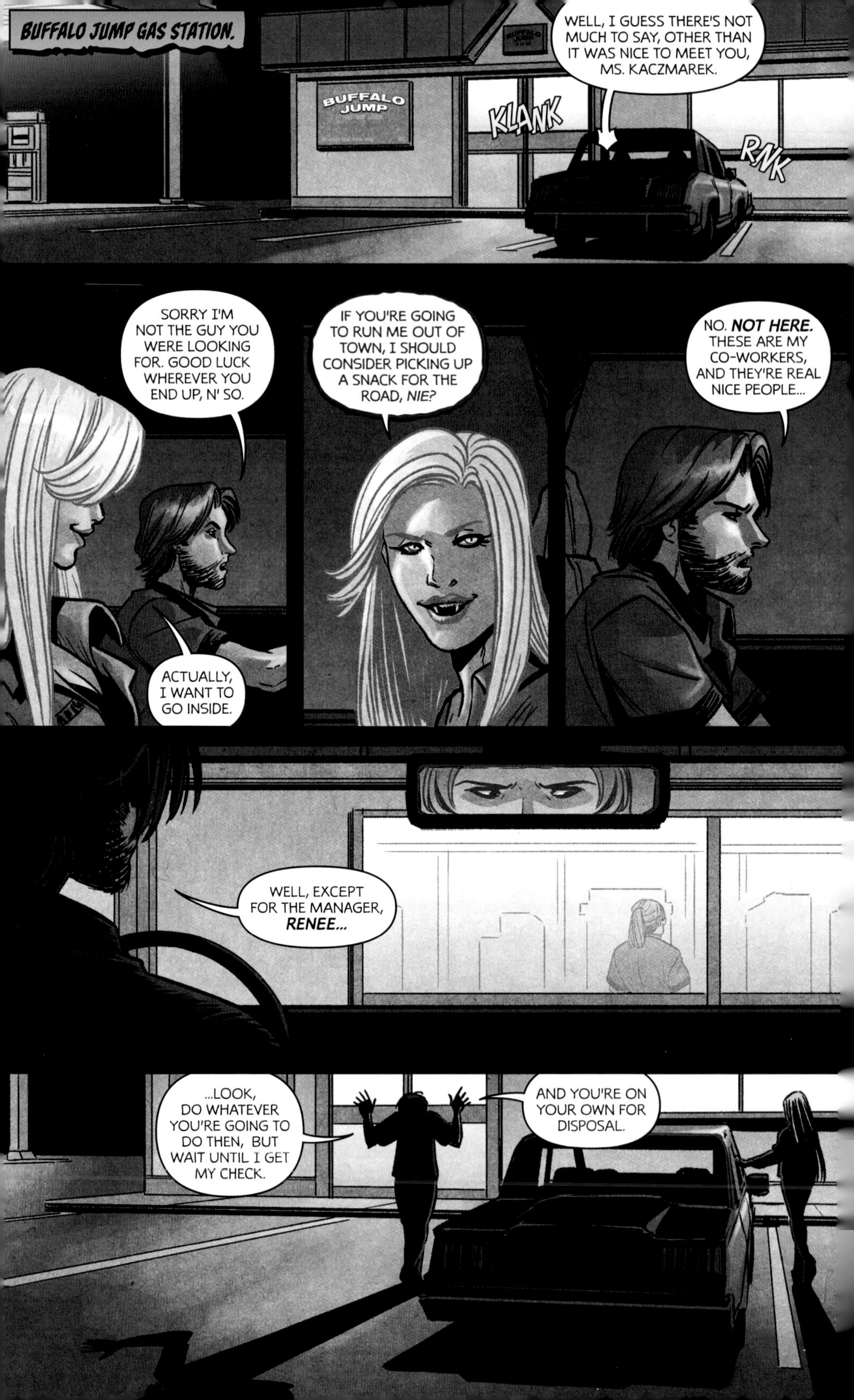
BUFFALO JUMP GAS STATION.
BUFFALO JUMP
WELL, I GUESS THERE'S NOT MUCH TO SAY, OTHER THAN IT WAS NICE TO MEET YOU, MS. KACZMAREK.
KLANK
RNK
SORRY I'M NOT THE GUY YOU WERE LOOKING FOR. GOOD LUCK WHEREVER YOU END UP, N' SO.
ACTUALLY, I WANT TO GO INSIDE.
IF YOU'RE GOING TO RUN ME OUT OF TOWN, I SHOULD CONSIDER PICKING UP A SNACK FOR THE ROAD, *NIE?*
NO. ***NOT HERE.*** THESE ARE MY CO-WORKERS, AND THEY'RE REAL NICE PEOPLE...
WELL, EXCEPT FOR THE MANAGER, ***RENEE...***
...LOOK, DO WHATEVER YOU'RE GOING TO DO THEN, BUT WAIT UNTIL I GET MY CHECK.
AND YOU'RE ON YOUR OWN FOR DISPOSAL.

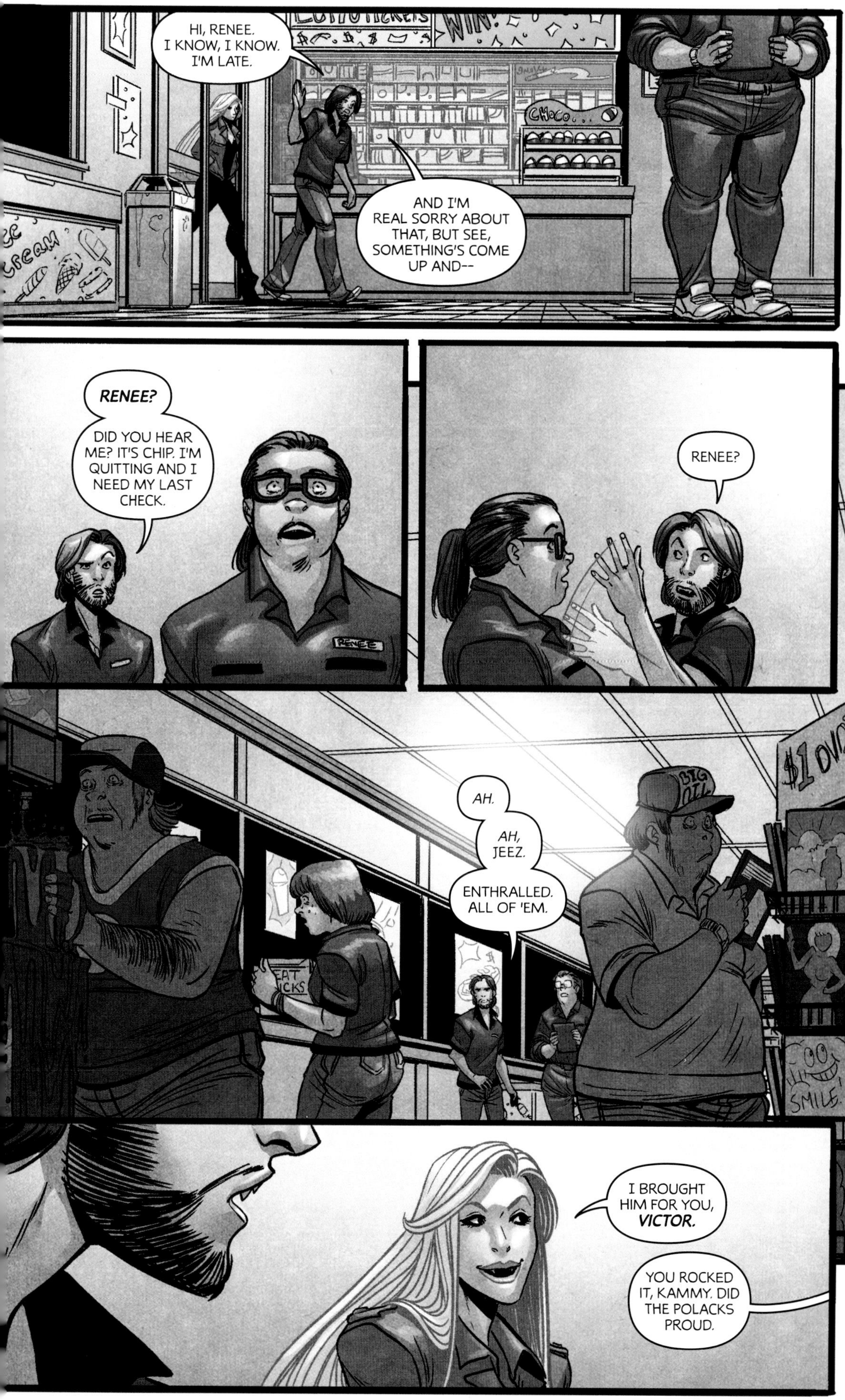
HI, RENEE. I KNOW, I KNOW. I'M LATE.
AND I'M REAL SORRY ABOUT THAT, BUT SEE, SOMETHING'S COME UP AND--
RENEE?
DID YOU HEAR ME? IT'S CHIP. I'M QUITTING AND I NEED MY LAST CHECK.
RENEE
RENEE?
AH.
AH, JEEZ.
ENTHRALLED. ALL OF 'EM.
$1 DVDs
SMILE
I BROUGHT HIM FOR YOU, VICTOR.
YOU ROCKED IT, KAMMY. DID THE POLACKS PROUD.

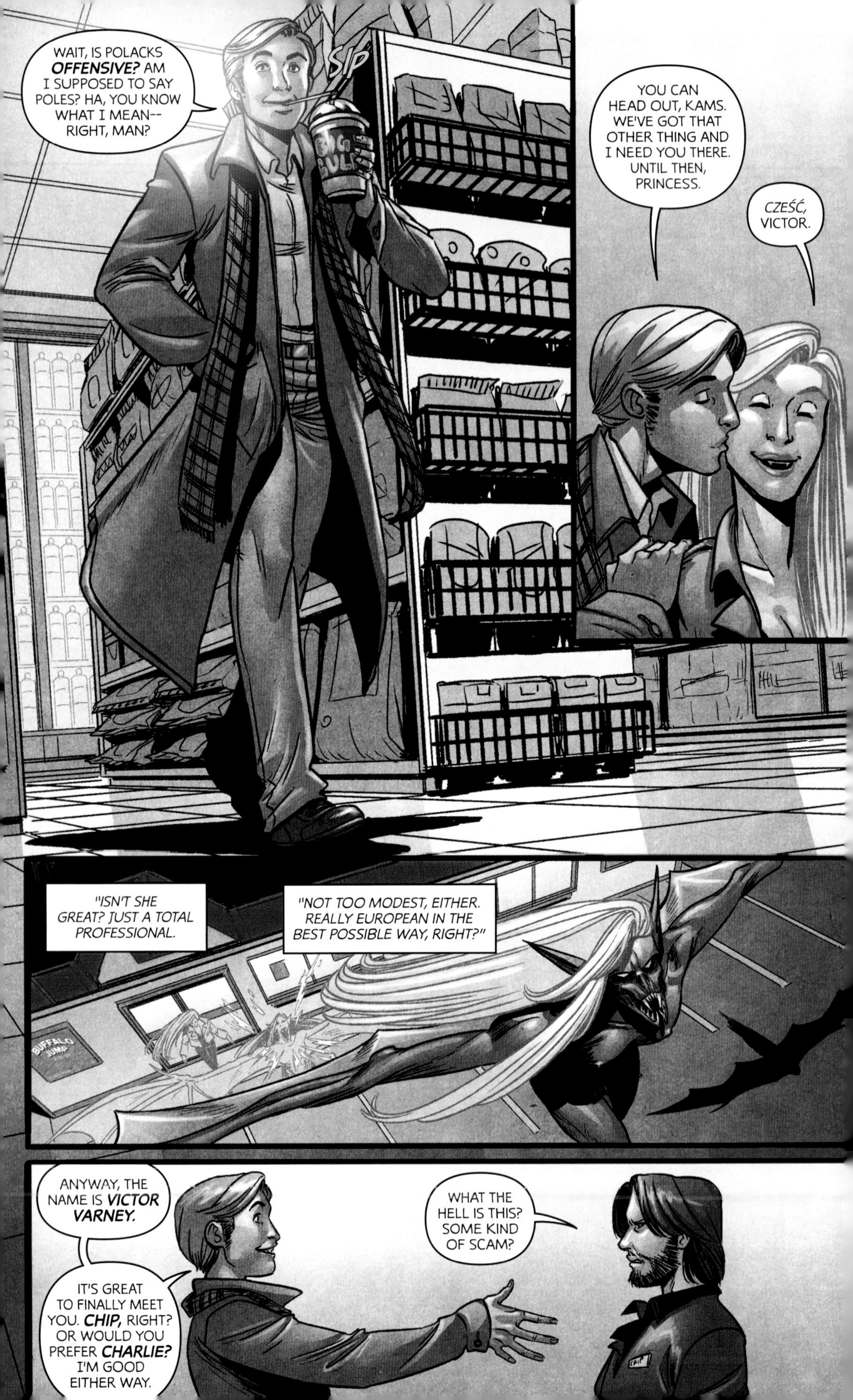
WAIT, IS POLACKS **OFFENSIVE?** AM I SUPPOSED TO SAY POLES? HA, YOU KNOW WHAT I MEAN-- RIGHT, MAN?
SIP
YOU CAN HEAD OUT, KAMS. WE'VE GOT THAT OTHER THING AND I NEED YOU THERE. UNTIL THEN, PRINCESS.
CZEŚĆ, VICTOR.
"ISN'T SHE GREAT? JUST A TOTAL PROFESSIONAL.
"NOT TOO MODEST, EITHER. REALLY EUROPEAN IN THE BEST POSSIBLE WAY, RIGHT?"
BUFFALO JUMP
ANYWAY, THE NAME IS **VICTOR VARNEY.**
IT'S GREAT TO FINALLY MEET YOU. **CHIP,** RIGHT? OR WOULD YOU PREFER **CHARLIE?** I'M GOOD EITHER WAY.
WHAT THE HELL IS THIS? SOME KIND OF SCAM?

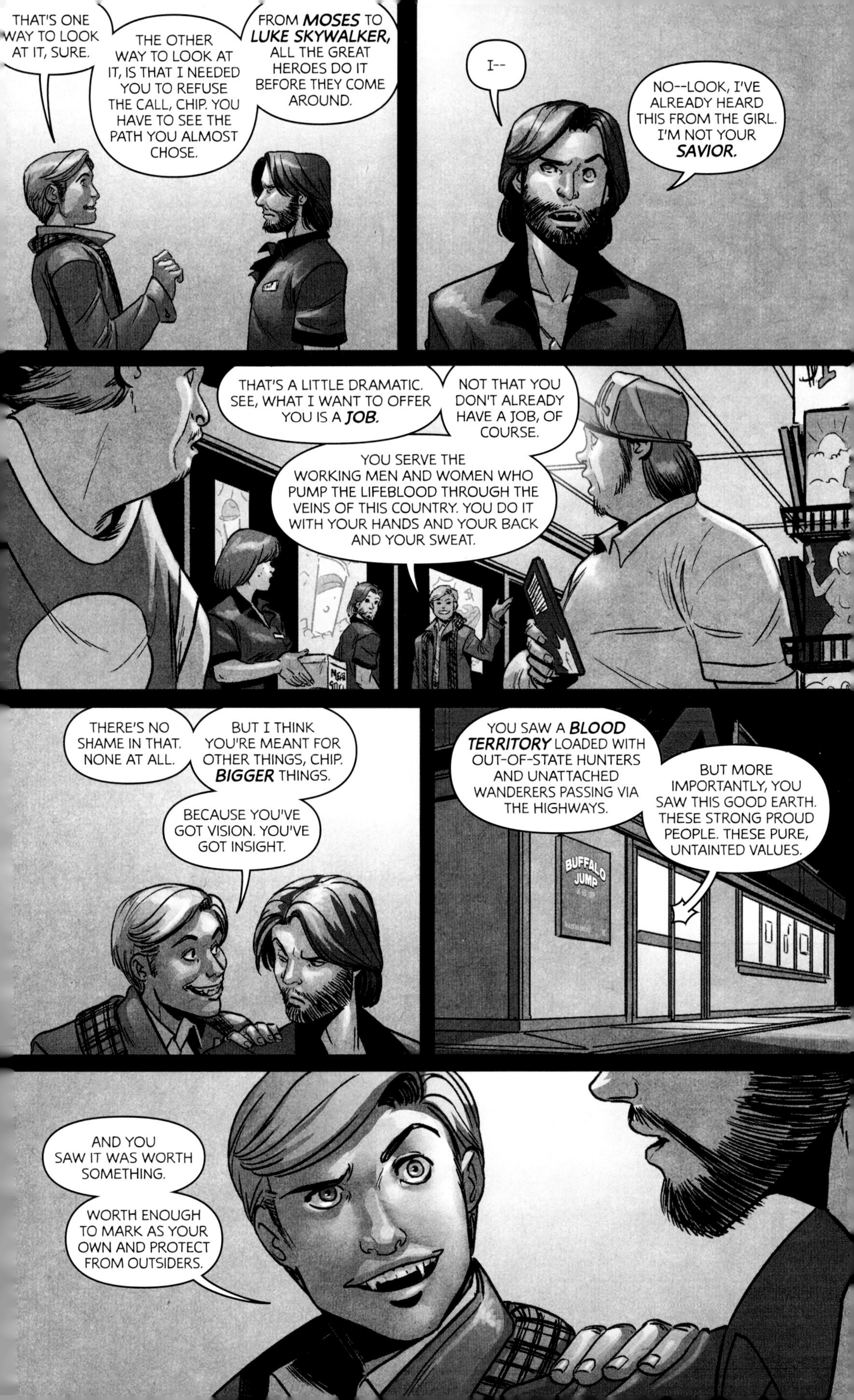
THAT'S ONE WAY TO LOOK AT IT, SURE.
THE OTHER WAY TO LOOK AT IT, IS THAT I NEEDED YOU TO REFUSE THE CALL, CHIP. YOU HAVE TO SEE THE PATH YOU ALMOST CHOSE.
FROM MOSES TO LUKE SKYWALKER, ALL THE GREAT HEROES DO IT BEFORE THEY COME AROUND.
I--
NO--LOOK, I'VE ALREADY HEARD THIS FROM THE GIRL. I'M NOT YOUR SAVIOR.
THAT'S A LITTLE DRAMATIC. SEE, WHAT I WANT TO OFFER YOU IS A JOB.
NOT THAT YOU DON'T ALREADY HAVE A JOB, OF COURSE.
YOU SERVE THE WORKING MEN AND WOMEN WHO PUMP THE LIFEBLOOD THROUGH THE VEINS OF THIS COUNTRY. YOU DO IT WITH YOUR HANDS AND YOUR BACK AND YOUR SWEAT.
THERE'S NO SHAME IN THAT. NONE AT ALL.
BUT I THINK YOU'RE MEANT FOR OTHER THINGS, CHIP. BIGGER THINGS.
BECAUSE YOU'VE GOT VISION. YOU'VE GOT INSIGHT.
YOU SAW A BLOOD TERRITORY LOADED WITH OUT-OF-STATE HUNTERS AND UNATTACHED WANDERERS PASSING VIA THE HIGHWAYS.
BUFFALO JUMP
BUT MORE IMPORTANTLY, YOU SAW THIS GOOD EARTH. THESE STRONG PROUD PEOPLE. THESE PURE, UNTAINTED VALUES.
AND YOU SAW IT WAS WORTH SOMETHING.
WORTH ENOUGH TO MARK AS YOUR OWN AND PROTECT FROM OUTSIDERS.

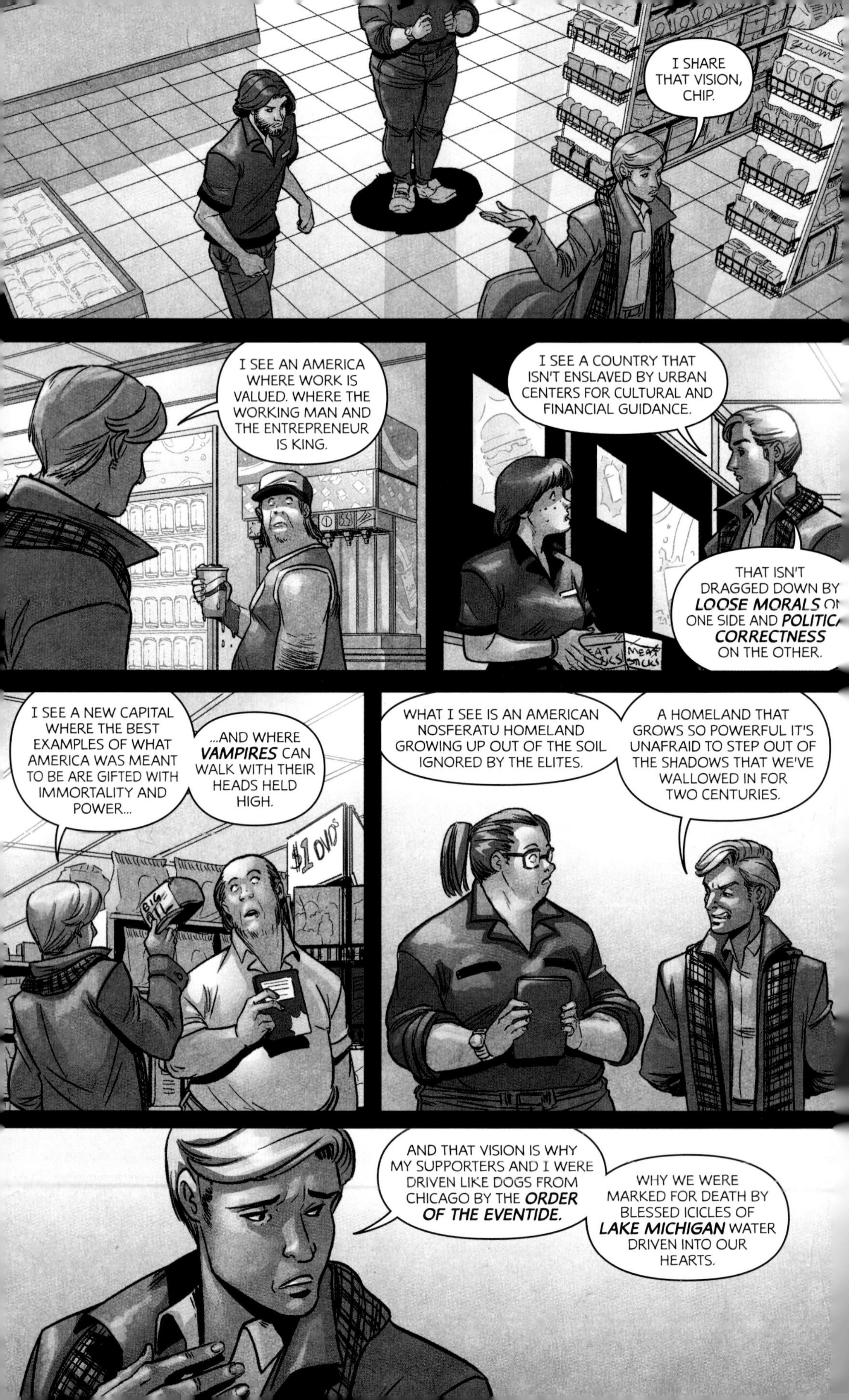
I SHARE THAT VISION, CHIP.
I SEE AN AMERICA WHERE WORK IS VALUED. WHERE THE WORKING MAN AND THE ENTREPRENEUR IS KING.
I SEE A COUNTRY THAT ISN'T ENSLAVED BY URBAN CENTERS FOR CULTURAL AND FINANCIAL GUIDANCE.
THAT ISN'T DRAGGED DOWN BY ***LOOSE MORALS*** ON ONE SIDE AND ***POLITICAL CORRECTNESS*** ON THE OTHER.
I SEE A NEW CAPITAL WHERE THE BEST EXAMPLES OF WHAT AMERICA WAS MEANT TO BE ARE GIFTED WITH IMMORTALITY AND POWER...
...AND WHERE ***VAMPIRES*** CAN WALK WITH THEIR HEADS HELD HIGH.
$1 DVDS
WHAT I SEE IS AN AMERICAN NOSFERATU HOMELAND GROWING UP OUT OF THE SOIL IGNORED BY THE ELITES.
A HOMELAND THAT GROWS SO POWERFUL IT'S UNAFRAID TO STEP OUT OF THE SHADOWS THAT WE'VE WALLOWED IN FOR TWO CENTURIES.
AND THAT VISION IS WHY MY SUPPORTERS AND I WERE DRIVEN LIKE DOGS FROM CHICAGO BY THE ***ORDER OF THE EVENTIDE.***
WHY WE WERE MARKED FOR DEATH BY BLESSED ICICLES OF ***LAKE MICHIGAN*** WATER DRIVEN INTO OUR HEARTS.

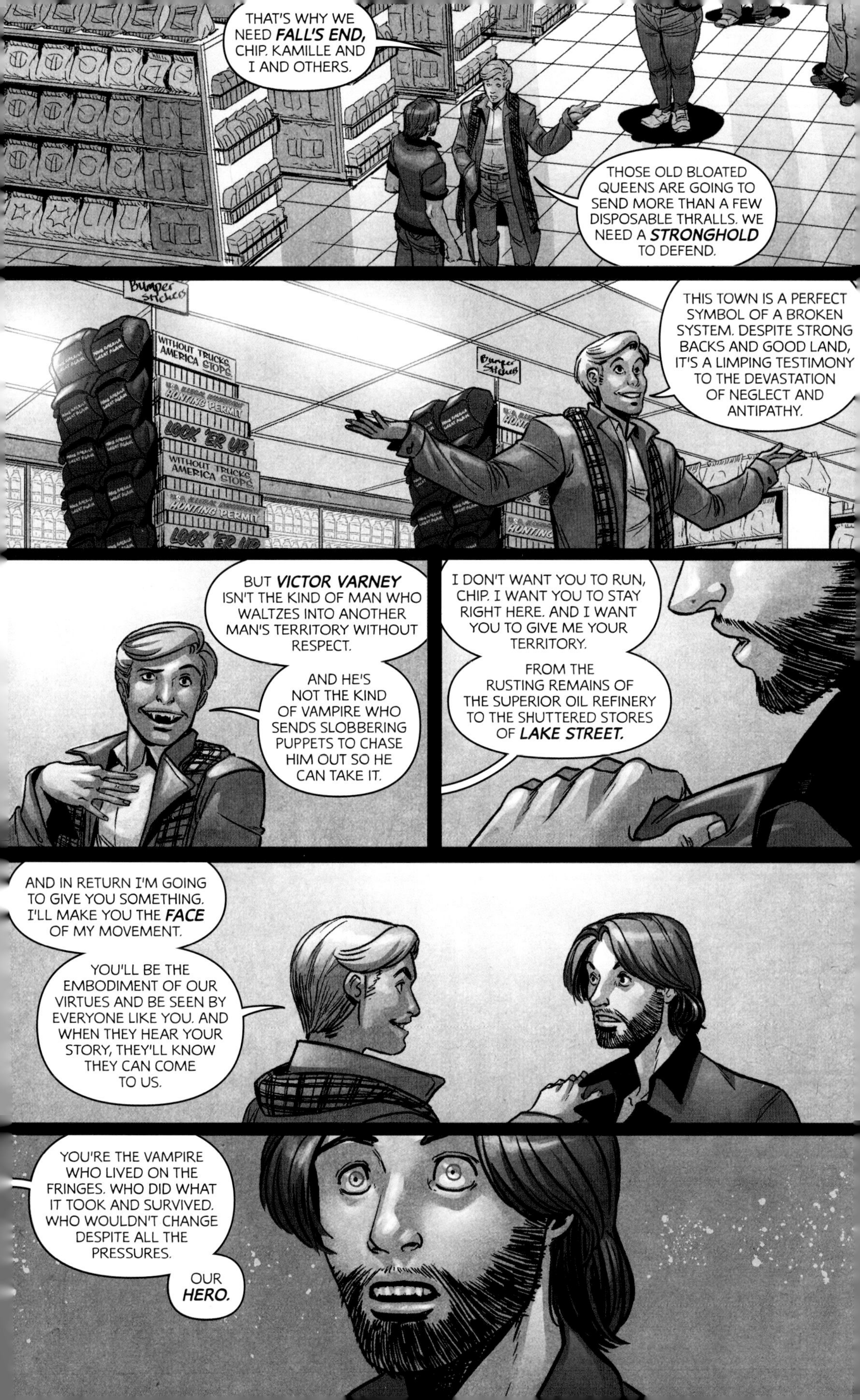

THAT'S WHY WE NEED FALL'S END, CHIP. KAMILLE AND I AND OTHERS.
THOSE OLD BLOATED QUEENS ARE GOING TO SEND MORE THAN A FEW DISPOSABLE THRALLS. WE NEED A STRONGHOLD TO DEFEND.
THIS TOWN IS A PERFECT SYMBOL OF A BROKEN SYSTEM. DESPITE STRONG BACKS AND GOOD LAND, IT'S A LIMPING TESTIMONY TO THE DEVASTATION OF NEGLECT AND ANTIPATHY.
BUT VICTOR VARNEY ISN'T THE KIND OF MAN WHO WALTZES INTO ANOTHER MAN'S TERRITORY WITHOUT RESPECT.
AND HE'S NOT THE KIND OF VAMPIRE WHO SENDS SLOBBERING PUPPETS TO CHASE HIM OUT SO HE CAN TAKE IT.
I DON'T WANT YOU TO RUN, CHIP. I WANT YOU TO STAY RIGHT HERE. AND I WANT YOU TO GIVE ME YOUR TERRITORY.
FROM THE RUSTING REMAINS OF THE SUPERIOR OIL REFINERY TO THE SHUTTERED STORES OF LAKE STREET.
AND IN RETURN I'M GOING TO GIVE YOU SOMETHING. I'LL MAKE YOU THE FACE OF MY MOVEMENT.
YOU'LL BE THE EMBODIMENT OF OUR VIRTUES AND BE SEEN BY EVERYONE LIKE YOU. AND WHEN THEY HEAR YOUR STORY, THEY'LL KNOW THEY CAN COME TO US.
YOU'RE THE VAMPIRE WHO LIVED ON THE FRINGES. WHO DID WHAT IT TOOK AND SURVIVED. WHO WOULDN'T CHANGE DESPITE ALL THE PRESSURES.
OUR HERO.

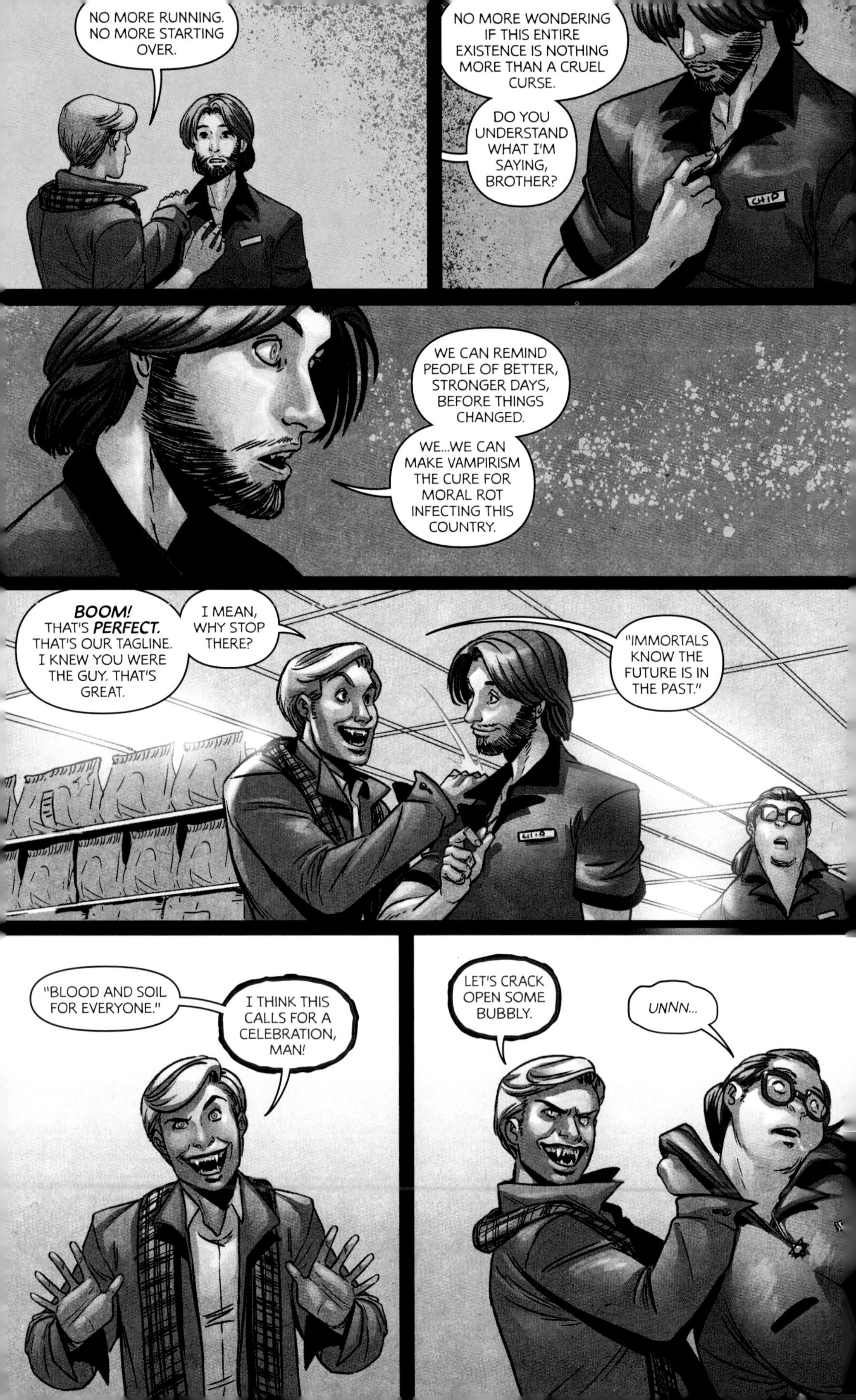
NO MORE RUNNING. NO MORE STARTING OVER.
NO MORE WONDERING IF THIS ENTIRE EXISTENCE IS NOTHING MORE THAN A CRUEL CURSE.
DO YOU UNDERSTAND WHAT I'M SAYING, BROTHER?
CHIP
WE CAN REMIND PEOPLE OF BETTER, STRONGER DAYS, BEFORE THINGS CHANGED.
WE...WE CAN MAKE VAMPIRISM THE CURE FOR MORAL ROT INFECTING THIS COUNTRY.
"IMMORTALS KNOW THE FUTURE IS IN THE PAST."
BOOM! THAT'S ***PERFECT.*** THAT'S OUR TAGLINE. I KNEW YOU WERE THE GUY. THAT'S GREAT.
I MEAN, WHY STOP THERE?
"BLOOD AND SOIL FOR EVERYONE."
I THINK THIS CALLS FOR A CELEBRATION, MAN!
LET'S CRACK OPEN SOME BUBBLY.
UNNN...

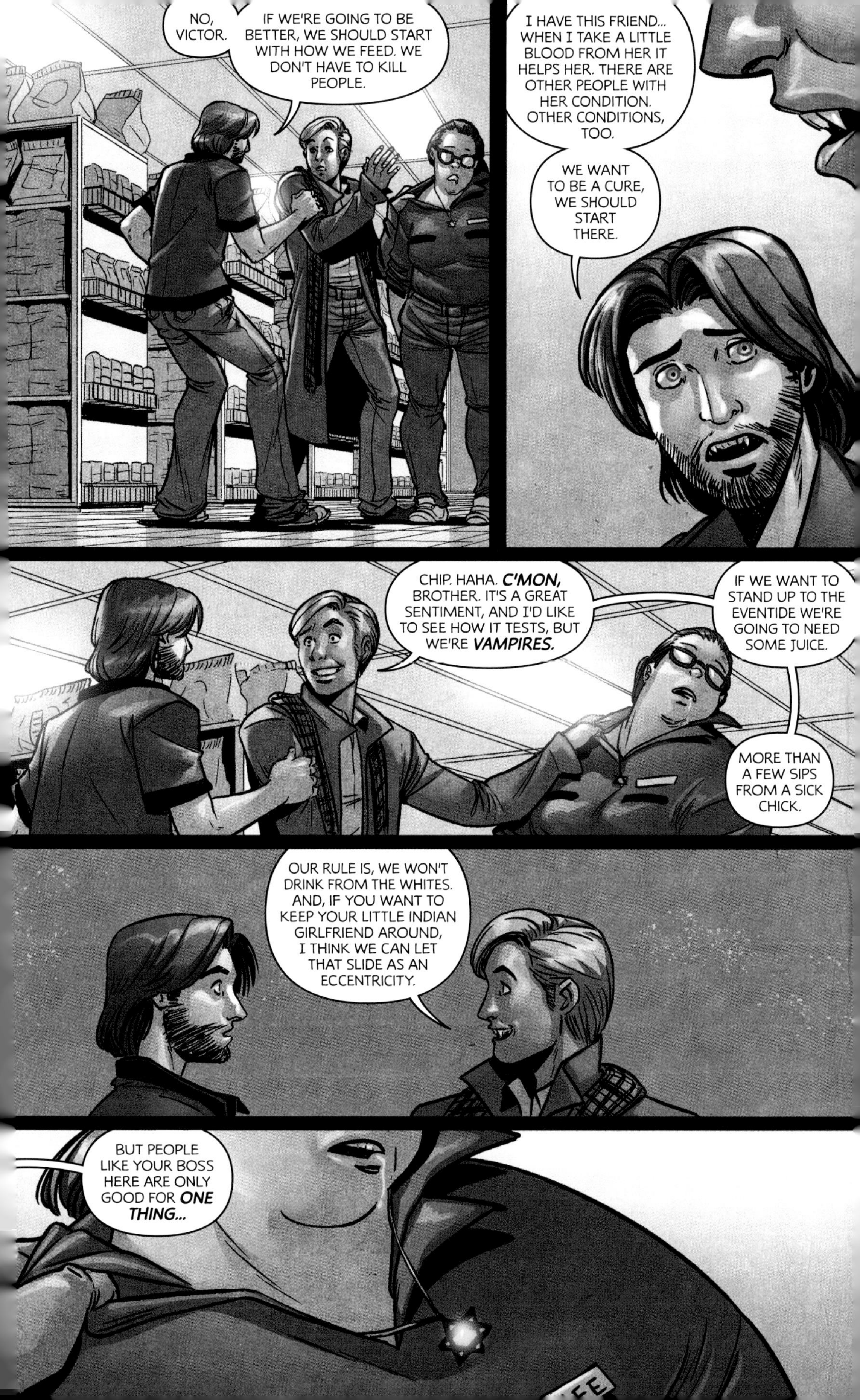
NO, VICTOR.
IF WE'RE GOING TO BE BETTER, WE SHOULD START WITH HOW WE FEED. WE DON'T HAVE TO KILL PEOPLE.
I HAVE THIS FRIEND... WHEN I TAKE A LITTLE BLOOD FROM HER IT HELPS HER. THERE ARE OTHER PEOPLE WITH HER CONDITION. OTHER CONDITIONS, TOO.
WE WANT TO BE A CURE, WE SHOULD START THERE.
CHIP. HAHA. **C'MON,** BROTHER. IT'S A GREAT SENTIMENT, AND I'D LIKE TO SEE HOW IT TESTS, BUT WE'RE ***VAMPIRES.***
IF WE WANT TO STAND UP TO THE EVENTIDE WE'RE GOING TO NEED SOME JUICE.
MORE THAN A FEW SIPS FROM A SICK CHICK.
OUR RULE IS, WE WON'T DRINK FROM THE WHITES. AND, IF YOU WANT TO KEEP YOUR LITTLE INDIAN GIRLFRIEND AROUND, I THINK WE CAN LET THAT SLIDE AS AN ECCENTRICITY.
BUT PEOPLE LIKE YOUR BOSS HERE ARE ONLY GOOD FOR ***ONE THING...***

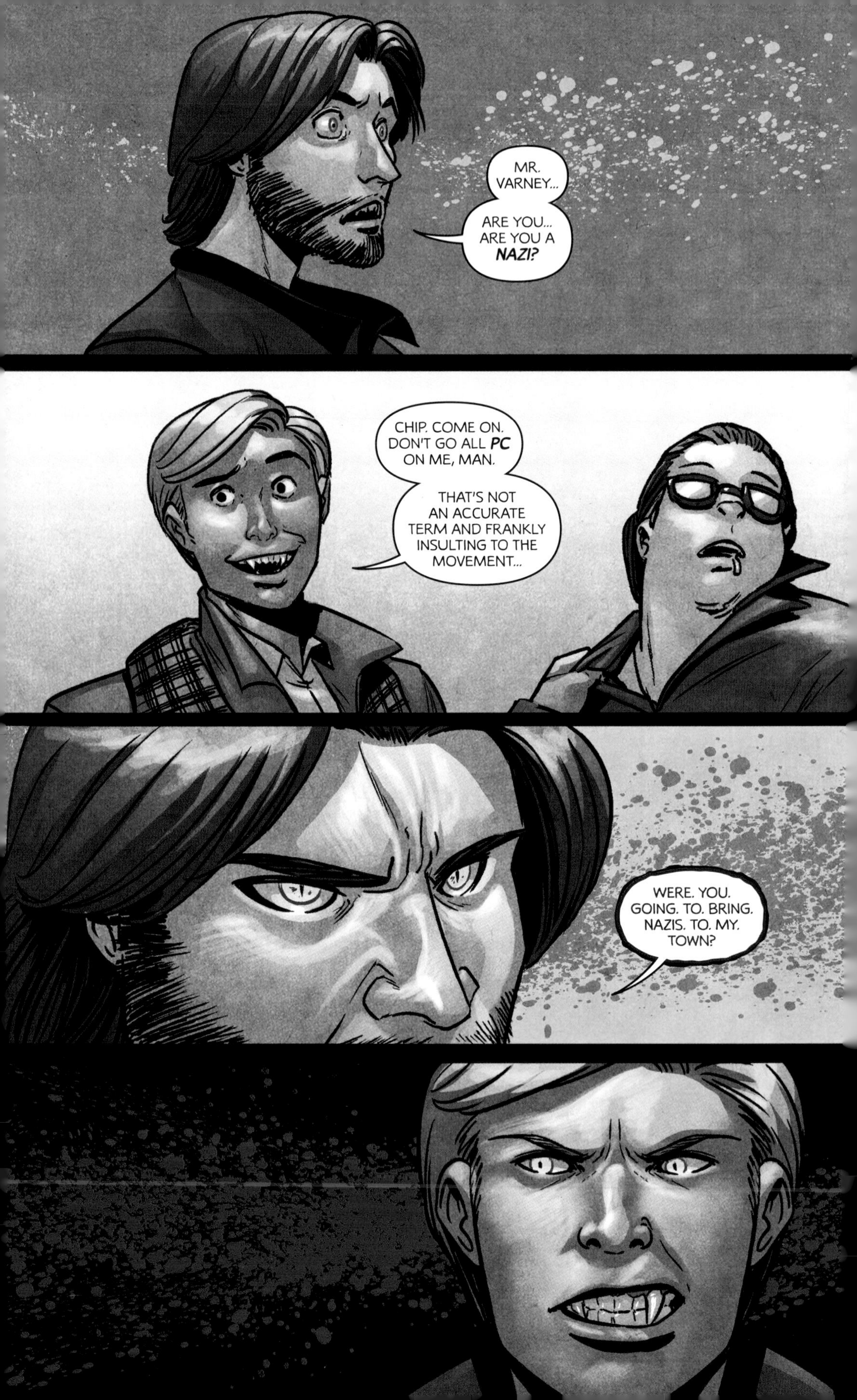
MR. VARNEY...
ARE YOU... ARE YOU A **NAZI?**
CHIP. COME ON. DON'T GO ALL **PC** ON ME, MAN.
THAT'S NOT AN ACCURATE TERM AND FRANKLY INSULTING TO THE MOVEMENT...
WERE. YOU. GOING. TO. BRING. NAZIS. TO. MY. TOWN?

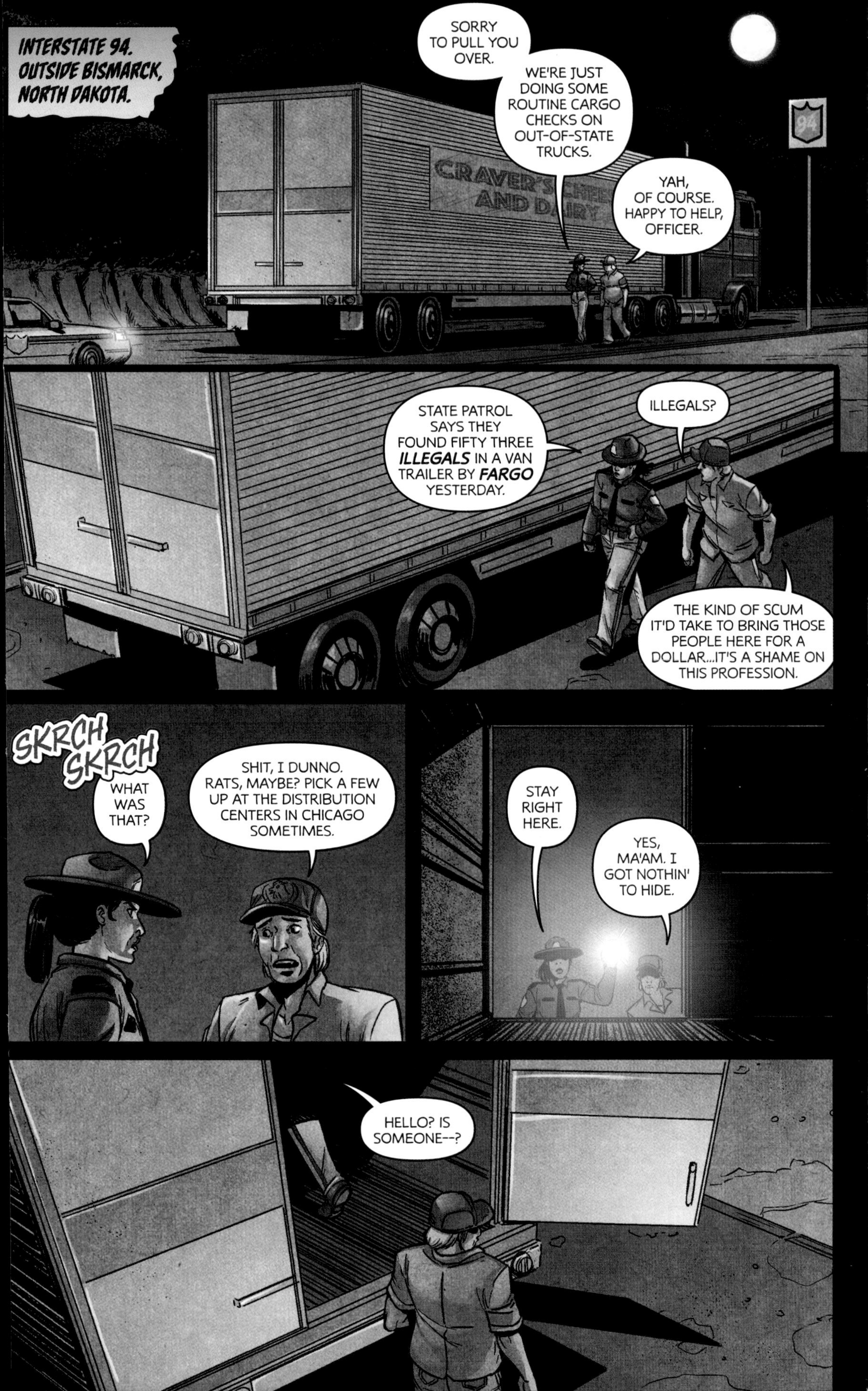
INTERSTATE 94. OUTSIDE BISMARCK, NORTH DAKOTA.
SORRY TO PULL YOU OVER.
WE'RE JUST DOING SOME ROUTINE CARGO CHECKS ON OUT-OF-STATE TRUCKS.
YAH, OF COURSE. HAPPY TO HELP, OFFICER.
94
CRAVER'S CHEE AND DAIRY
STATE PATROL SAYS THEY FOUND FIFTY THREE ILLEGALS IN A VAN TRAILER BY FARGO YESTERDAY.
ILLEGALS?
THE KIND OF SCUM IT'D TAKE TO BRING THOSE PEOPLE HERE FOR A DOLLAR...IT'S A SHAME ON THIS PROFESSION.
SKRCH SKRCH
WHAT WAS THAT?
SHIT, I DUNNO. RATS, MAYBE? PICK A FEW UP AT THE DISTRIBUTION CENTERS IN CHICAGO SOMETIMES.
STAY RIGHT HERE.
YES, MA'AM. I GOT NOTHIN' TO HIDE.
HELLO? IS SOMEONE--?

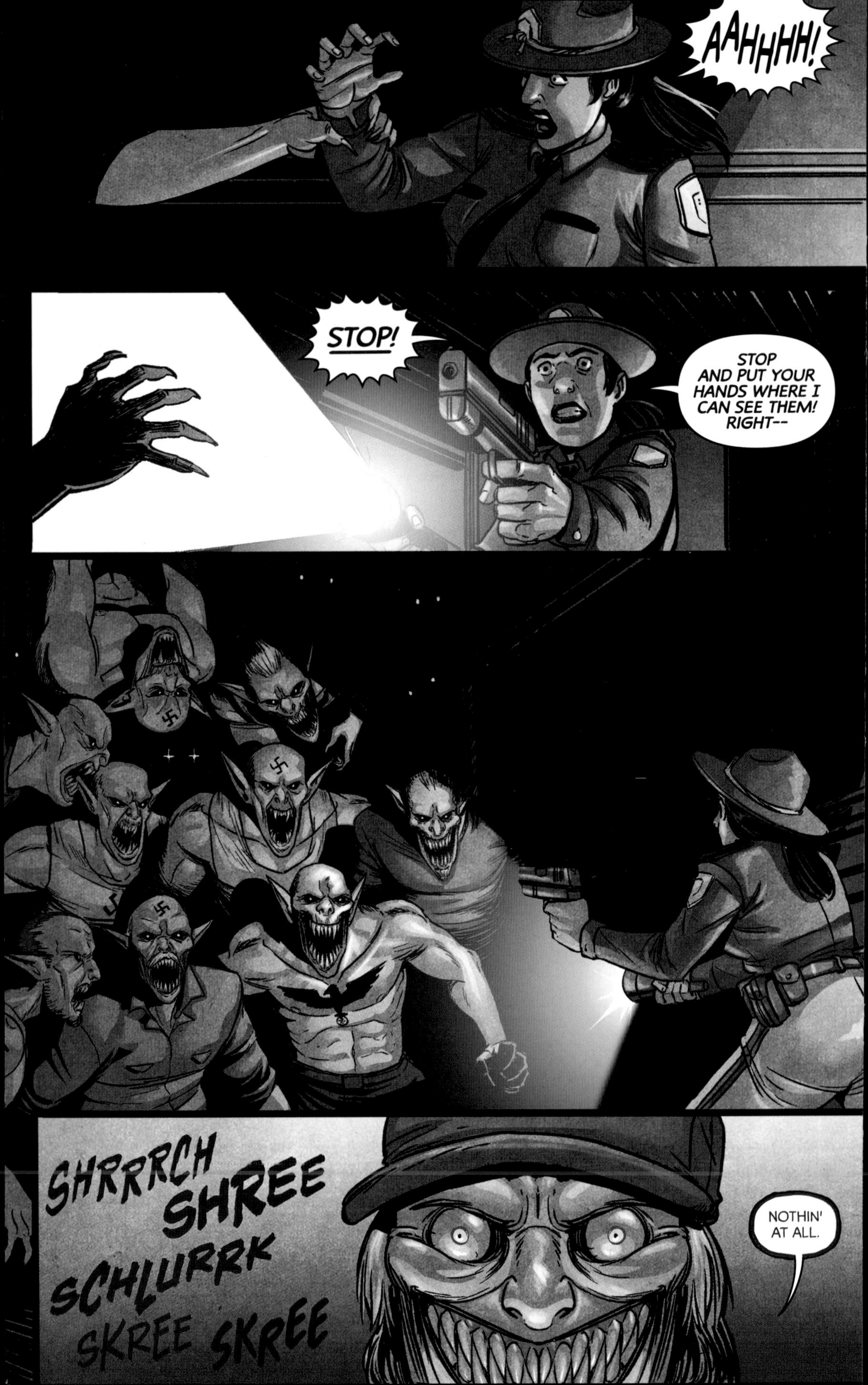
AAHHHH!
STOP!
STOP AND PUT YOUR HANDS WHERE I CAN SEE THEM! RIGHT--
SHRRRCH SHREE SCHLURRK SKREE SKREE
NOTHIN' AT ALL.

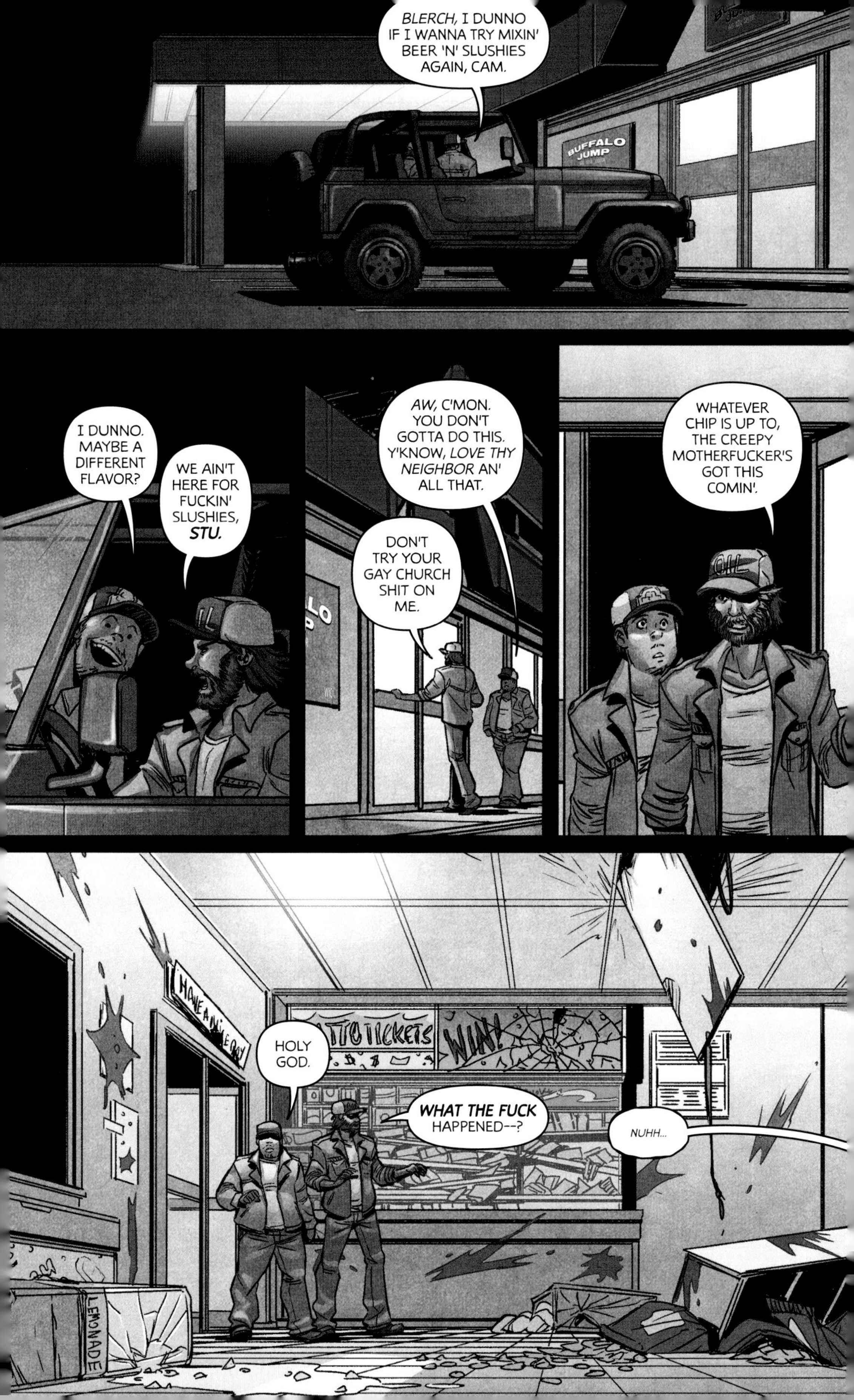
BLERCH, I DUNNO IF I WANNA TRY MIXIN' BEER 'N' SLUSHIES AGAIN, CAM.
BUFFALO JUMP
I DUNNO. MAYBE A DIFFERENT FLAVOR?
WE AIN'T HERE FOR FUCKIN' SLUSHIES, STU.
AW, C'MON. YOU DON'T GOTTA DO THIS. Y'KNOW, LOVE THY NEIGHBOR AN' ALL THAT.
DON'T TRY YOUR GAY CHURCH SHIT ON ME.
WHATEVER CHIP IS UP TO, THE CREEPY MOTHERFUCKER'S GOT THIS COMIN'.
WIN!
HOLY GOD.
WHAT THE FUCK HAPPENED--?
NUHH...
LEMONADE

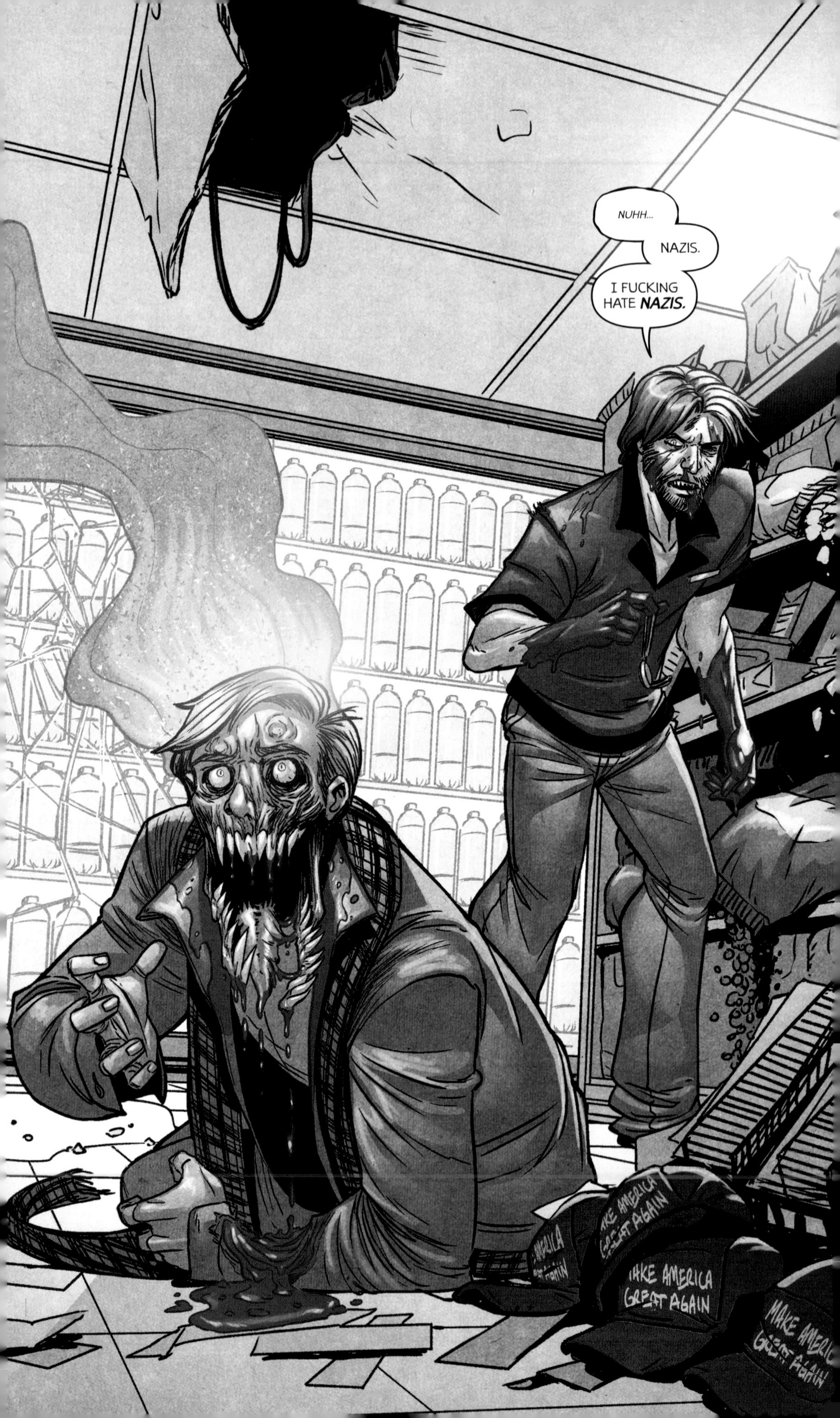
NUHH...
NAZIS.
I FUCKING HATE NAZIS.
MAKE AMERICA GREAT AGAIN
MAKE AMERICA GREAT AGAIN
MAKE AMERICA

3

A LETTER HOME

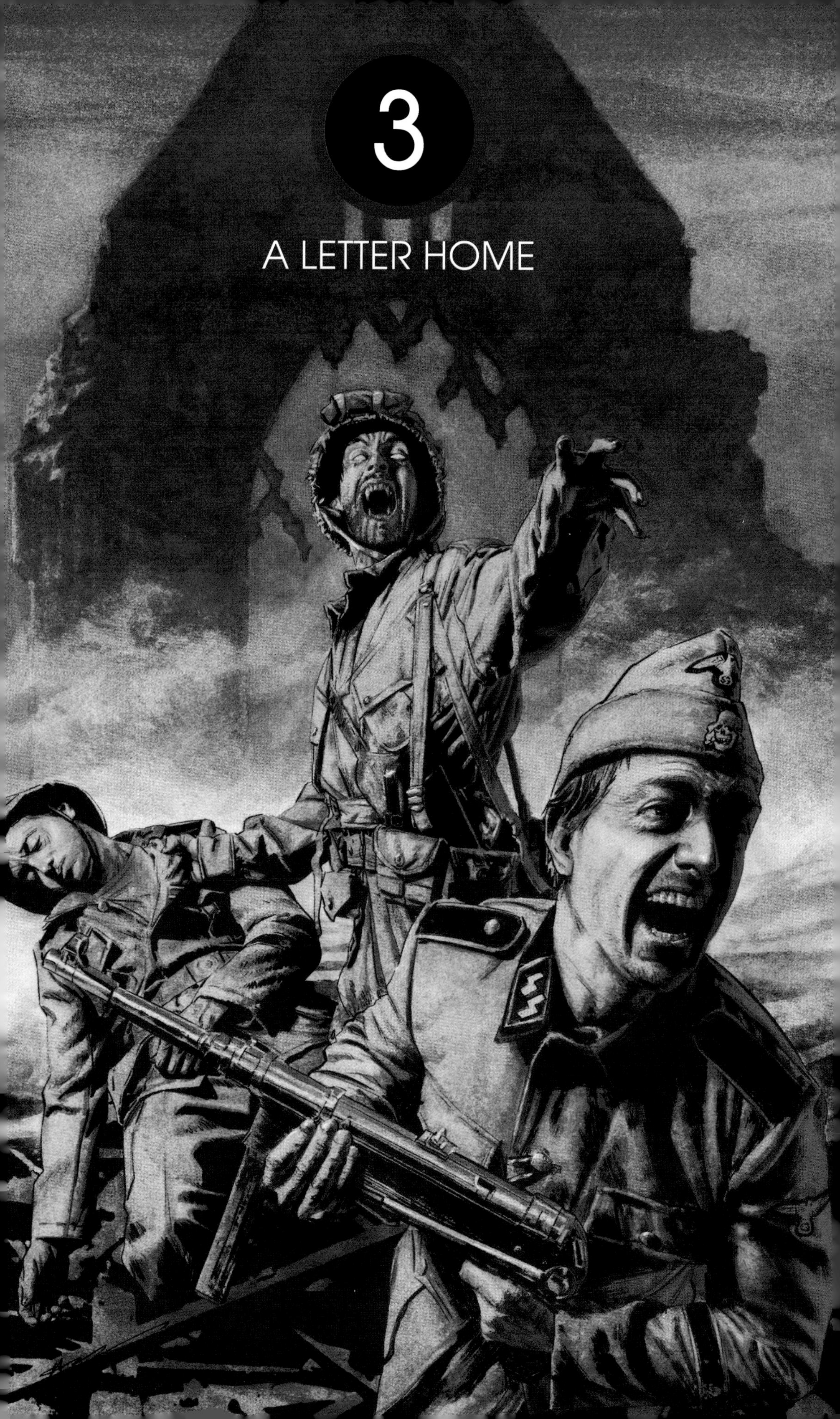

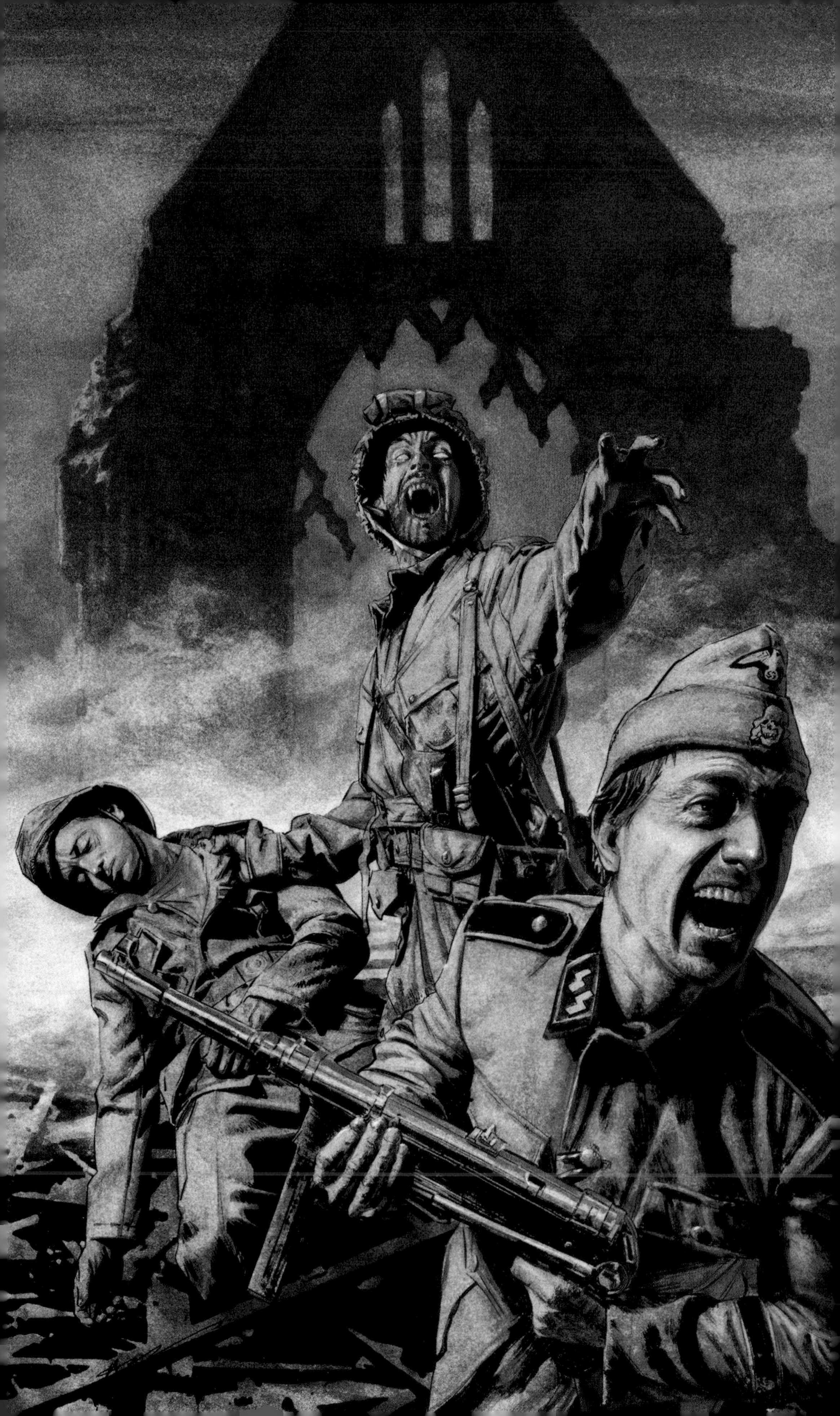

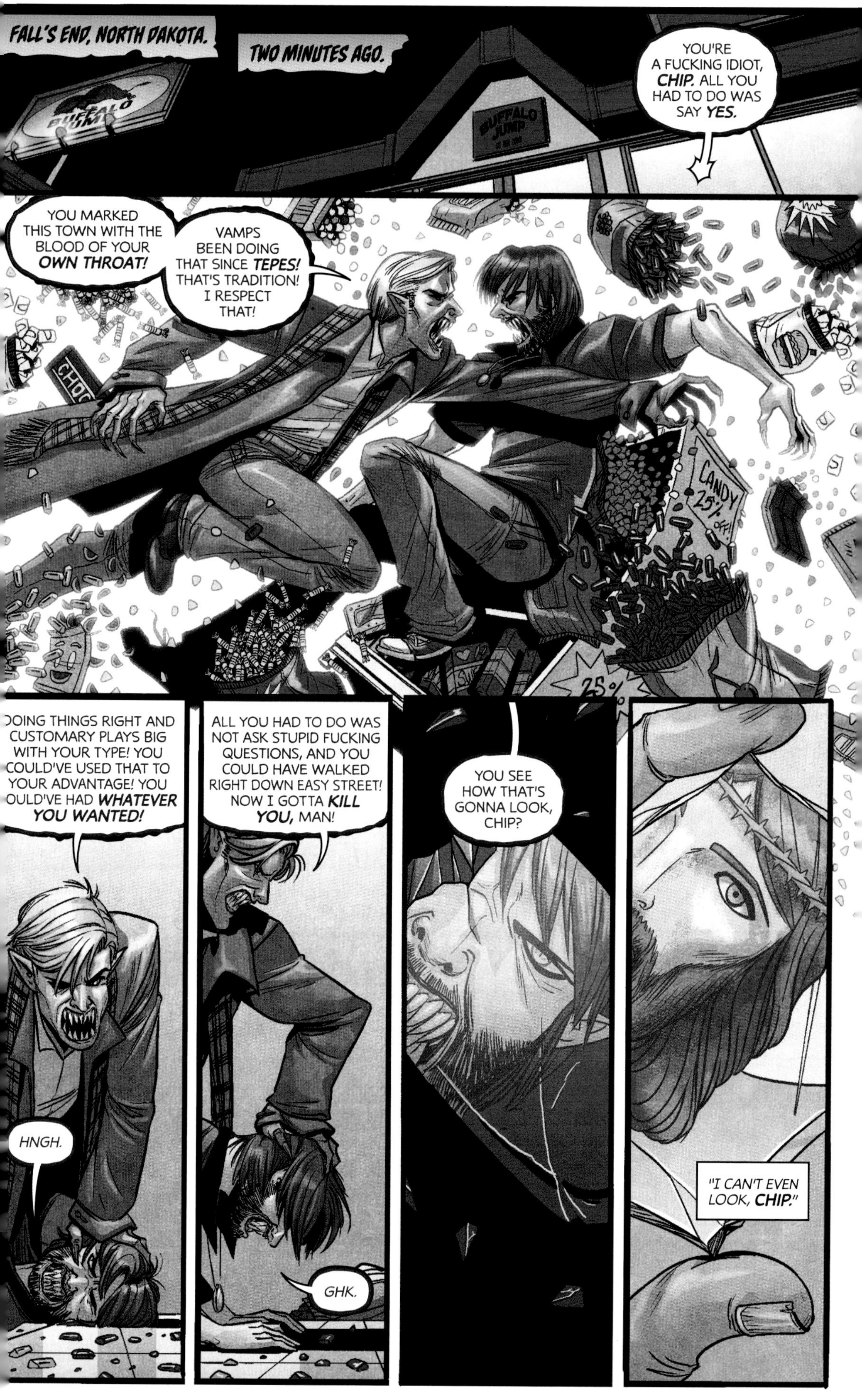
FALL'S END, NORTH DAKOTA.
TWO MINUTES AGO.
YOU'RE A FUCKING IDIOT, CHIP. ALL YOU HAD TO DO WAS SAY YES.
YOU MARKED THIS TOWN WITH THE BLOOD OF YOUR OWN THROAT!
VAMPS BEEN DOING THAT SINCE TEPES! THAT'S TRADITION! I RESPECT THAT!
CANDY 25% OFF!
DOING THINGS RIGHT AND CUSTOMARY PLAYS BIG WITH YOUR TYPE! YOU COULD'VE USED THAT TO YOUR ADVANTAGE! YOU COULD'VE HAD WHATEVER YOU WANTED!
HNGH.
ALL YOU HAD TO DO WAS NOT ASK STUPID FUCKING QUESTIONS, AND YOU COULD HAVE WALKED RIGHT DOWN EASY STREET! NOW I GOTTA KILL YOU, MAN!
GHK.
YOU SEE HOW THAT'S GONNA LOOK, CHIP?
"I CAN'T EVEN LOOK, CHIP."

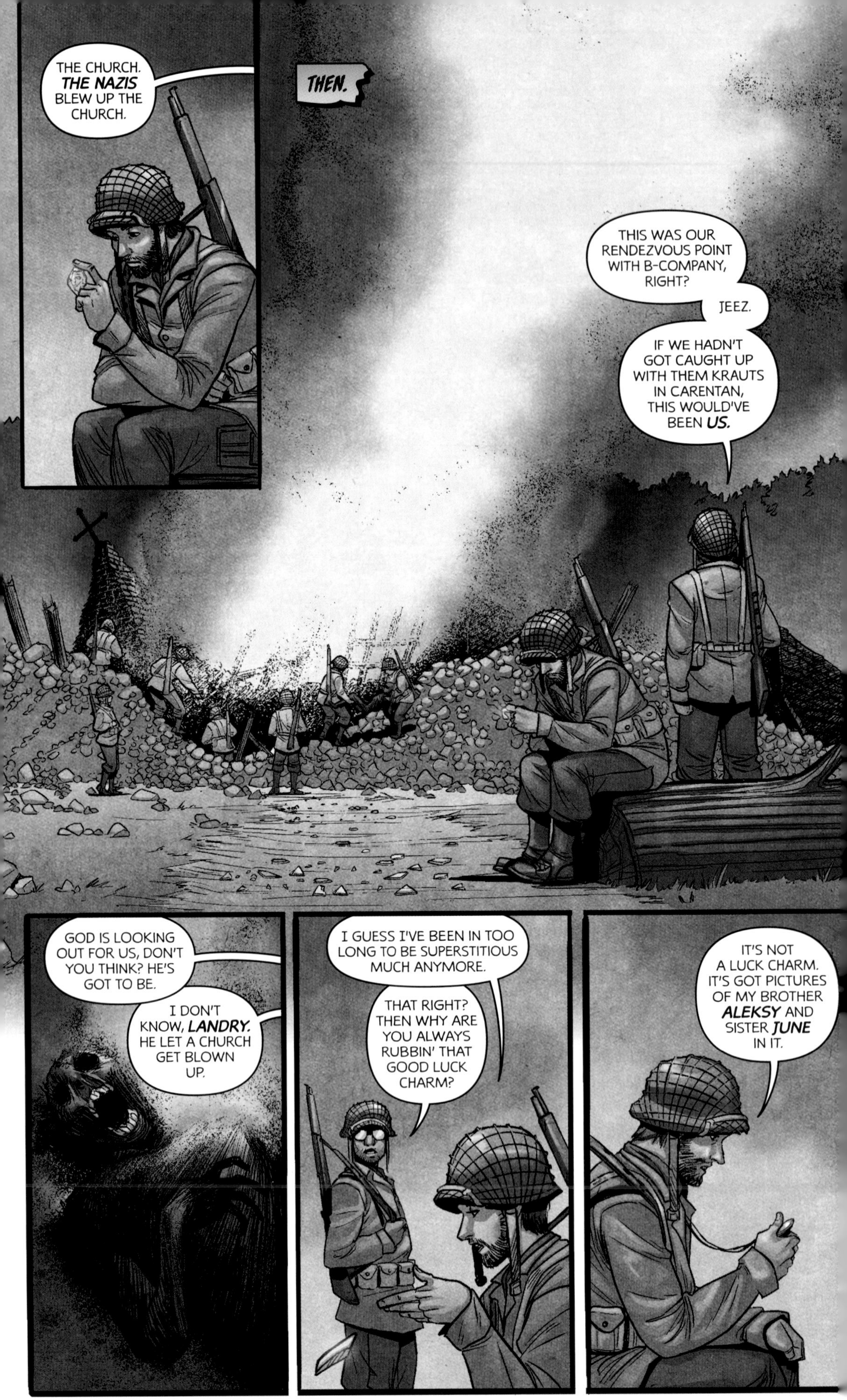
THE CHURCH. THE NAZIS BLEW UP THE CHURCH.
THEN.
THIS WAS OUR RENDEZVOUS POINT WITH B-COMPANY, RIGHT?
JEEZ.
IF WE HADN'T GOT CAUGHT UP WITH THEM KRAUTS IN CARENTAN, THIS WOULD'VE BEEN US.
GOD IS LOOKING OUT FOR US, DON'T YOU THINK? HE'S GOT TO BE.
I DON'T KNOW, LANDRY. HE LET A CHURCH GET BLOWN UP.
I GUESS I'VE BEEN IN TOO LONG TO BE SUPERSTITIOUS MUCH ANYMORE.
THAT RIGHT? THEN WHY ARE YOU ALWAYS RUBBIN' THAT GOOD LUCK CHARM?
IT'S NOT A LUCK CHARM. IT'S GOT PICTURES OF MY BROTHER ALEKSY AND SISTER JUNE IN IT.

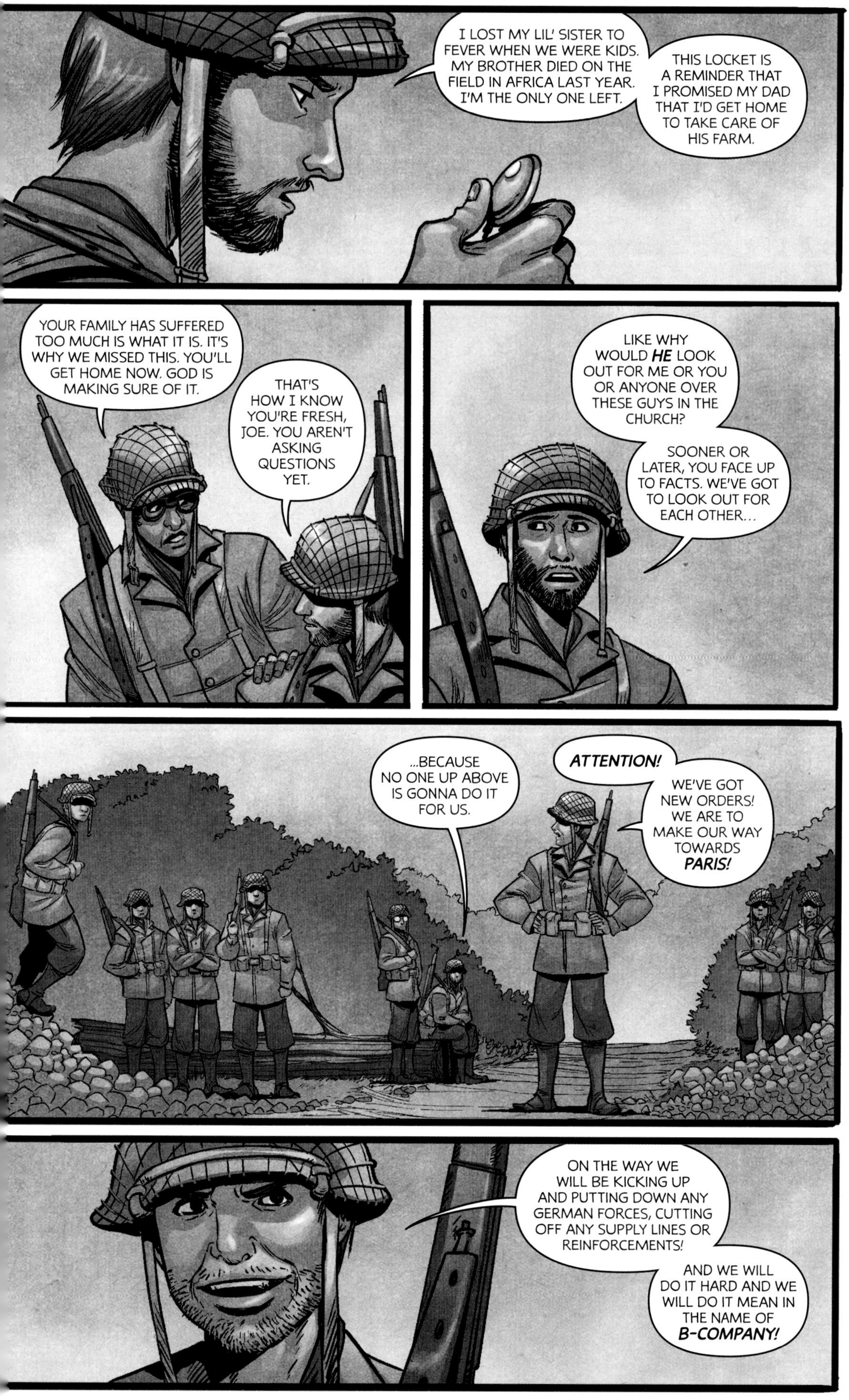

I LOST MY LIL' SISTER TO FEVER WHEN WE WERE KIDS. MY BROTHER DIED ON THE FIELD IN AFRICA LAST YEAR. I'M THE ONLY ONE LEFT.
THIS LOCKET IS A REMINDER THAT I PROMISED MY DAD THAT I'D GET HOME TO TAKE CARE OF HIS FARM.
YOUR FAMILY HAS SUFFERED TOO MUCH IS WHAT IT IS. IT'S WHY WE MISSED THIS. YOU'LL GET HOME NOW. GOD IS MAKING SURE OF IT.
THAT'S HOW I KNOW YOU'RE FRESH, JOE. YOU AREN'T ASKING QUESTIONS YET.
LIKE WHY WOULD *HE* LOOK OUT FOR ME OR YOU OR ANYONE OVER THESE GUYS IN THE CHURCH?
SOONER OR LATER, YOU FACE UP TO FACTS. WE'VE GOT TO LOOK OUT FOR EACH OTHER...
...BECAUSE NO ONE UP ABOVE IS GONNA DO IT FOR US.
ATTENTION!
WE'VE GOT NEW ORDERS! WE ARE TO MAKE OUR WAY TOWARDS ***PARIS!***
ON THE WAY WE WILL BE KICKING UP AND PUTTING DOWN ANY GERMAN FORCES, CUTTING OFF ANY SUPPLY LINES OR REINFORCEMENTS!
AND WE WILL DO IT HARD AND WE WILL DO IT MEAN IN THE NAME OF ***B-COMPANY!***

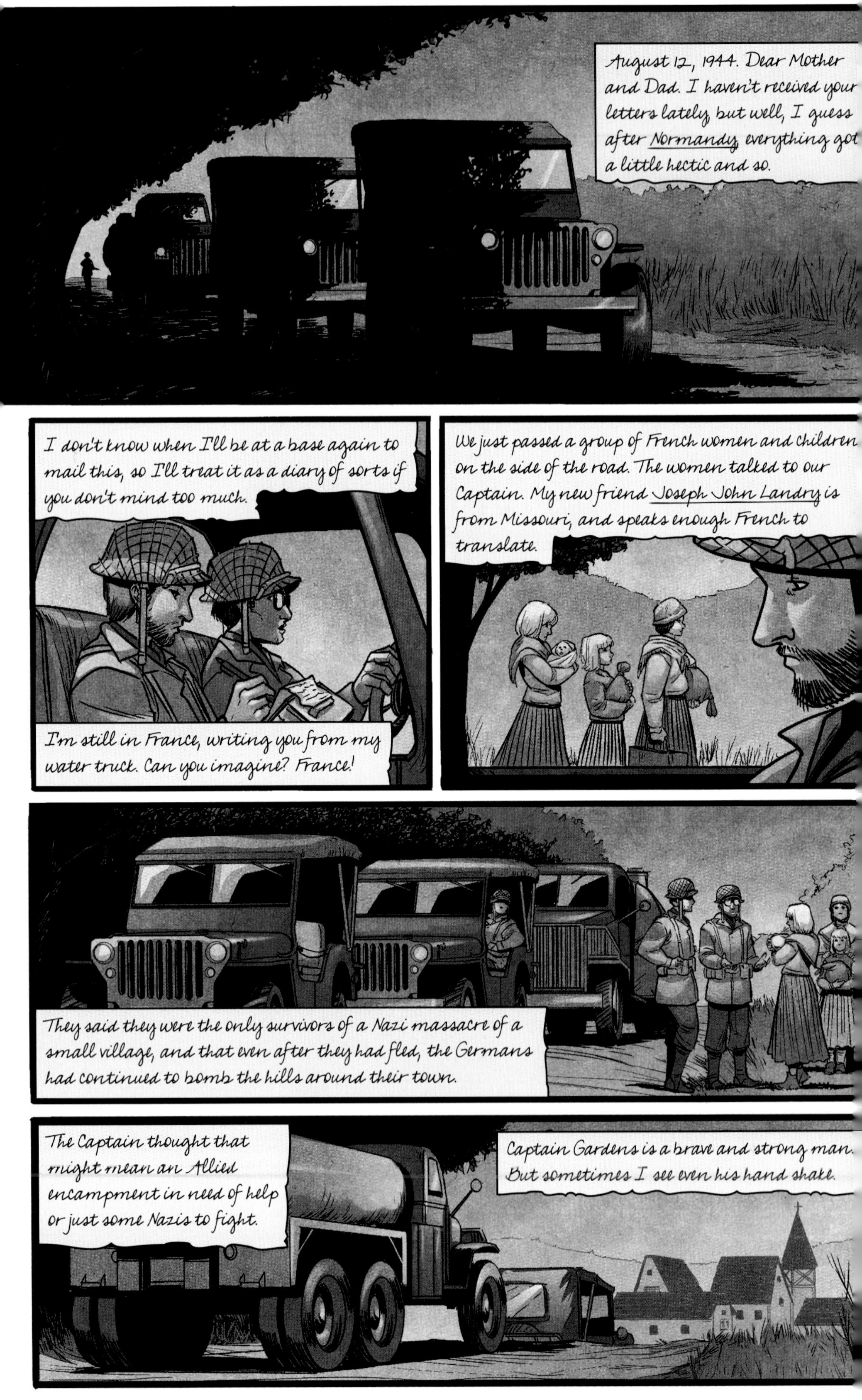
August 12, 1944. Dear Mother and Dad. I haven't received your letters lately, but well, I guess after Normandy everything got a little hectic and so.
I don't know when I'll be at a base again to mail this, so I'll treat it as a diary of sorts if you don't mind too much.
I'm still in France, writing you from my water truck. Can you imagine? France!
We just passed a group of French women and children on the side of the road. The women talked to our Captain. My new friend Joseph John Landry is from Missouri, and speaks enough French to translate.
They said they were the only survivors of a Nazi massacre of a small village, and that even after they had fled, the Germans had continued to bomb the hills around their town.
The Captain thought that might mean an Allied encampment in need of help or just some Nazis to fight.
Captain Gardens is a brave and strong man. But sometimes I see even his hand shake.

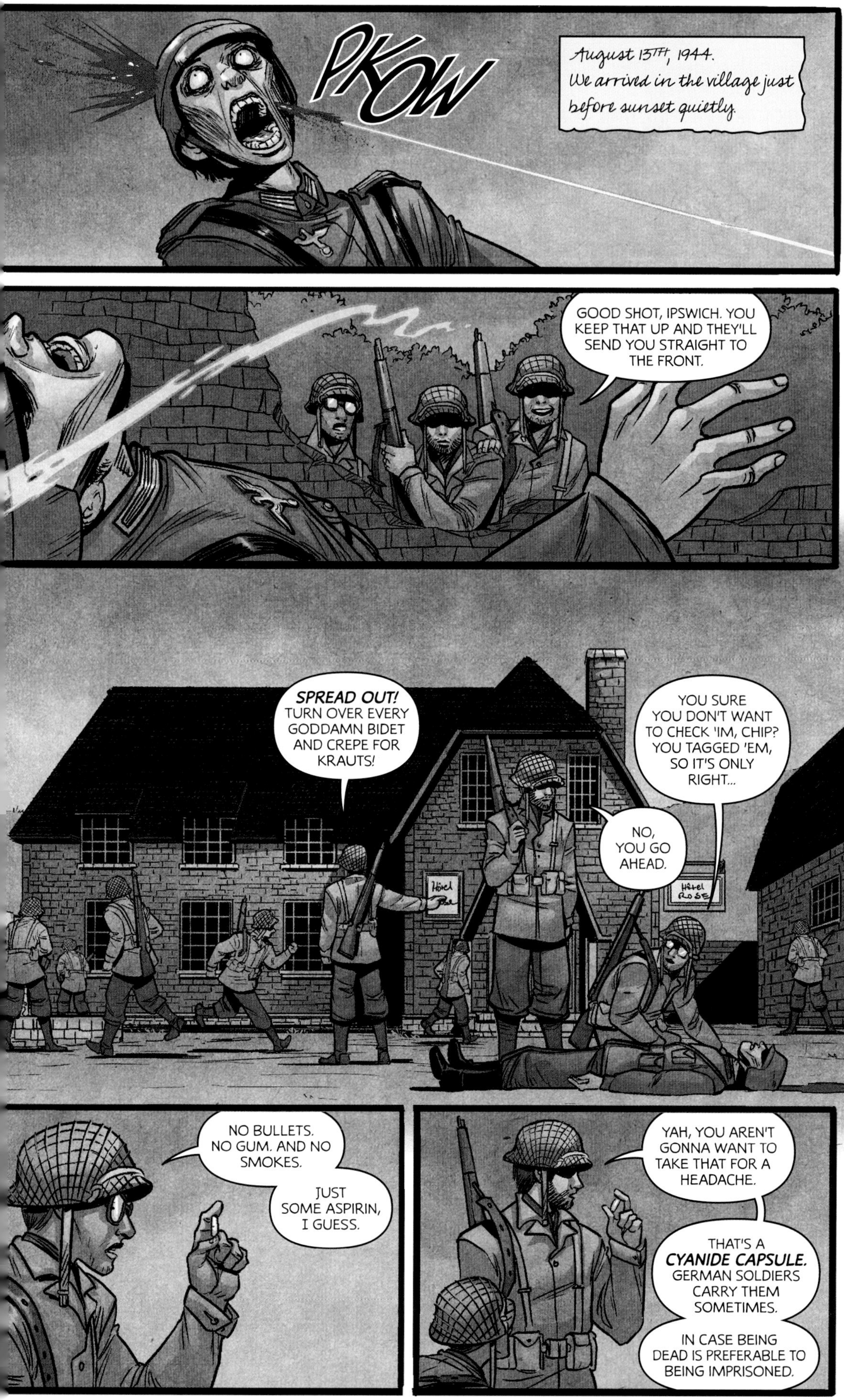
PKOW
August 13TH, 1944.
We arrived in the village just before sunset quietly.
GOOD SHOT, IPSWICH. YOU KEEP THAT UP AND THEY'LL SEND YOU STRAIGHT TO THE FRONT.
SPREAD OUT! TURN OVER EVERY GODDAMN BIDET AND CREPE FOR KRAUTS!
YOU SURE YOU DON'T WANT TO CHECK 'IM, CHIP? YOU TAGGED 'EM, SO IT'S ONLY RIGHT...
NO, YOU GO AHEAD.
Hôtel Rose
NO BULLETS. NO GUM. AND NO SMOKES.
JUST SOME ASPIRIN, I GUESS.
YAH, YOU AREN'T GONNA WANT TO TAKE THAT FOR A HEADACHE.
THAT'S A CYANIDE CAPSULE. GERMAN SOLDIERS CARRY THEM SOMETIMES.
IN CASE BEING DEAD IS PREFERABLE TO BEING IMPRISONED.

MUST'VE BEEN A DESERTER. CITY BOY FROM BERLIN MAYBE, 'CUZ BY THE LOOK OF HIM HE DIDN'T KNOW HOW TO HUNT.

CAPTAIN, SIR, I DON'T THINK HE WAS STARVING.

HE'S JUST... *SCRAWNY.*

ONE NAZI... IT JUST SEEMS SUSPICIOUS.

IT SEEMS FORTUITOUS. NO NAZIS IS NO NAZIS FAR AS I'M CONCERNED. NOW, YOU SEE WHAT I SEE, IPSWICH?

The sergeant gave the town an all-clear, as rain started to fall. Captain Gardens said we'd spread out and look for Allied camps in the morning.

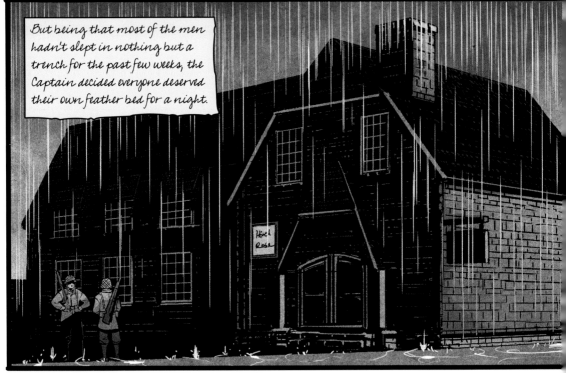

But being that most of the men hadn't slept in nothing but a trench for the past few weeks, the Captain decided everyone deserved their own feather bed for a night.

AND DON'T DRINK ANY WATER OUT OF THE FAUCET! ALL I NEED IS A BUNCH OF *CHOLERA SHITS* MESSIN' UP MY NIGHT!

AND DON'T TOUCH THE GODDAMN WINE BARRELS, EITHER!

YOU LEAVE THOSE TO YOUR CAPTAIN.

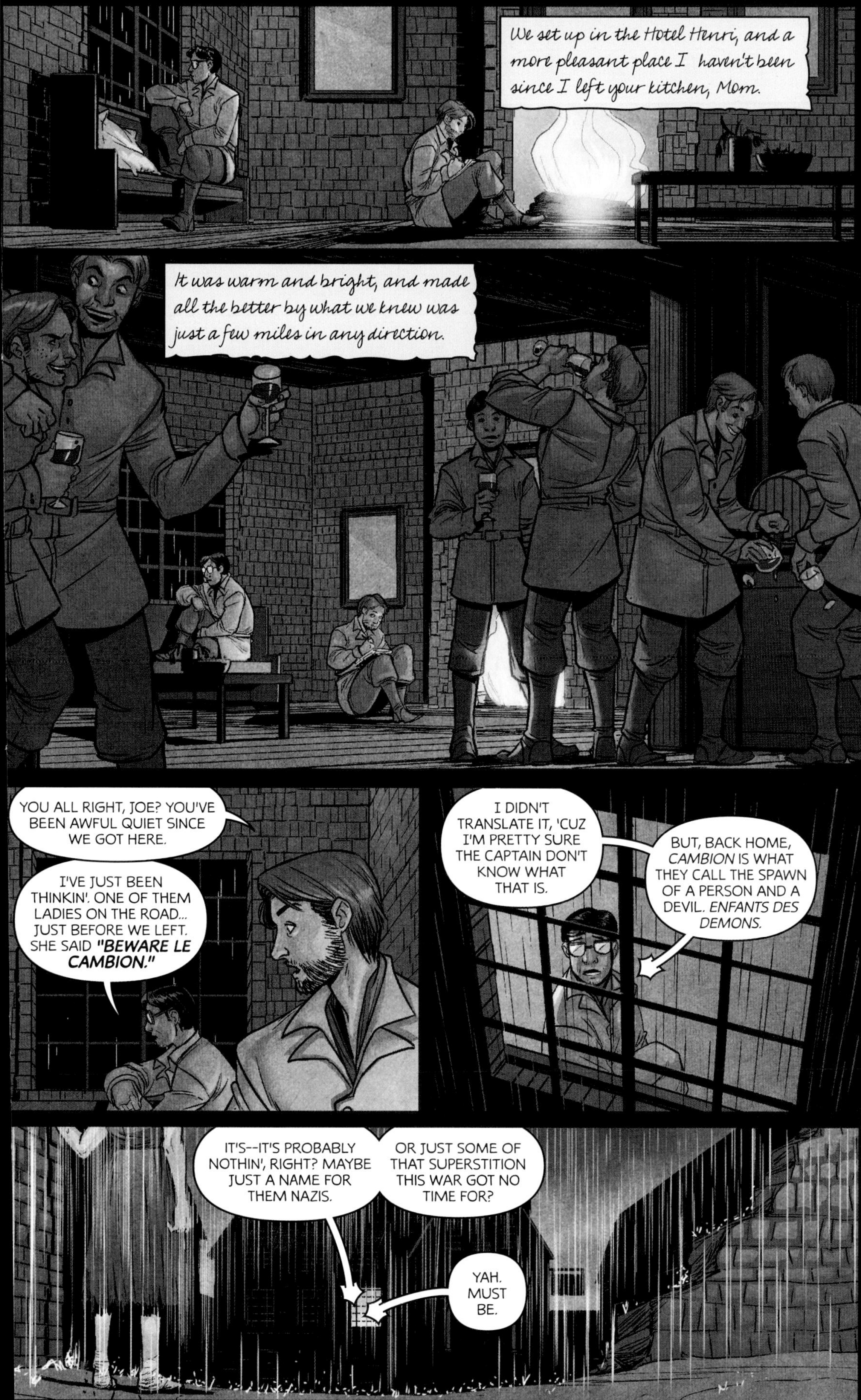
We set up in the Hotel Henri, and a more pleasant place I haven't been since I left your kitchen, Mom.
It was warm and bright, and made all the better by what we knew was just a few miles in any direction.
YOU ALL RIGHT, JOE? YOU'VE BEEN AWFUL QUIET SINCE WE GOT HERE.
I'VE JUST BEEN THINKIN'. ONE OF THEM LADIES ON THE ROAD... JUST BEFORE WE LEFT. SHE SAID "BEWARE LE CAMBION."
I DIDN'T TRANSLATE IT, 'CUZ I'M PRETTY SURE THE CAPTAIN DON'T KNOW WHAT THAT IS.
BUT, BACK HOME, CAMBION IS WHAT THEY CALL THE SPAWN OF A PERSON AND A DEVIL. ENFANTS DES DEMONS.
IT'S--IT'S PROBABLY NOTHIN', RIGHT? MAYBE JUST A NAME FOR THEM NAZIS.
OR JUST SOME OF THAT SUPERSTITION THIS WAR GOT NO TIME FOR?
YAH. MUST BE.

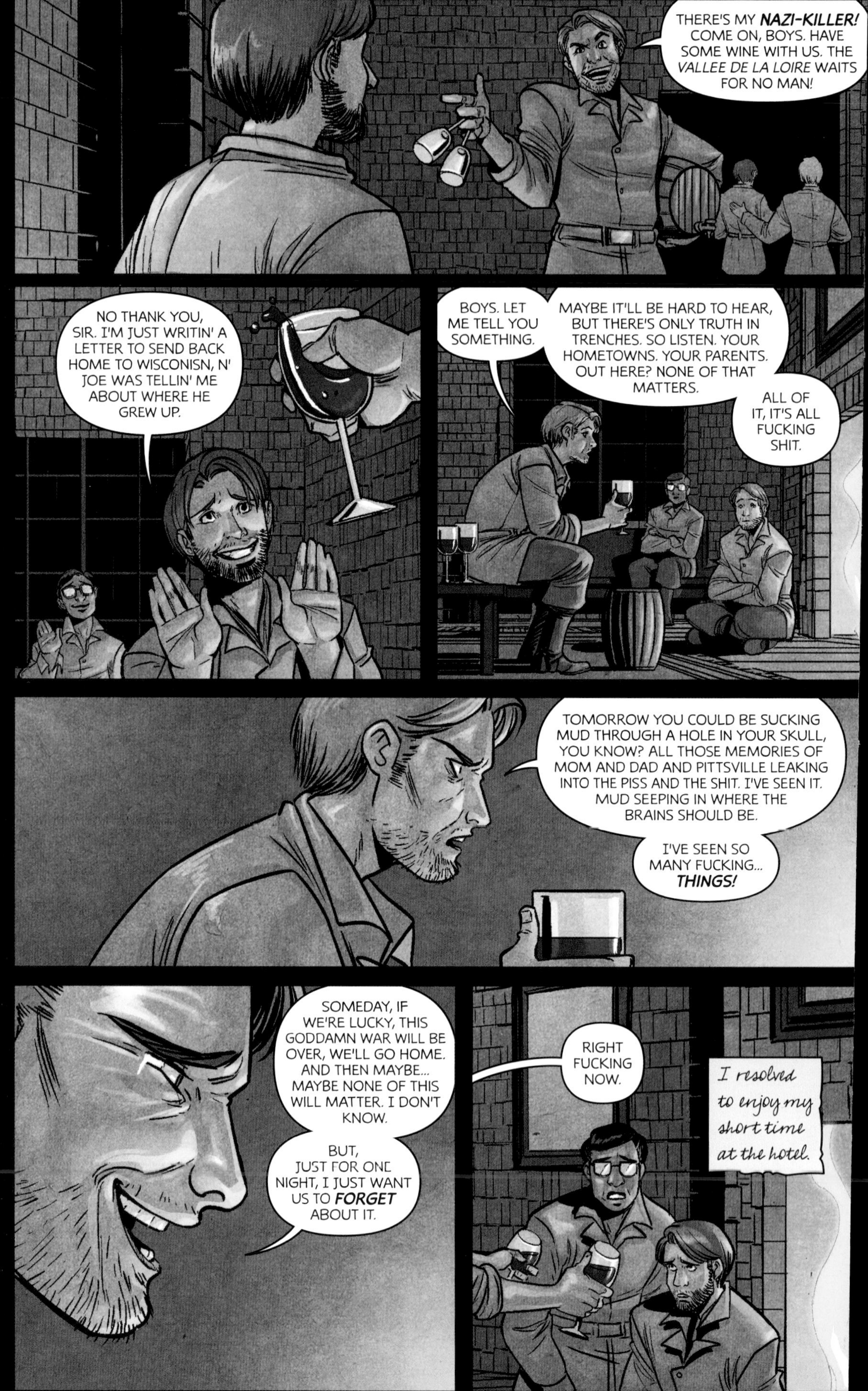
THERE'S MY **NAZI-KILLER!** COME ON, BOYS. HAVE SOME WINE WITH US. THE *VALLEE DE LA LOIRE* WAITS FOR NO MAN!
NO THANK YOU, SIR. I'M JUST WRITIN' A LETTER TO SEND BACK HOME TO WISCONISN, N' JOE WAS TELLIN' ME ABOUT WHERE HE GREW UP.
BOYS. LET ME TELL YOU SOMETHING.
MAYBE IT'LL BE HARD TO HEAR, BUT THERE'S ONLY TRUTH IN TRENCHES. SO LISTEN. YOUR HOMETOWNS. YOUR PARENTS. OUT HERE? NONE OF THAT MATTERS.
ALL OF IT, IT'S ALL FUCKING SHIT.
TOMORROW YOU COULD BE SUCKING MUD THROUGH A HOLE IN YOUR SKULL, YOU KNOW? ALL THOSE MEMORIES OF MOM AND DAD AND PITTSVILLE LEAKING INTO THE PISS AND THE SHIT. I'VE SEEN IT. MUD SEEPING IN WHERE THE BRAINS SHOULD BE.
I'VE SEEN SO MANY FUCKING... ***THINGS!***
SOMEDAY, IF WE'RE LUCKY, THIS GODDAMN WAR WILL BE OVER, WE'LL GO HOME. AND THEN MAYBE... MAYBE NONE OF THIS WILL MATTER. I DON'T KNOW.
BUT, JUST FOR ONE NIGHT, I JUST WANT US TO ***FORGET*** ABOUT IT.
RIGHT FUCKING NOW.
I resolved to enjoy my short time at the hotel.

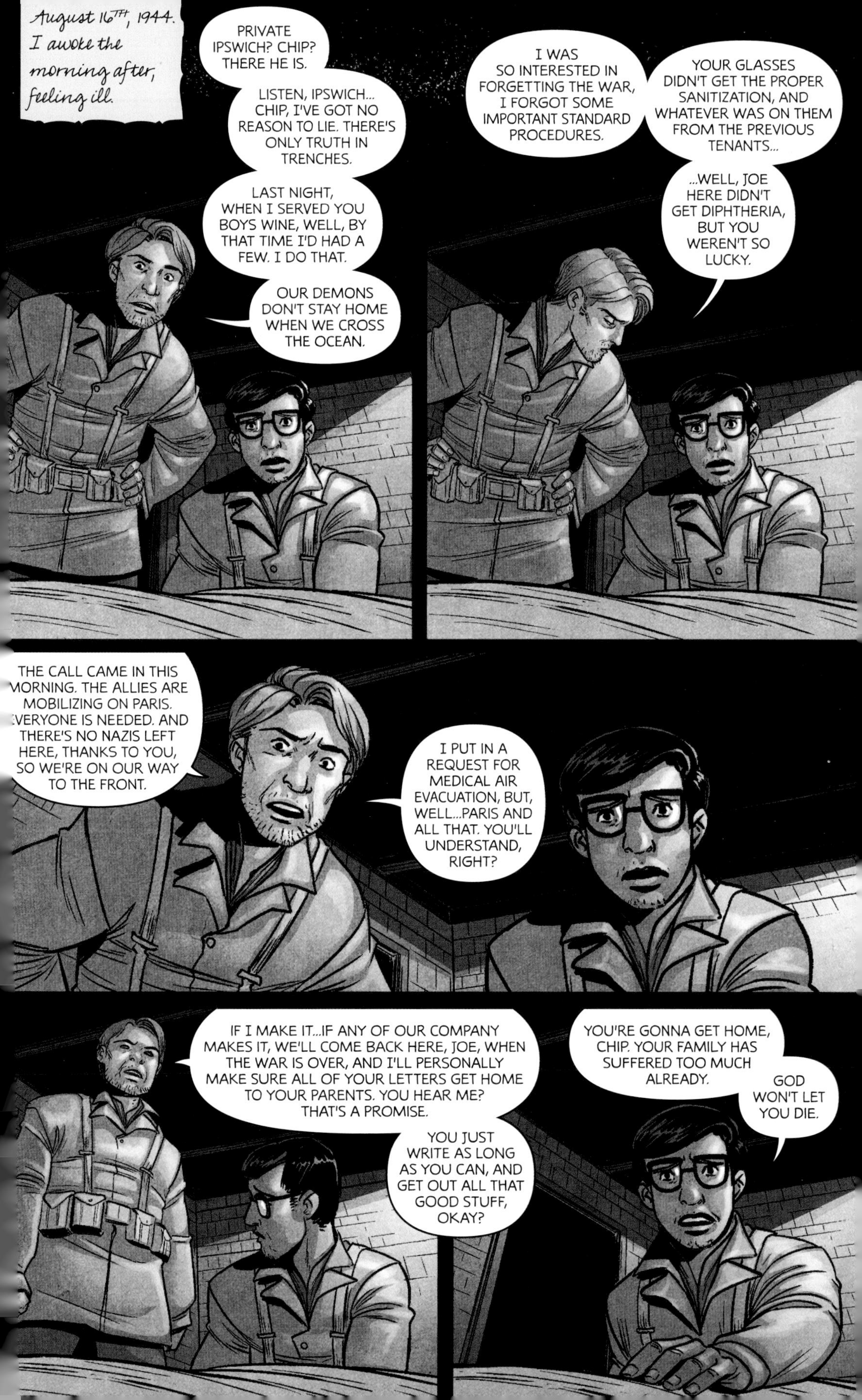
August 16TH, 1944. I awoke the morning after, feeling ill.
PRIVATE IPSWICH? CHIP? THERE HE IS.
LISTEN, IPSWICH... CHIP, I'VE GOT NO REASON TO LIE. THERE'S ONLY TRUTH IN TRENCHES.
LAST NIGHT, WHEN I SERVED YOU BOYS WINE, WELL, BY THAT TIME I'D HAD A FEW. I DO THAT.
OUR DEMONS DON'T STAY HOME WHEN WE CROSS THE OCEAN.
I WAS SO INTERESTED IN FORGETTING THE WAR, I FORGOT SOME IMPORTANT STANDARD PROCEDURES.
YOUR GLASSES DIDN'T GET THE PROPER SANITIZATION, AND WHATEVER WAS ON THEM FROM THE PREVIOUS TENANTS...
...WELL, JOE HERE DIDN'T GET DIPHTHERIA, BUT YOU WEREN'T SO LUCKY.
THE CALL CAME IN THIS MORNING. THE ALLIES ARE MOBILIZING ON PARIS. VERYONE IS NEEDED. AND THERE'S NO NAZIS LEFT HERE, THANKS TO YOU, SO WE'RE ON OUR WAY TO THE FRONT.
I PUT IN A REQUEST FOR MEDICAL AIR EVACUATION, BUT, WELL...PARIS AND ALL THAT. YOU'LL UNDERSTAND, RIGHT?
IF I MAKE IT...IF ANY OF OUR COMPANY MAKES IT, WE'LL COME BACK HERE, JOE, WHEN THE WAR IS OVER, AND I'LL PERSONALLY MAKE SURE ALL OF YOUR LETTERS GET HOME TO YOUR PARENTS. YOU HEAR ME? THAT'S A PROMISE.
YOU JUST WRITE AS LONG AS YOU CAN, AND GET OUT ALL THAT GOOD STUFF, OKAY?
YOU'RE GONNA GET HOME, CHIP. YOUR FAMILY HAS SUFFERED TOO MUCH ALREADY.
GOD WON'T LET YOU DIE.

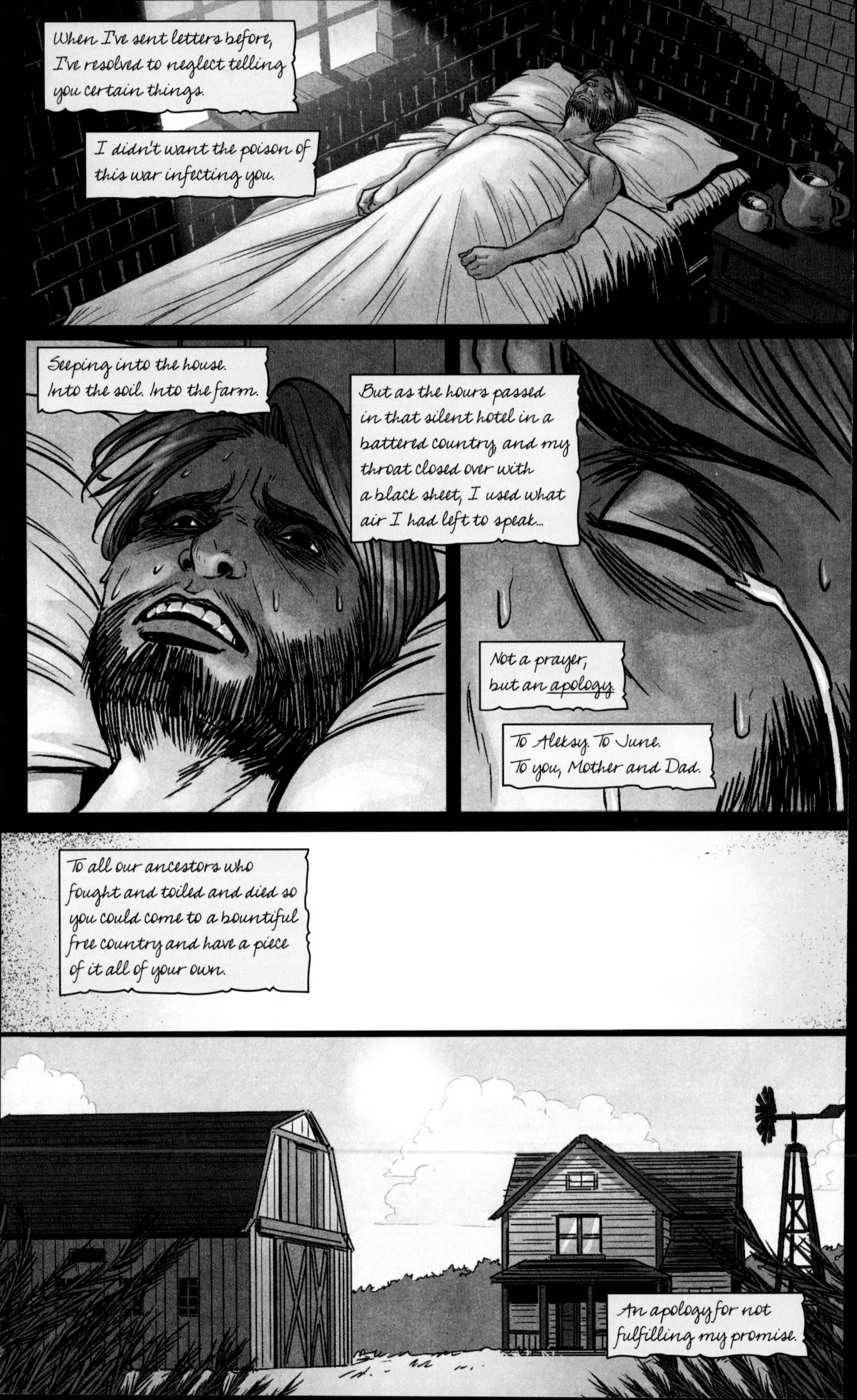
When I've sent letters before, I've resolved to neglect telling you certain things.
I didn't want the poison of this war infecting you.
Seeping into the house. Into the soil. Into the farm.
But as the hours passed in that silent hotel in a battered country, and my throat closed over with a black sheet, I used what air I had left to speak...
Not a prayer, but an apology.
To Aleksy. To June. To you, Mother and Dad.
To all our ancestors who fought and toiled and died so you could come to a bountiful free country and have a piece of it all of your own.
An apology for not fulfilling my promise.

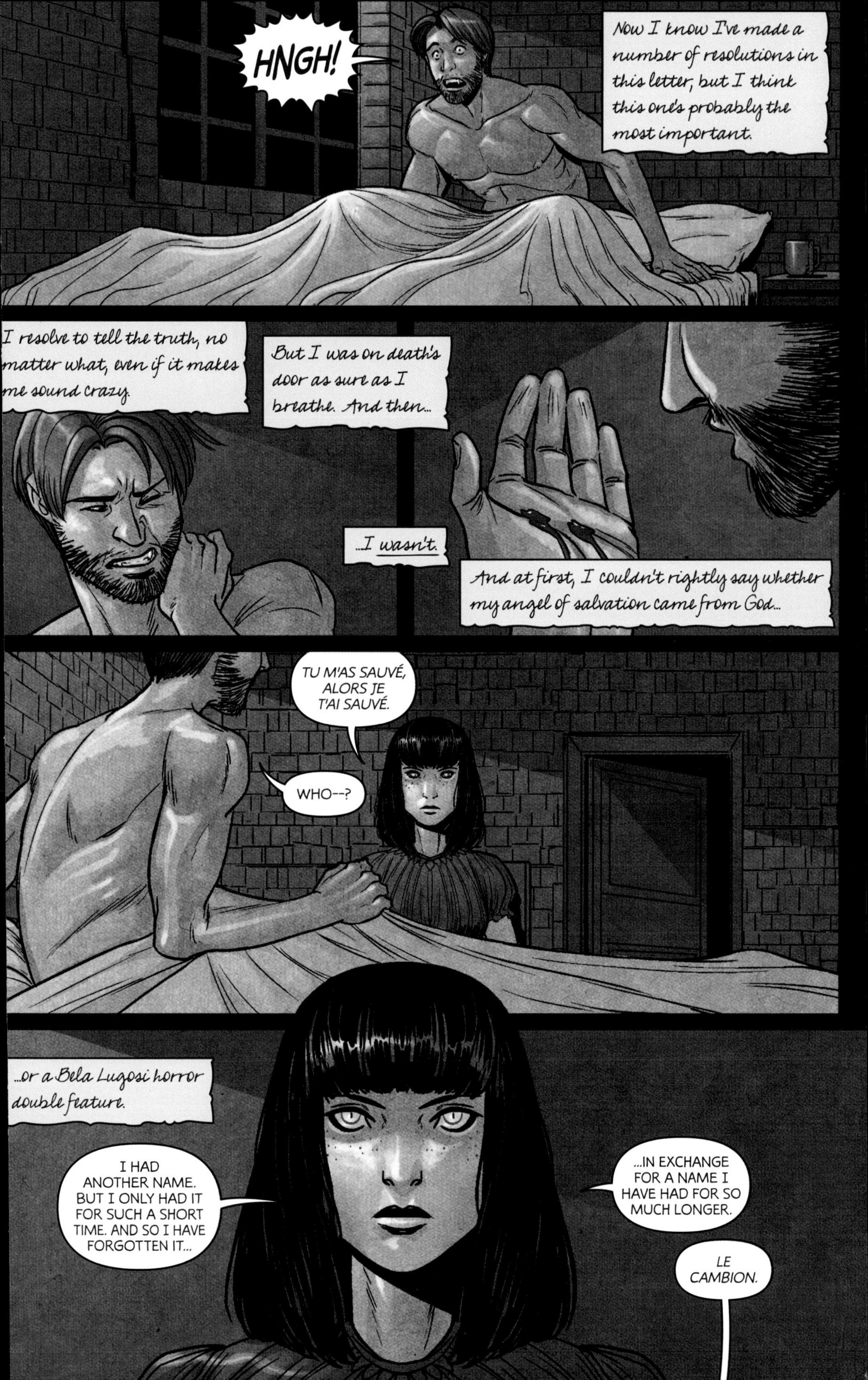
HNGH!
Now I know I've made a number of resolutions in this letter, but I think this one's probably the most important.
I resolve to tell the truth, no matter what, even if it makes me sound crazy.
But I was on death's door as sure as I breathe. And then...
...I wasn't.
And at first, I couldn't rightly say whether my angel of salvation came from God...
TU M'AS SAUVÉ, ALORS JE T'AI SAUVÉ.
WHO--?
...or a Bela Lugosi horror double feature.
I HAD ANOTHER NAME. BUT I ONLY HAD IT FOR SUCH A SHORT TIME. AND SO I HAVE FORGOTTEN IT...
...IN EXCHANGE FOR A NAME I HAVE HAD FOR SO MUCH LONGER.
LE CAMBION.

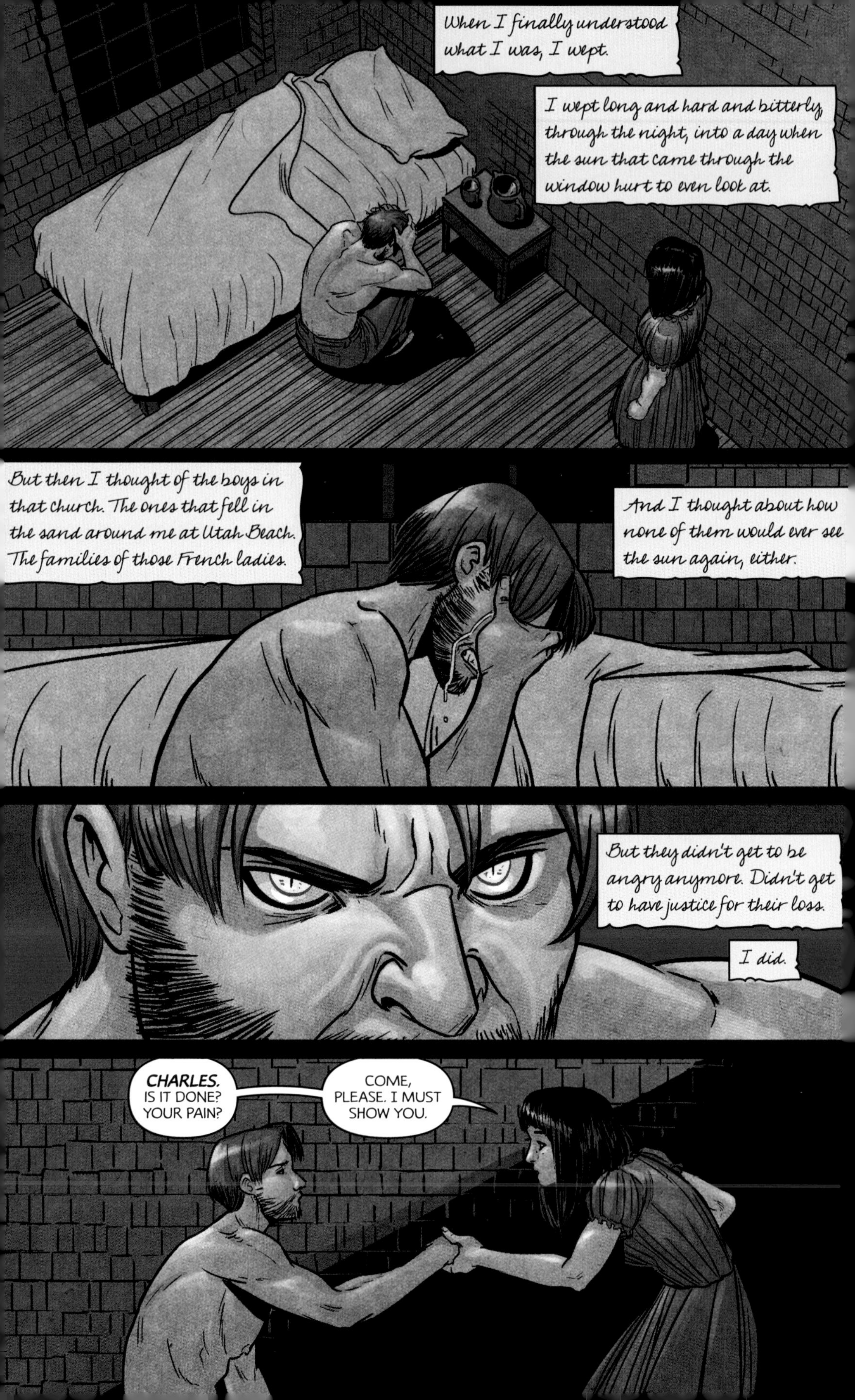
When I finally understood what I was, I wept.
I wept long and hard and bitterly through the night, into a day when the sun that came through the window hurt to even look at.
But then I thought of the boys in that church. The ones that fell in the sand around me at Utah Beach. The families of those French ladies.
And I thought about how none of them would ever see the sun again, either.
But they didn't get to be angry anymore. Didn't get to have justice for their loss.
I did.
CHARLES. IS IT DONE? YOUR PAIN?
COME, PLEASE. I MUST SHOW YOU.

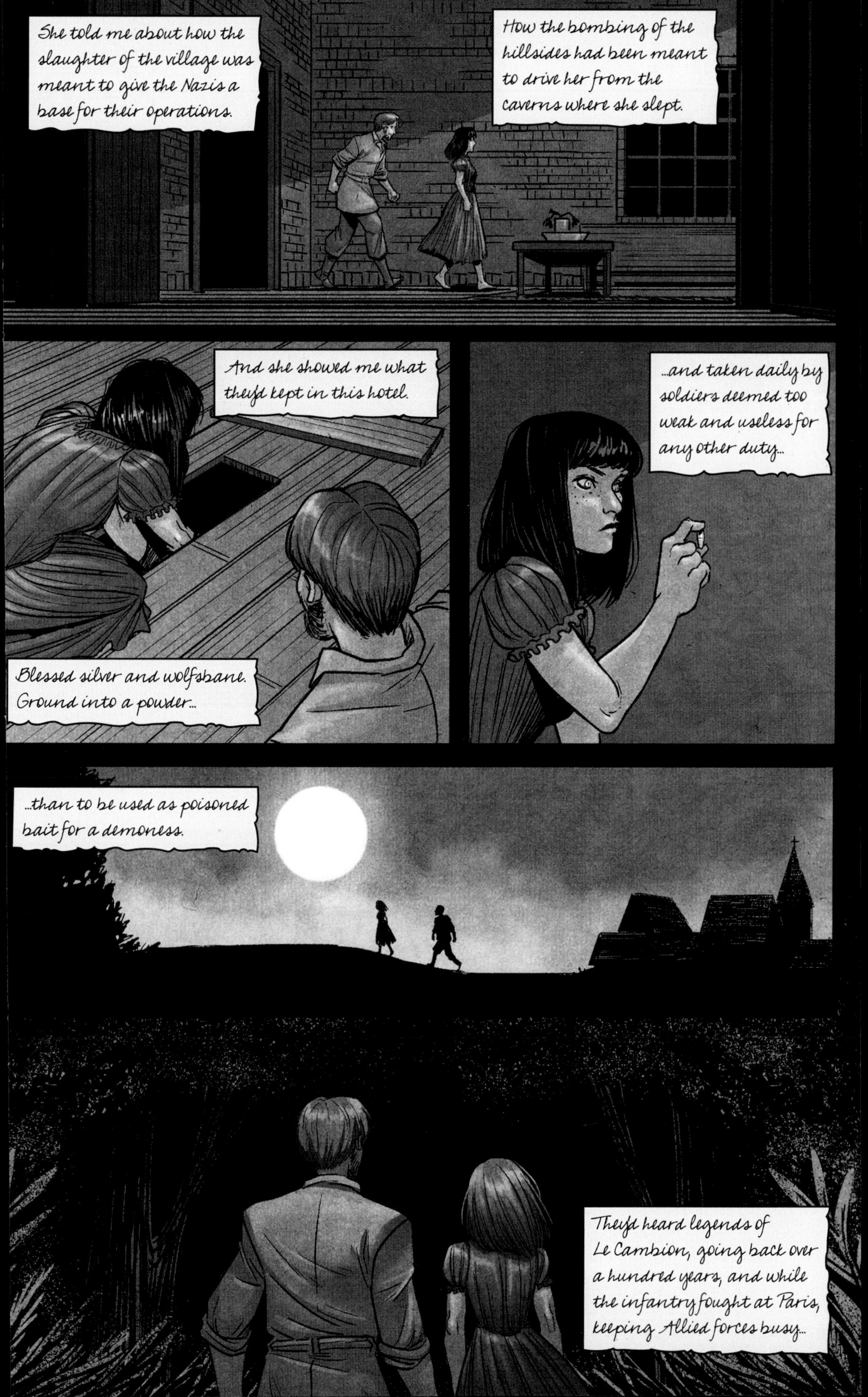
She told me about how the slaughter of the village was meant to give the Nazis a base for their operations.
How the bombing of the hillsides had been meant to drive her from the caverns where she slept.
And she showed me what they'd kept in this hotel.
Blessed silver and wolfsbane. Ground into a powder...
...and taken daily by soldiers deemed too weak and useless for any other duty...
...than to be used as poisoned bait for a demoness.
They'd heard legends of Le Cambion, going back over a hundred years, and while the infantry fought at Paris, keeping Allied forces busy...

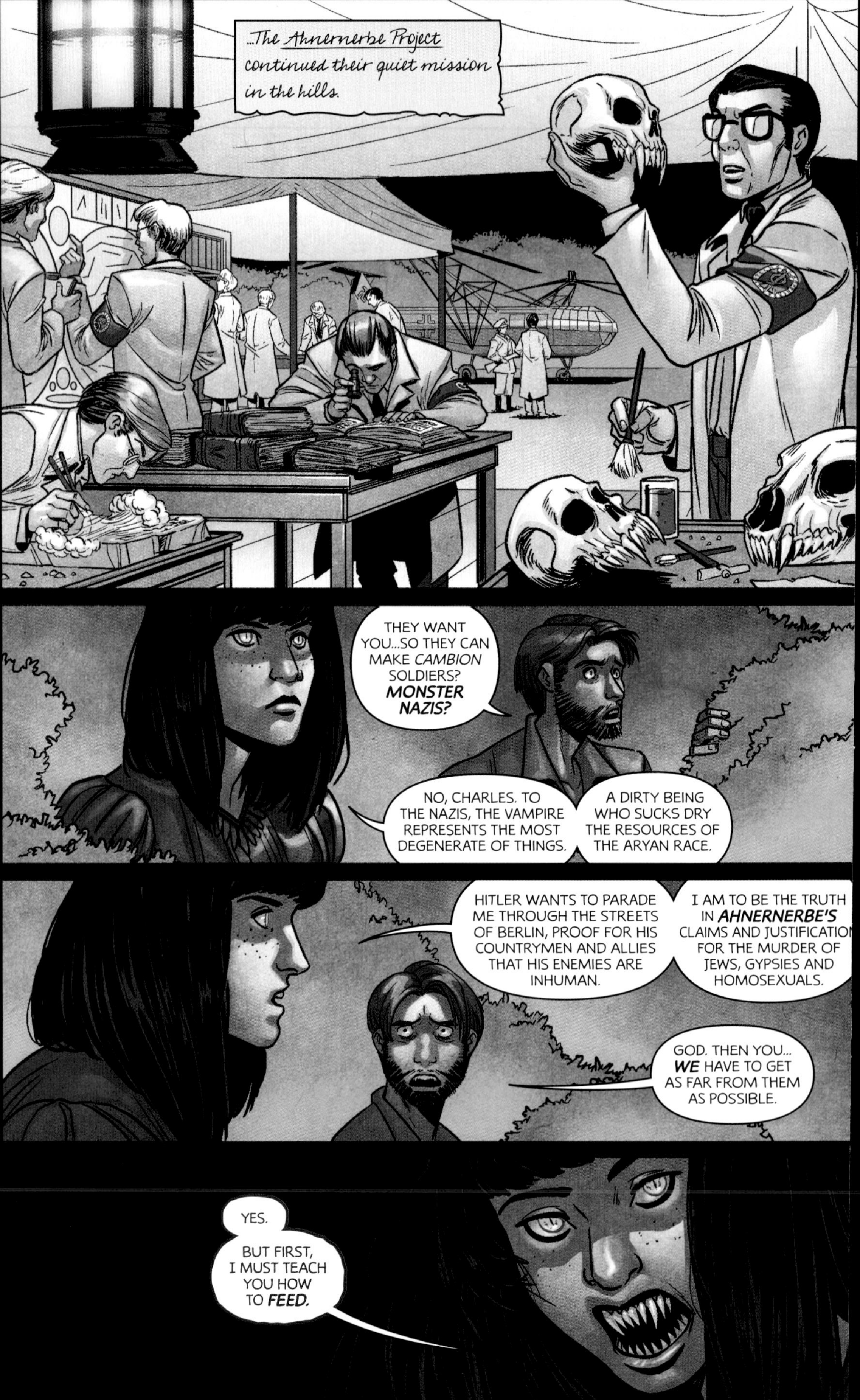

...The Ahnernerbe Project continued their quiet mission in the hills.
THEY WANT YOU...SO THEY CAN MAKE *CAMBION* SOLDIERS? ***MONSTER NAZIS?***
NO, CHARLES. TO THE NAZIS, THE VAMPIRE REPRESENTS THE MOST DEGENERATE OF THINGS.
A DIRTY BEING WHO SUCKS DRY THE RESOURCES OF THE ARYAN RACE.
HITLER WANTS TO PARADE ME THROUGH THE STREETS OF BERLIN, PROOF FOR HIS COUNTRYMEN AND ALLIES THAT HIS ENEMIES ARE INHUMAN.
I AM TO BE THE TRUTH IN ***AHNERNERBE'S*** CLAIMS AND JUSTIFICATION FOR THE MURDER OF JEWS, GYPSIES AND HOMOSEXUALS.
GOD. THEN YOU... ***WE*** HAVE TO GET AS FAR FROM THEM AS POSSIBLE.
YES.
BUT FIRST, I MUST TEACH YOU HOW TO ***FEED.***

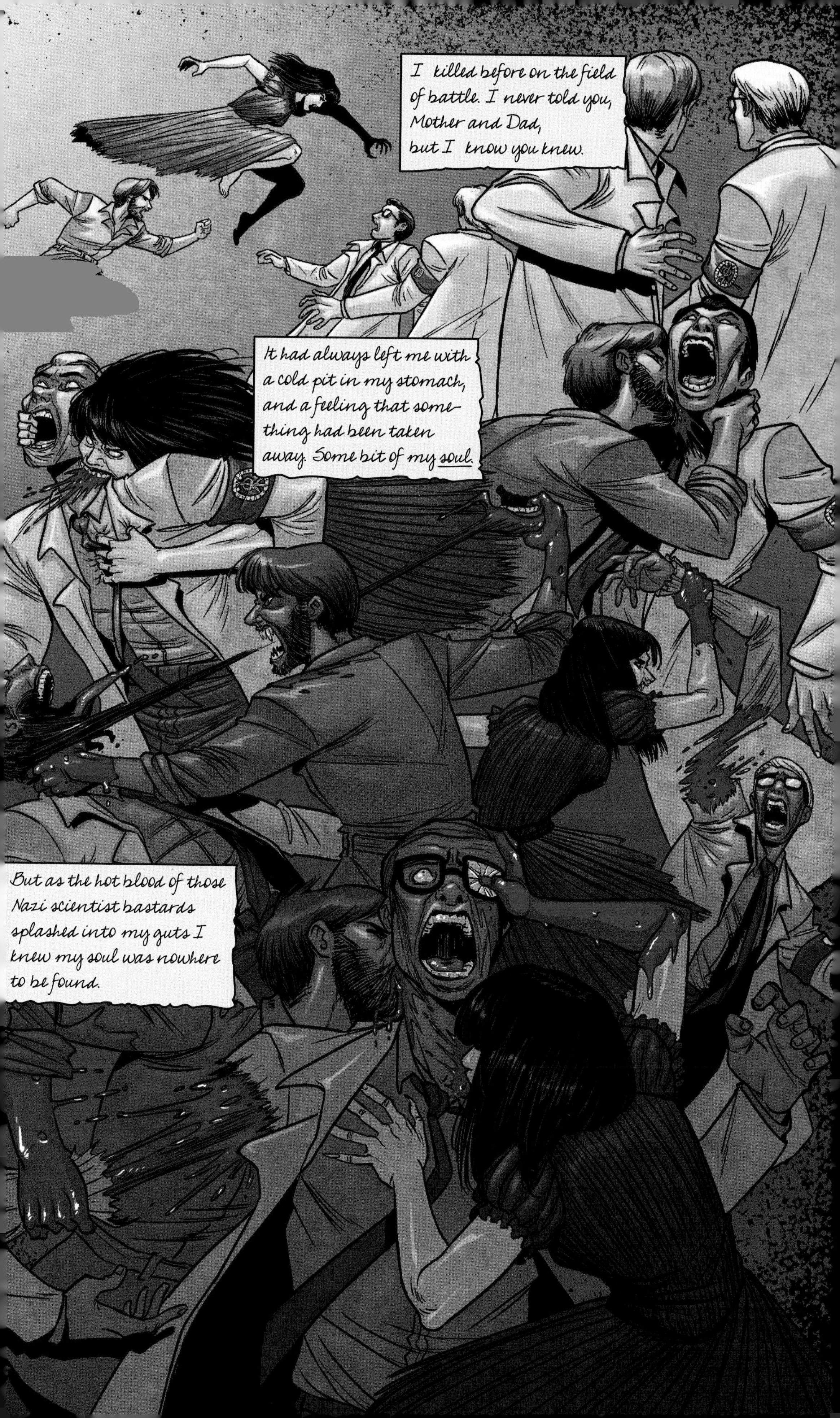
I killed before on the field of battle. I never told you, Mother and Dad, but I know you knew.
It had always left me with a cold pit in my stomach, and a feeling that something had been taken away. Some bit of my soul.
But as the hot blood of those Nazi scientist bastards splashed into my guts I knew my soul was nowhere to be found.

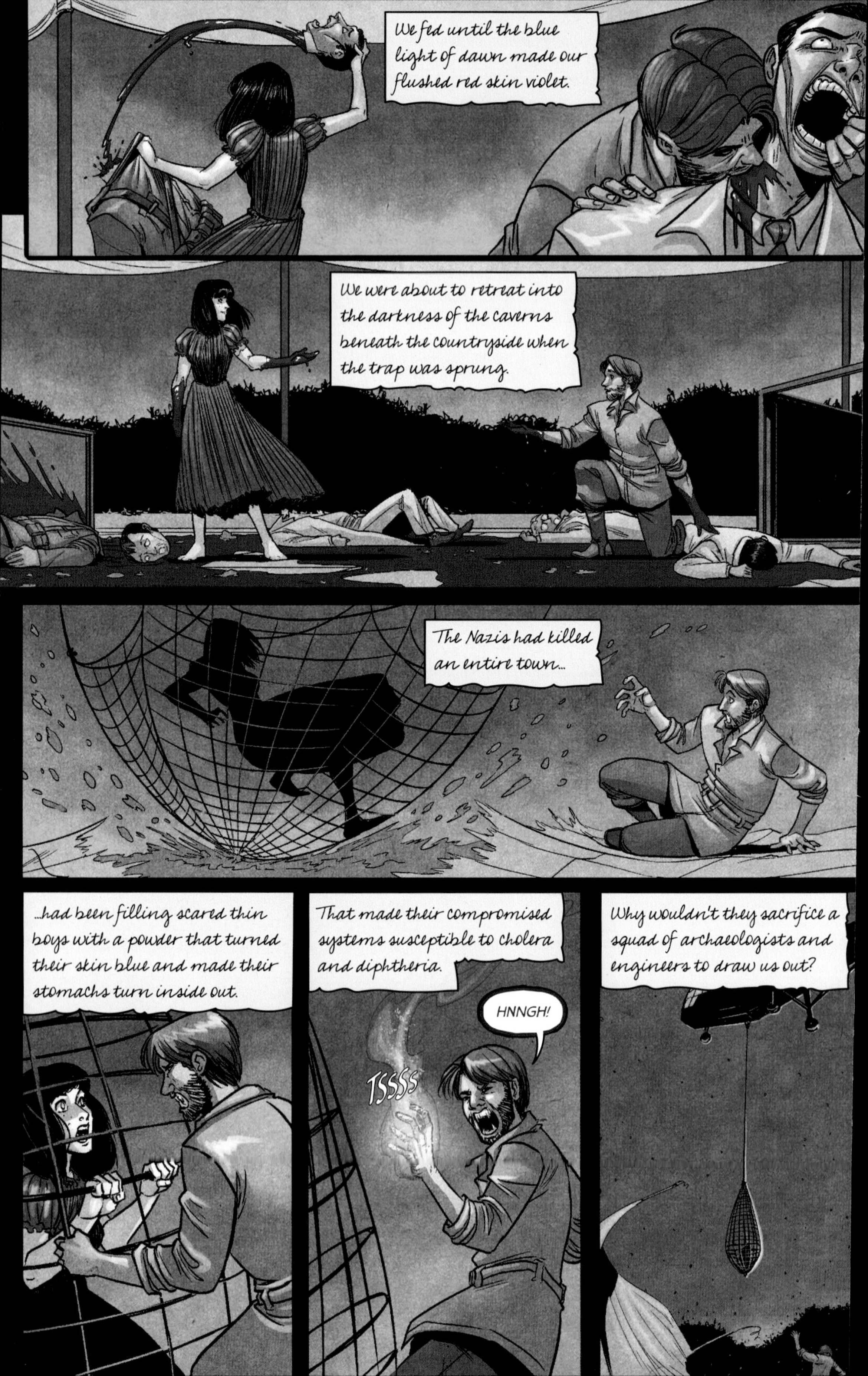
We fed until the blue light of dawn made our flushed red skin violet.
We were about to retreat into the darkness of the caverns beneath the countryside when the trap was sprung.
The Nazis had killed an entire town...
...had been filling scared thin boys with a powder that turned their skin blue and made their stomachs turn inside out.
That made their compromised systems susceptible to cholera and diphtheria.
HNNGH!
TSSSS
Why wouldn't they sacrifice a squad of archaeologists and engineers to draw us out?

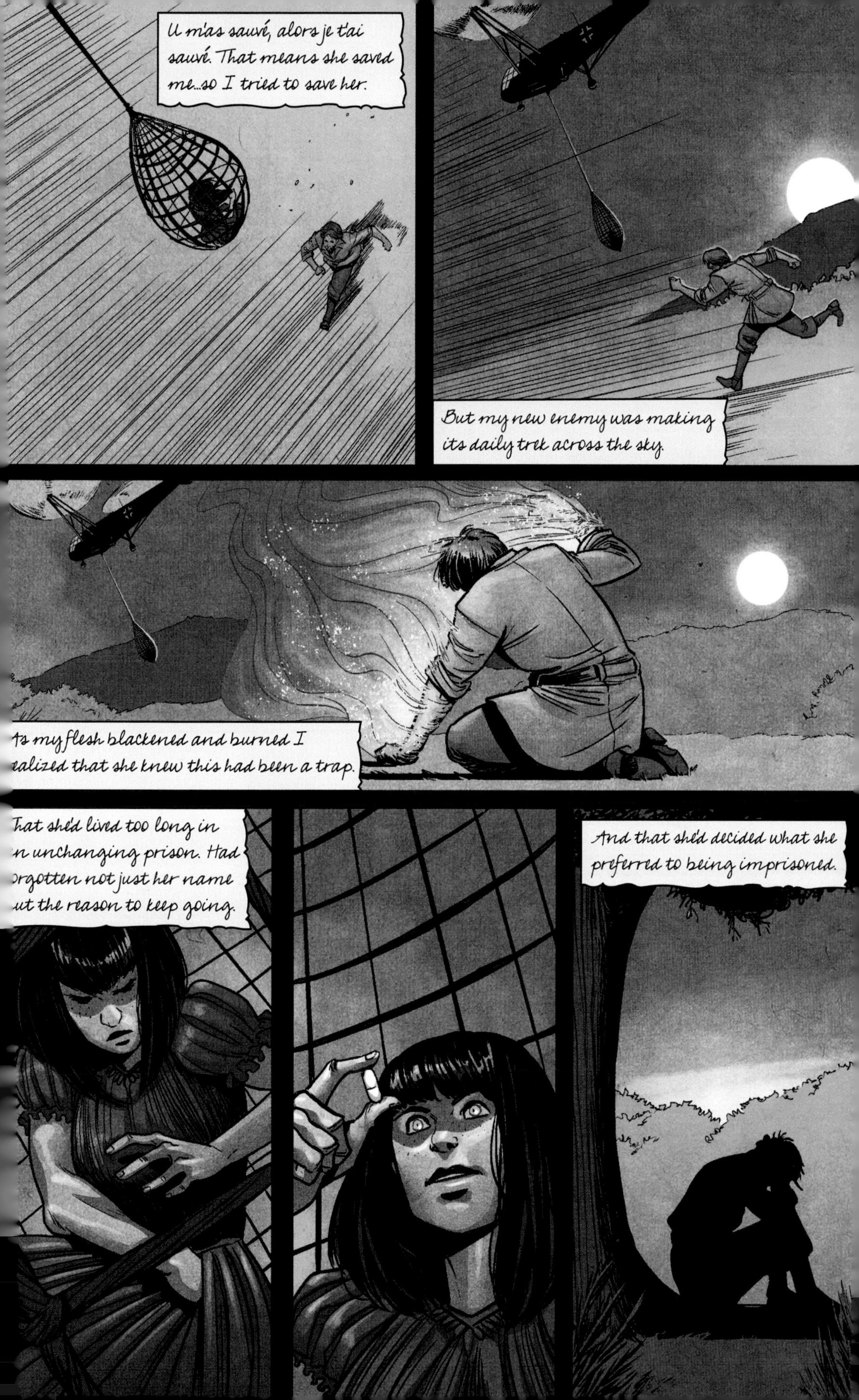
U m'as sauvé, alors je t'ai sauvé. That means she saved me...so I tried to save her.
But my new enemy was making its daily trek across the sky.
s my flesh blackened and burned I ealized that she knew this had been a trap.
hat she'd lived too long in n unchanging prison. Had orgotten not just her name ut the reason to keep going.
And that she'd decided what she preferred to being imprisoned.

CHIP

Mr. & Mrs.
Harry Ipswich
219 N Legner Ln
Knowlton, WI

September 28TH, 1944.
I wanted to keep fighting
from the shadows. To sink
my teeth into Hitler's
throat. But I would be
giving him what he
wanted most of all.

I resolved that I'd live as long
as it wasn't a prison I came
back to America. To the farm.

But I didn't come
back to you.

You'd already suffered so
much. You'd already lost
June and Aleksy.

And it wasn't God who
brought me home.

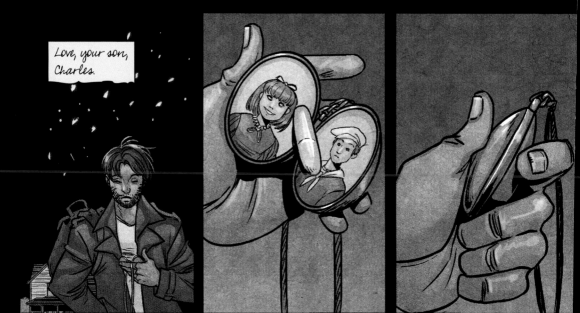

Love, your son,
Charles.

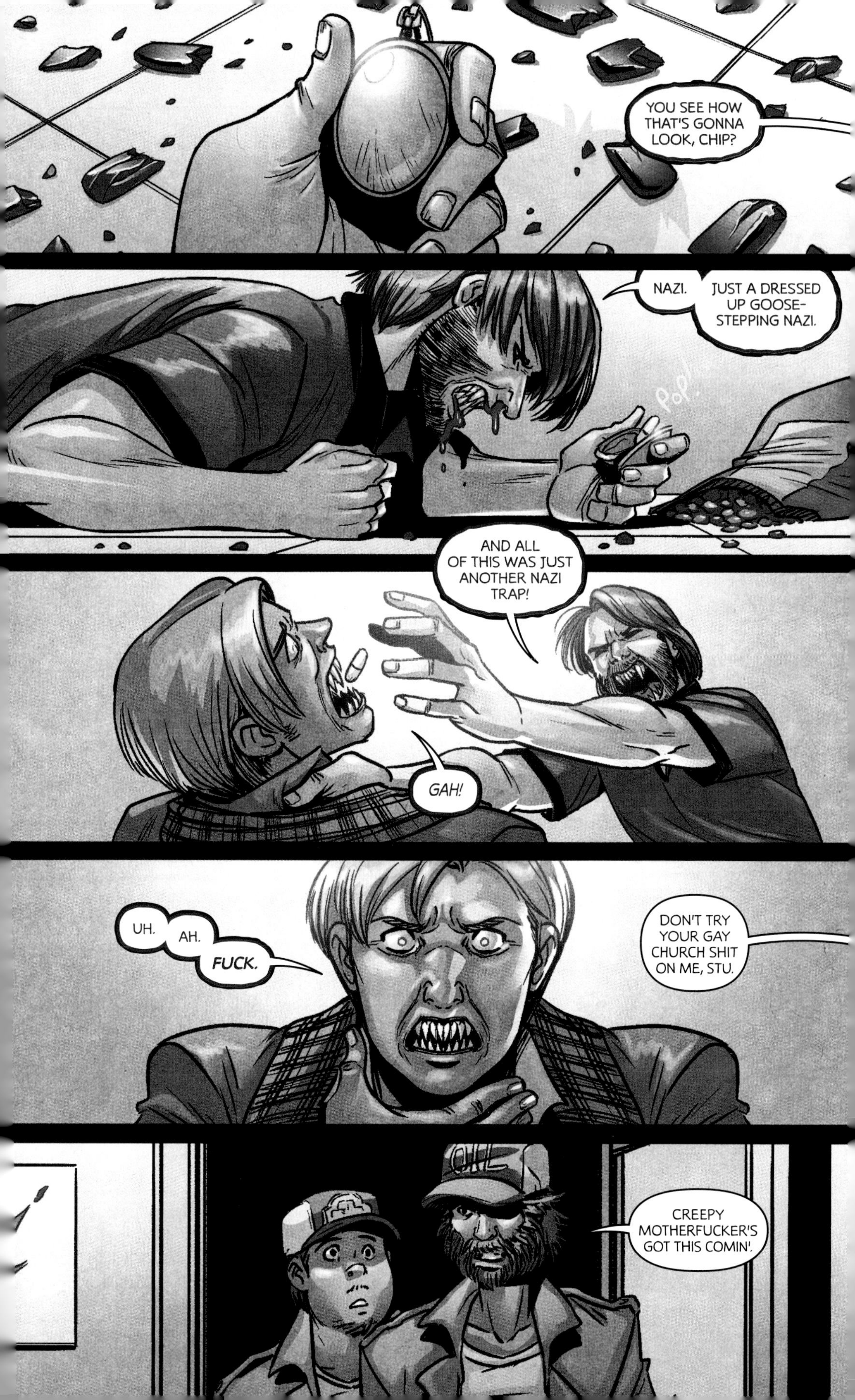
YOU SEE HOW THAT'S GONNA LOOK, CHIP?
NAZI.
JUST A DRESSED UP GOOSE-STEPPING NAZI.
POP!
AND ALL OF THIS WAS JUST ANOTHER NAZI TRAP!
GAH!
UH.
AH.
FUCK.
DON'T TRY YOUR GAY CHURCH SHIT ON ME, STU.
CREEPY MOTHERFUCKER'S GOT THIS COMIN'.

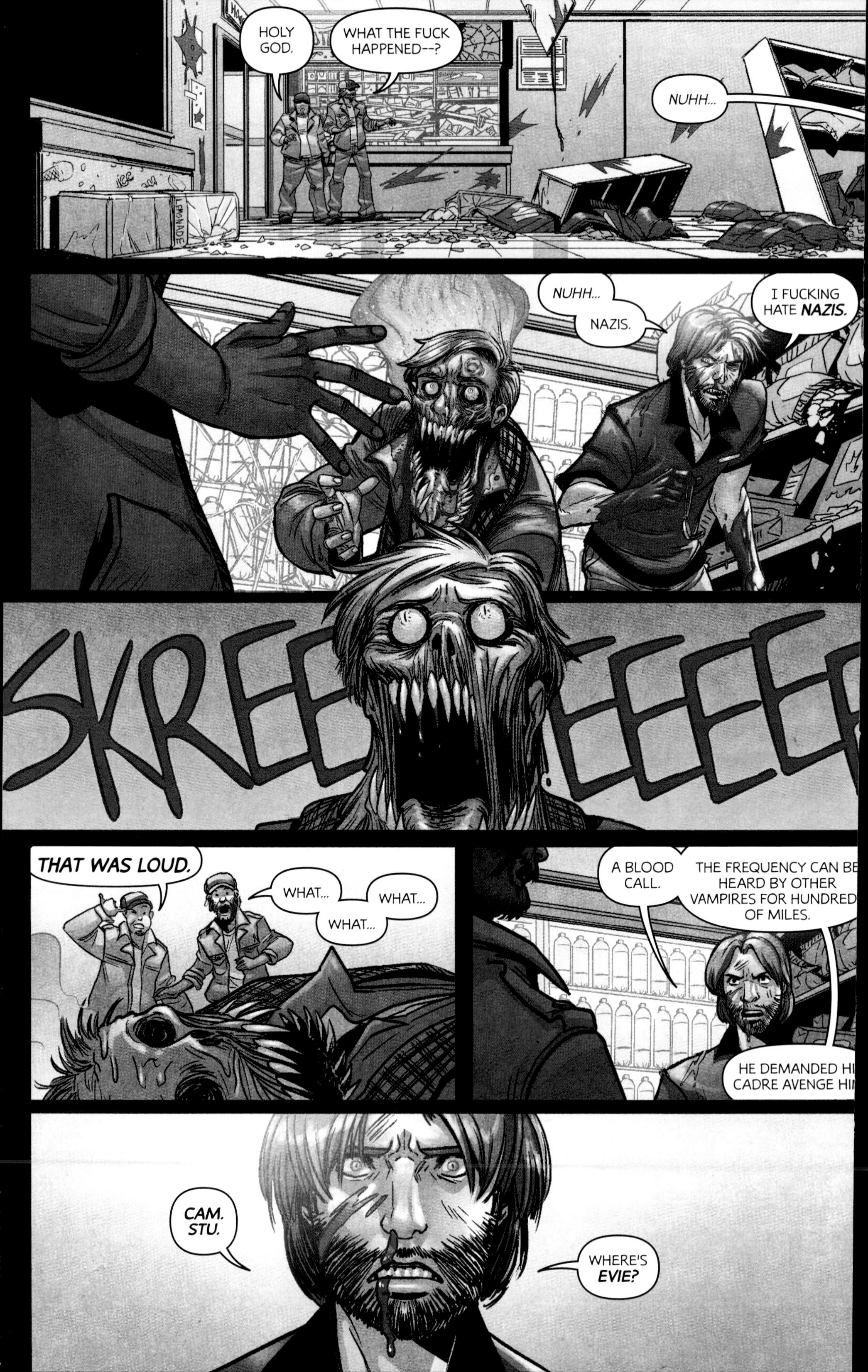
HOLY GOD.
WHAT THE FUCK HAPPENED--?
NUHH...
LEMONADE
NUHH...
NAZIS.
I FUCKING HATE NAZIS.
SKREEEEEEEE
THAT WAS LOUD.
WHAT...
WHAT...
WHAT...
A BLOOD CALL.
THE FREQUENCY CAN BE HEARD BY OTHER VAMPIRES FOR HUNDRED OF MILES.
HE DEMANDED HI CADRE AVENGE HI
CAM. STU.
WHERE'S EVIE?

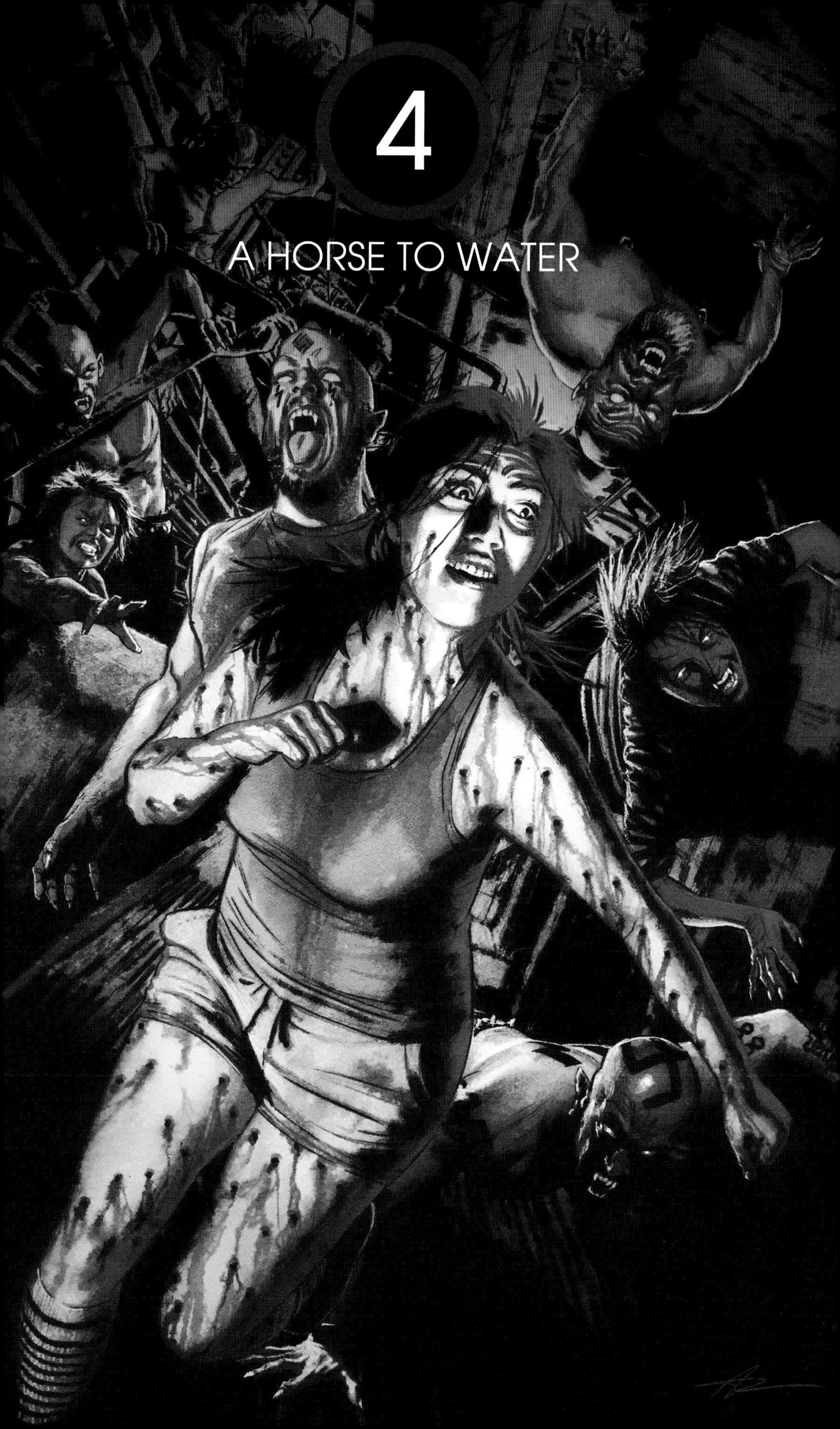
4
A HORSE TO WATER

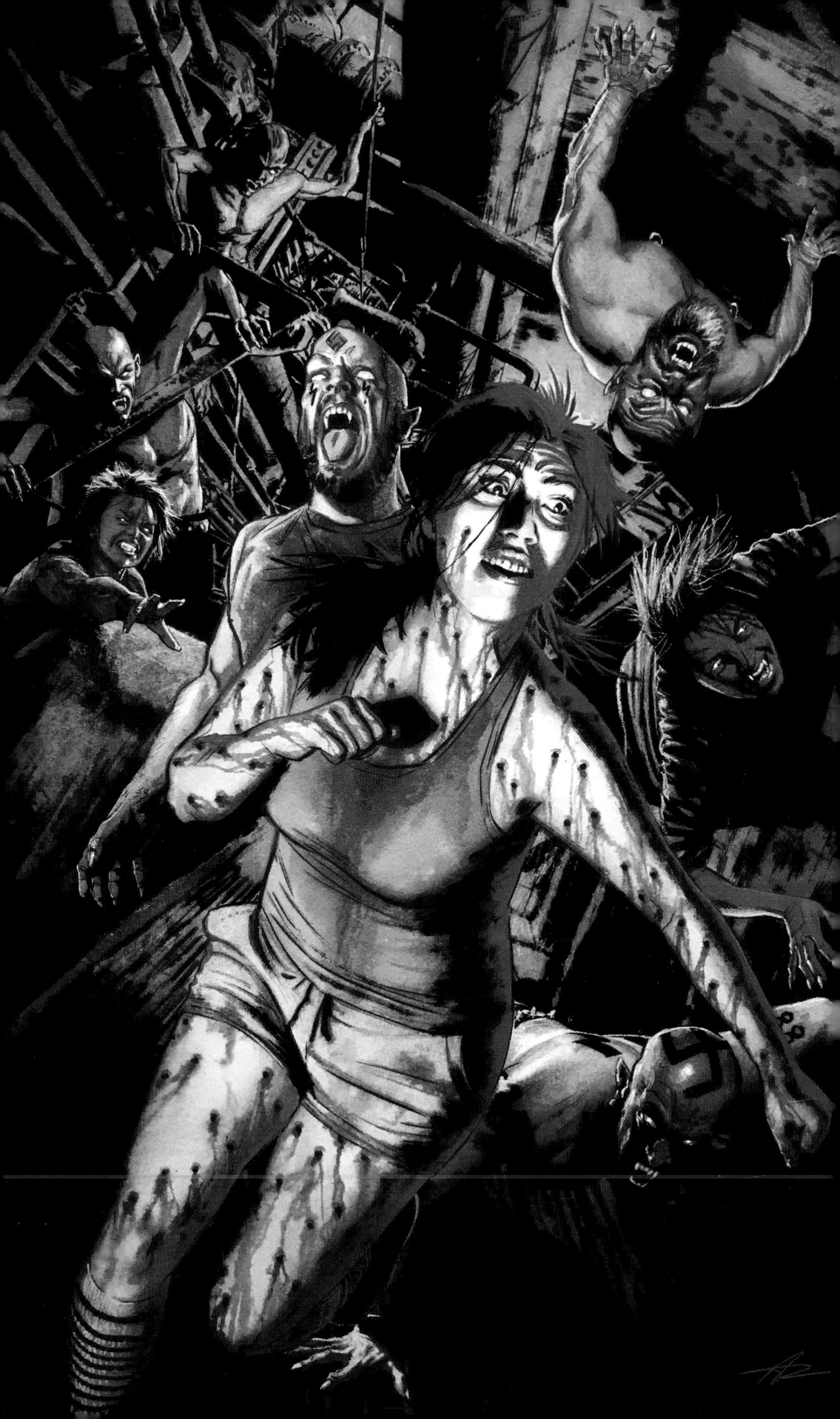

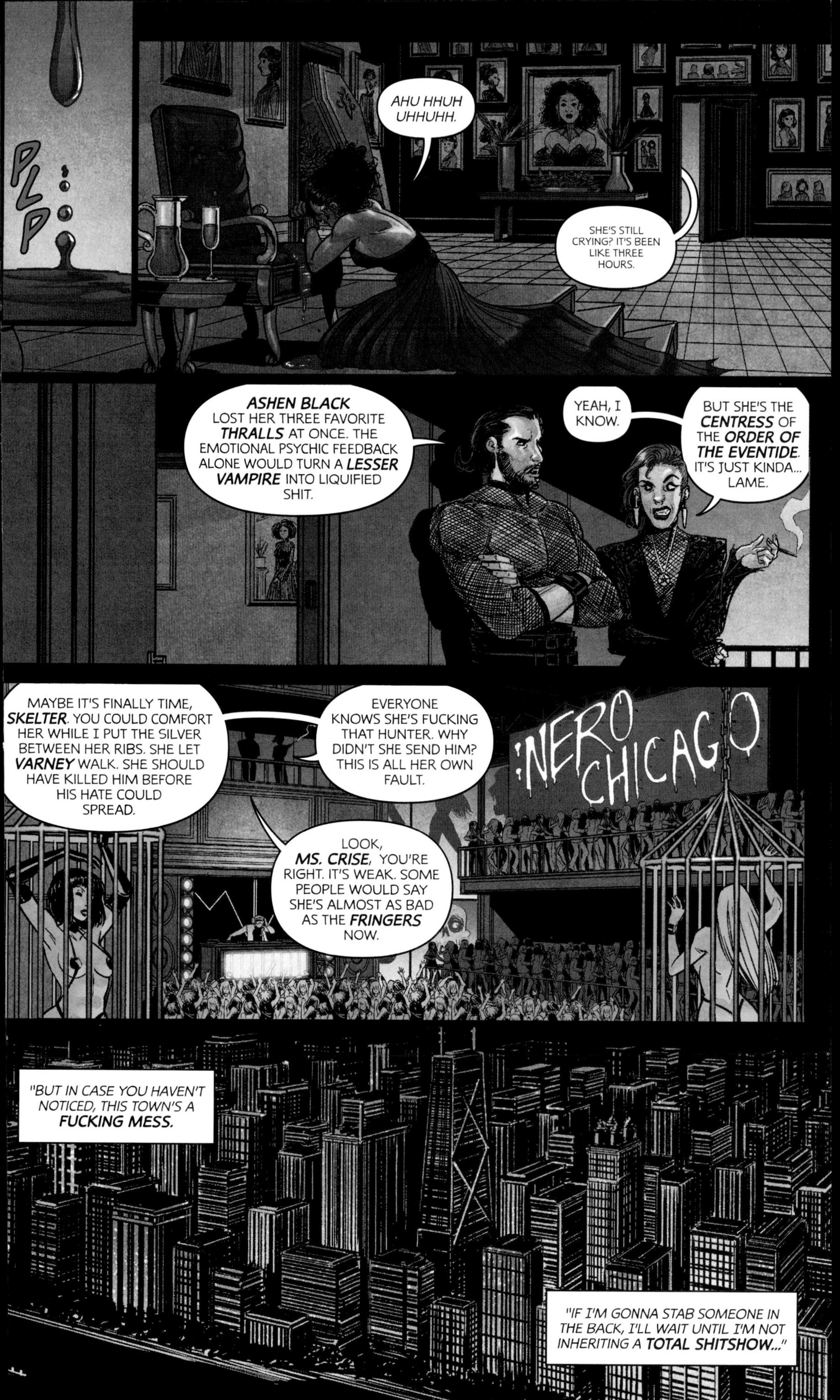
PLP
AHU HHUH UHHUHH.
SHE'S STILL CRYING? IT'S BEEN LIKE THREE HOURS.
ASHEN BLACK LOST HER THREE FAVORITE THRALLS AT ONCE. THE EMOTIONAL PSYCHIC FEEDBACK ALONE WOULD TURN A LESSER VAMPIRE INTO LIQUIFIED SHIT.
YEAH, I KNOW.
BUT SHE'S THE CENTRESS OF THE ORDER OF THE EVENTIDE. IT'S JUST KINDA... LAME.
EVERYONE KNOWS SHE'S FUCKING THAT HUNTER. WHY DIDN'T SHE SEND HIM? THIS IS ALL HER OWN FAULT.
NERO CHICAGO
MAYBE IT'S FINALLY TIME, SKELTER. YOU COULD COMFORT HER WHILE I PUT THE SILVER BETWEEN HER RIBS. SHE LET VARNEY WALK. SHE SHOULD HAVE KILLED HIM BEFORE HIS HATE COULD SPREAD.
LOOK, MS. CRISE, YOU'RE RIGHT. IT'S WEAK. SOME PEOPLE WOULD SAY SHE'S ALMOST AS BAD AS THE FRINGERS NOW.
"BUT IN CASE YOU HAVEN'T NOTICED, THIS TOWN'S A FUCKING MESS.
"IF I'M GONNA STAB SOMEONE IN THE BACK, I'LL WAIT UNTIL I'M NOT INHERITING A TOTAL SHITSHOW..."

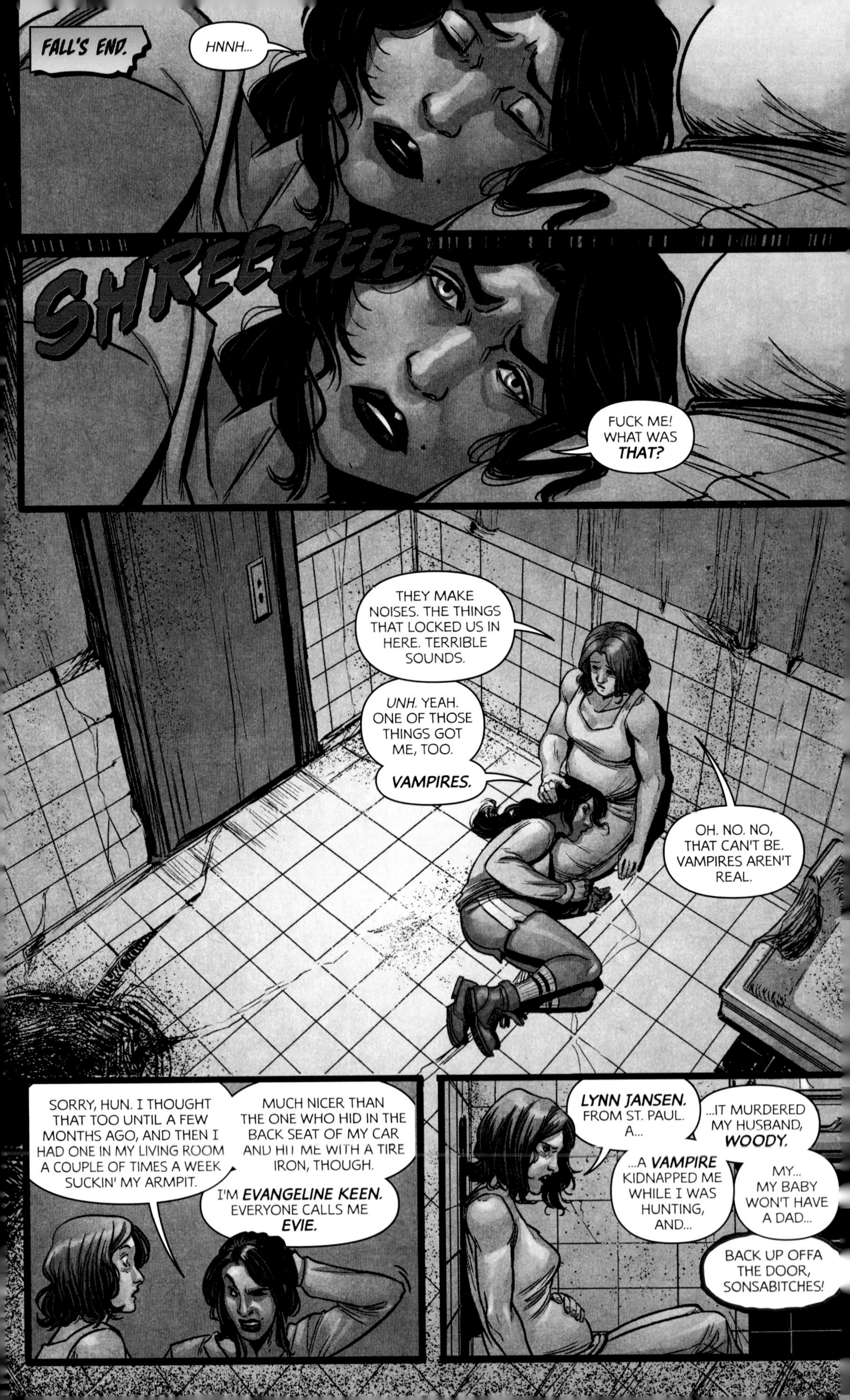
FALL'S END.
HNNH...
SHREEEEEEEE
FUCK ME! WHAT WAS THAT?
THEY MAKE NOISES. THE THINGS THAT LOCKED US IN HERE. TERRIBLE SOUNDS.
UNH. YEAH. ONE OF THOSE THINGS GOT ME, TOO.
VAMPIRES.
OH. NO. NO, THAT CAN'T BE. VAMPIRES AREN'T REAL.
SORRY, HUN. I THOUGHT THAT TOO UNTIL A FEW MONTHS AGO, AND THEN I HAD ONE IN MY LIVING ROOM A COUPLE OF TIMES A WEEK SUCKIN' MY ARMPIT.
MUCH NICER THAN THE ONE WHO HID IN THE BACK SEAT OF MY CAR AND HIT ME WITH A TIRE IRON, THOUGH.
I'M EVANGELINE KEEN. EVERYONE CALLS ME EVIE.
LYNN JANSEN. FROM ST. PAUL. A...
...A VAMPIRE KIDNAPPED ME WHILE I WAS HUNTING, AND...
...IT MURDERED MY HUSBAND, WOODY.
MY... MY BABY WON'T HAVE A DAD...
BACK UP OFFA THE DOOR, SONSABITCHES!

'CUZ **TOAD WARRIOR'S** COMIN'!

A GOOD MAN JUST DIED, AN' THE BOSS LADY'S IN A SCREAMIN' ANGUISH KIND OF MOOD, SO I'M BRINGING HER A SNACK--

--BUT NOT YOU, *INJUN.*

YRRAA!

'CUZ NOTHIN' CHASES BAD VIBES LIKE SOME INFANT JUICE.

C'MON, MONGREL-MAKER. WE CAN DO THIS WITH YOU ALIVE OR YOU CAN JOIN YOUR MUD-HUBBY IN THE **DAKOTA DIRT.**

OH, GOD.

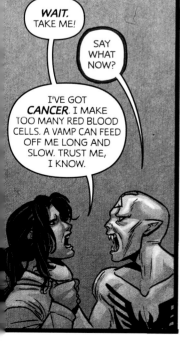

WAIT. TAKE ME!

SAY WHAT NOW?

I'VE GOT *CANCER.* I MAKE TOO MANY RED BLOOD CELLS. A VAMP CAN FEED OFF ME LONG AND SLOW. TRUST ME, I KNOW.

SNFF SNFF

WELL, I AIN'T MUCH INTO EATIN' CANCERS, BUT THE LADY'S REAL HIGH FALUTIN' TYPE. SHE LOVES A DELICACY.

CHILL FOR NOW, *RACE-TRAITOR.*

BUT I'LL BE BACK FOR YOU WHEN THE BOYS GET HERE.

OH, NO, EVIE. I'M SORRY...

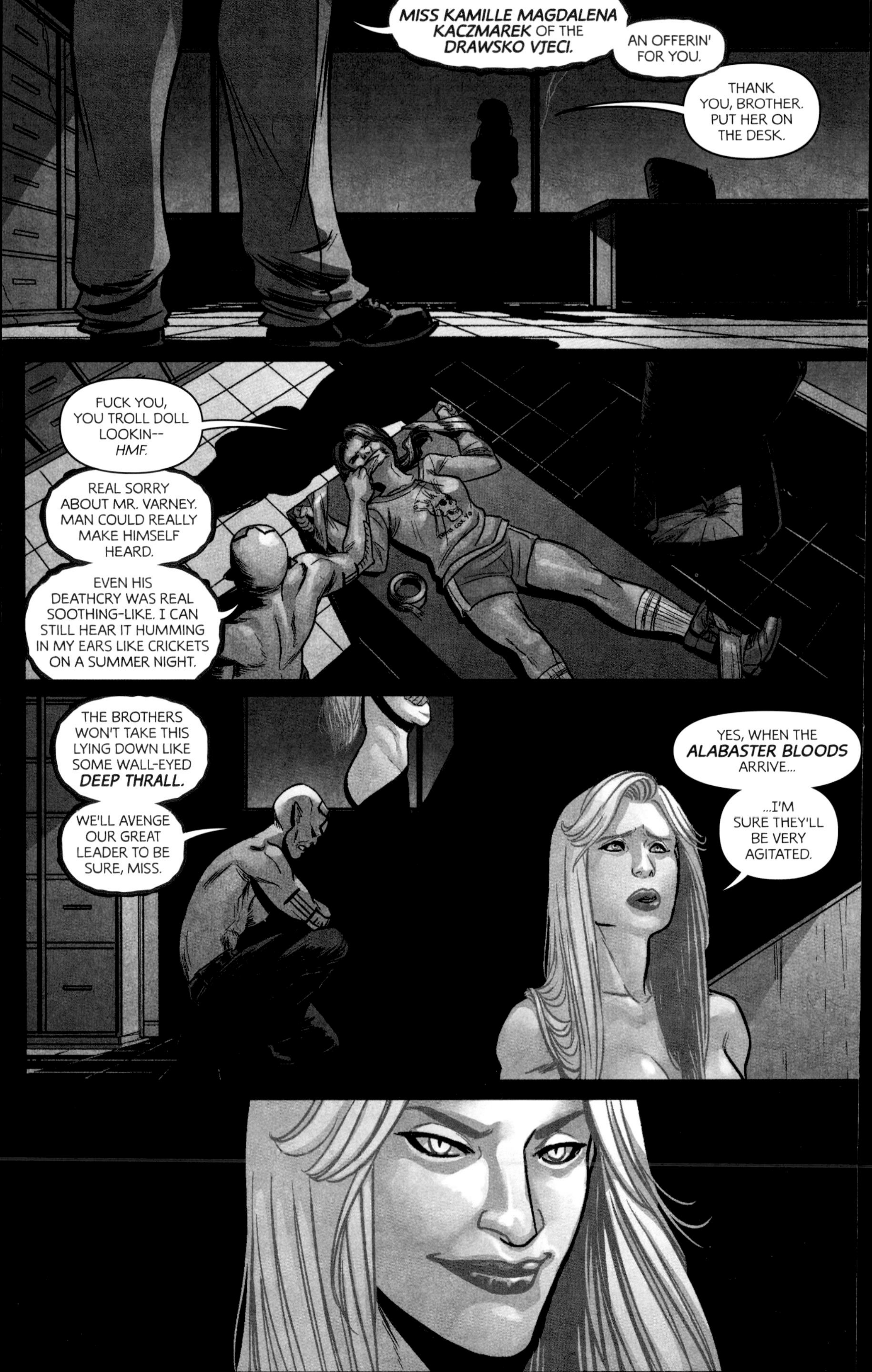
MISS KAMILLE MAGDALENA KACZMAREK OF THE DRAWSKO VJECI.
AN OFFERIN' FOR YOU.
THANK YOU, BROTHER. PUT HER ON THE DESK.
FUCK YOU, YOU TROLL DOLL LOOKIN-- HMF.
REAL SORRY ABOUT MR. VARNEY. MAN COULD REALLY MAKE HIMSELF HEARD.
EVEN HIS DEATHCRY WAS REAL SOOTHING-LIKE. I CAN STILL HEAR IT HUMMING IN MY EARS LIKE CRICKETS ON A SUMMER NIGHT.
THE BROTHERS WON'T TAKE THIS LYING DOWN LIKE SOME WALL-EYED DEEP THRALL.
WE'LL AVENGE OUR GREAT LEADER TO BE SURE, MISS.
YES, WHEN THE ALABASTER BLOODS ARRIVE...
...I'M SURE THEY'LL BE VERY AGITATED.

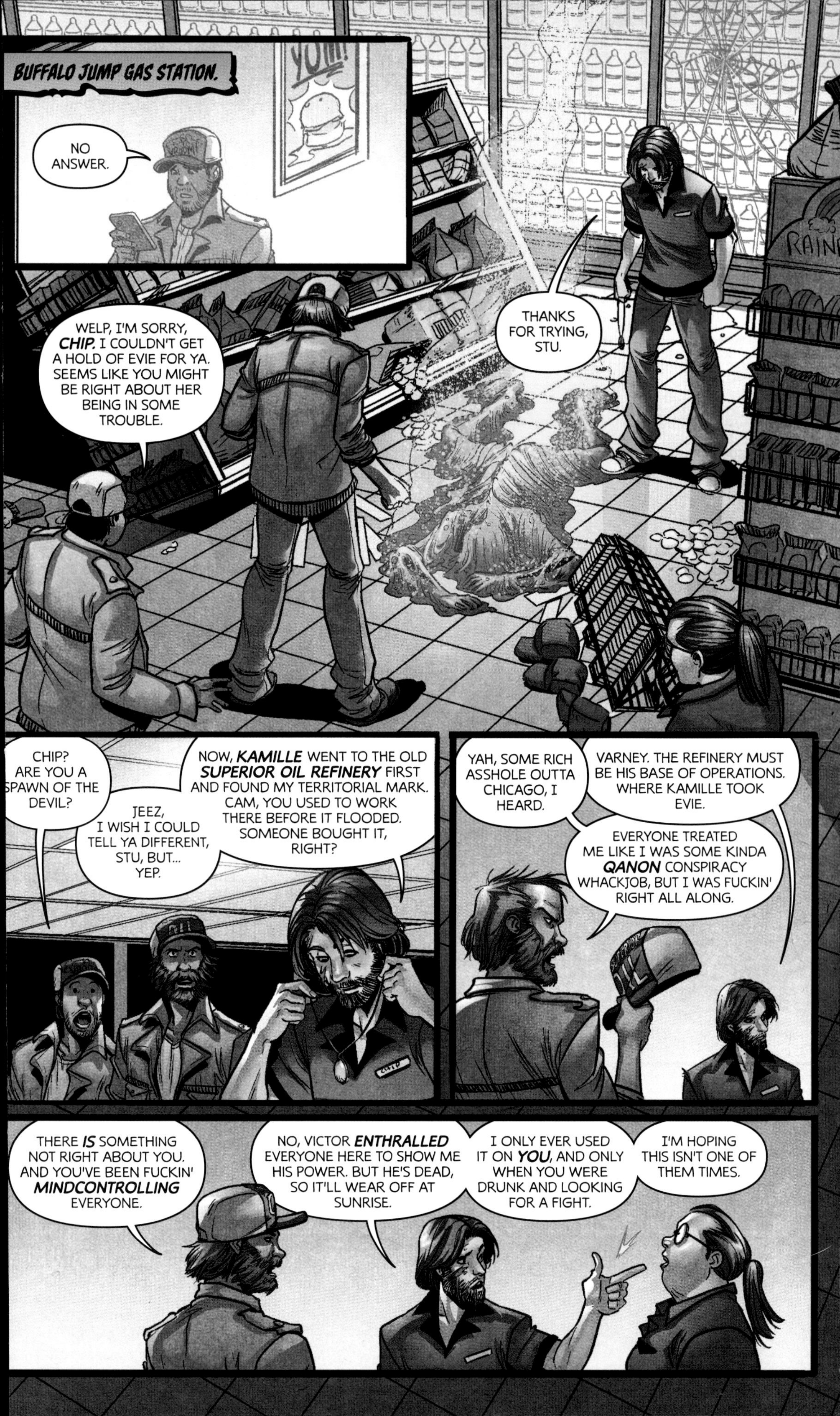
BUFFALO JUMP GAS STATION.
NO ANSWER.
WELP, I'M SORRY, CHIP. I COULDN'T GET A HOLD OF EVIE FOR YA. SEEMS LIKE YOU MIGHT BE RIGHT ABOUT HER BEING IN SOME TROUBLE.
THANKS FOR TRYING, STU.
CHIP? ARE YOU A SPAWN OF THE DEVIL?
JEEZ, I WISH I COULD TELL YA DIFFERENT, STU, BUT... YEP.
NOW, KAMILLE WENT TO THE OLD SUPERIOR OIL REFINERY FIRST AND FOUND MY TERRITORIAL MARK. CAM, YOU USED TO WORK THERE BEFORE IT FLOODED. SOMEONE BOUGHT IT, RIGHT?
YAH, SOME RICH ASSHOLE OUTTA CHICAGO, I HEARD.
VARNEY. THE REFINERY MUST BE HIS BASE OF OPERATIONS. WHERE KAMILLE TOOK EVIE.
EVERYONE TREATED ME LIKE I WAS SOME KINDA QANON CONSPIRACY WHACKJOB, BUT I WAS FUCKIN' RIGHT ALL ALONG.
THERE IS SOMETHING NOT RIGHT ABOUT YOU. AND YOU'VE BEEN FUCKIN' MINDCONTROLLING EVERYONE.
NO, VICTOR ENTHRALLED EVERYONE HERE TO SHOW ME HIS POWER. BUT HE'S DEAD, SO IT'LL WEAR OFF AT SUNRISE.
I ONLY EVER USED IT ON YOU, AND ONLY WHEN YOU WERE DRUNK AND LOOKING FOR A FIGHT.
I'M HOPING THIS ISN'T ONE OF THEM TIMES.

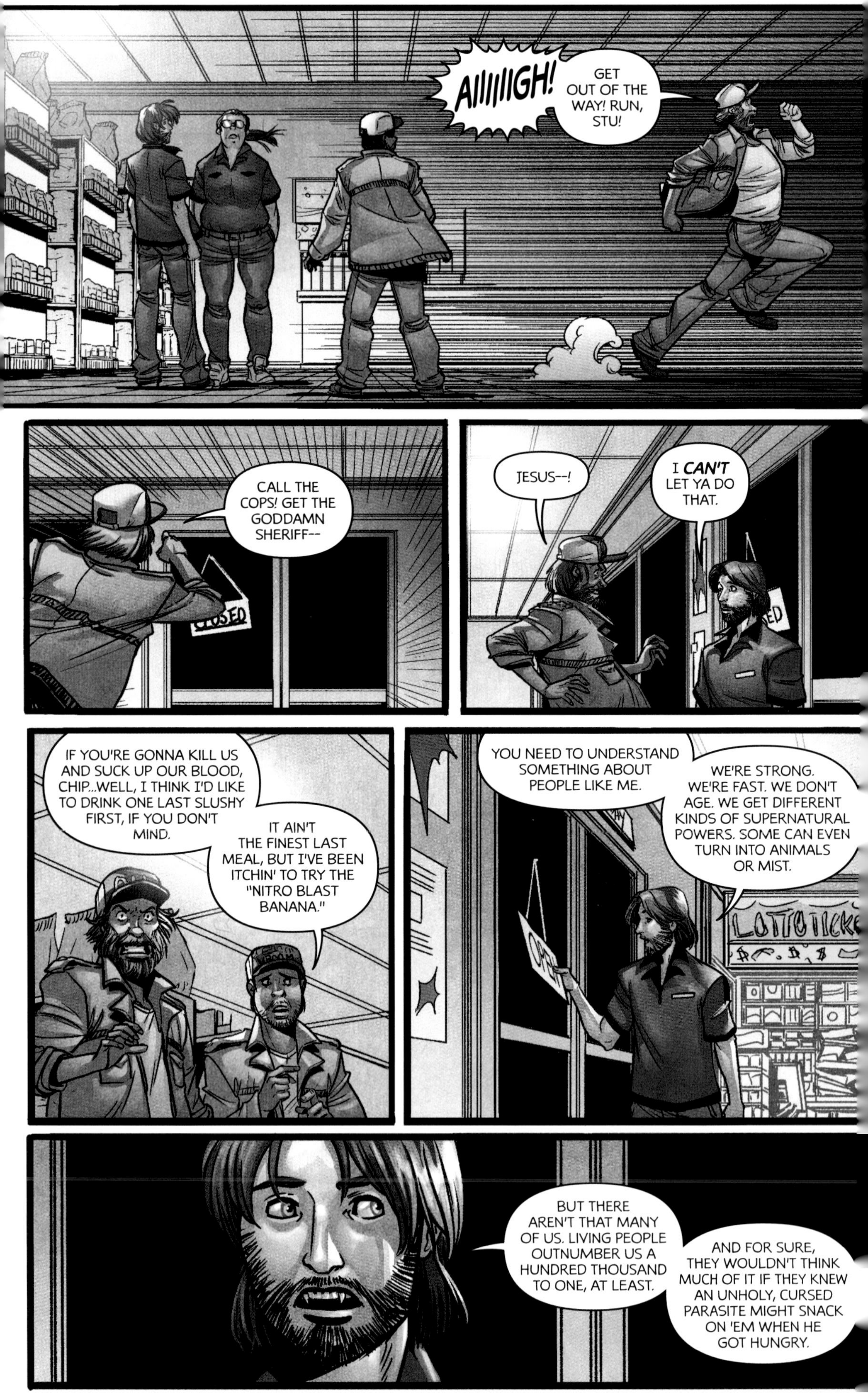
AIIIIIIGH!
GET OUT OF THE WAY! RUN, STU!
CALL THE COPS! GET THE GODDAMN SHERIFF--
CLOSED
JESUS--!
I *CAN'T* LET YA DO THAT.
IF YOU'RE GONNA KILL US AND SUCK UP OUR BLOOD, CHIP...WELL, I THINK I'D LIKE TO DRINK ONE LAST SLUSHY FIRST, IF YOU DON'T MIND.
IT AIN'T THE FINEST LAST MEAL, BUT I'VE BEEN ITCHIN' TO TRY THE "NITRO BLAST BANANA."
YOU NEED TO UNDERSTAND SOMETHING ABOUT PEOPLE LIKE ME.
WE'RE STRONG. WE'RE FAST. WE DON'T AGE. WE GET DIFFERENT KINDS OF SUPERNATURAL POWERS. SOME CAN EVEN TURN INTO ANIMALS OR MIST.
BUT THERE AREN'T THAT MANY OF US. LIVING PEOPLE OUTNUMBER US A HUNDRED THOUSAND TO ONE, AT LEAST.
AND FOR SURE, THEY WOULDN'T THINK MUCH OF IT IF THEY KNEW AN UNHOLY, CURSED PARASITE MIGHT SNACK ON 'EM WHEN HE GOT HUNGRY.

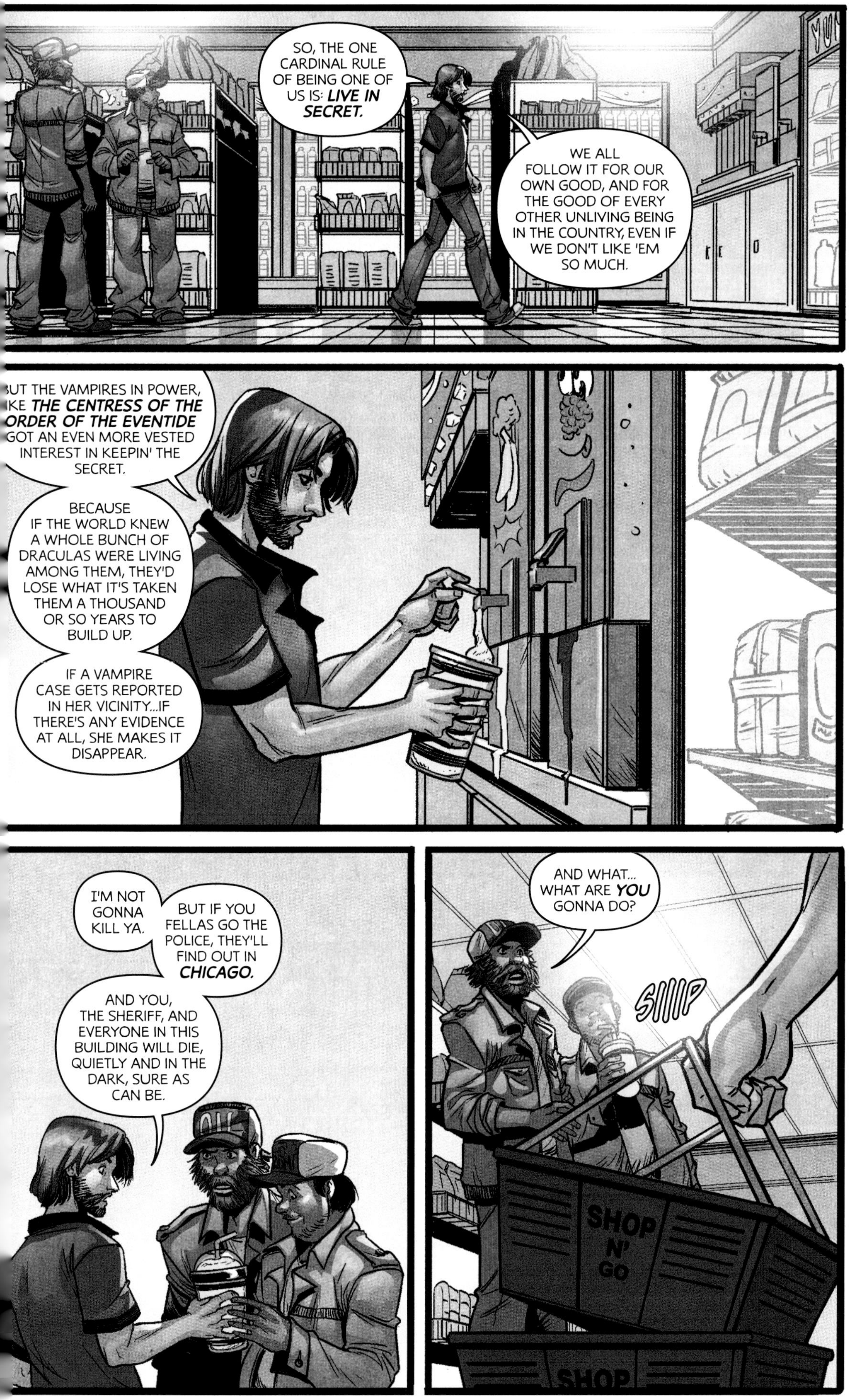

SO, THE ONE CARDINAL RULE OF BEING ONE OF US IS: ***LIVE IN SECRET.***
WE ALL FOLLOW IT FOR OUR OWN GOOD, AND FOR THE GOOD OF EVERY OTHER UNLIVING BEING IN THE COUNTRY, EVEN IF WE DON'T LIKE 'EM SO MUCH.
UT THE VAMPIRES IN POWER, KE ***THE CENTRESS OF THE ORDER OF THE EVENTIDE*** GOT AN EVEN MORE VESTED INTEREST IN KEEPIN' THE SECRET.
BECAUSE IF THE WORLD KNEW A WHOLE BUNCH OF DRACULAS WERE LIVING AMONG THEM, THEY'D LOSE WHAT IT'S TAKEN THEM A THOUSAND OR SO YEARS TO BUILD UP.
IF A VAMPIRE CASE GETS REPORTED IN HER VICINITY...IF THERE'S ANY EVIDENCE AT ALL, SHE MAKES IT DISAPPEAR.
I'M NOT GONNA KILL YA.
BUT IF YOU FELLAS GO THE POLICE, THEY'LL FIND OUT IN ***CHICAGO.***
AND YOU, THE SHERIFF, AND EVERYONE IN THIS BUILDING WILL DIE, QUIETLY AND IN THE DARK, SURE AS CAN BE.
AND WHAT... WHAT ARE ***YOU*** GONNA DO?
SIIIP
SHOP N' GO
SHOP

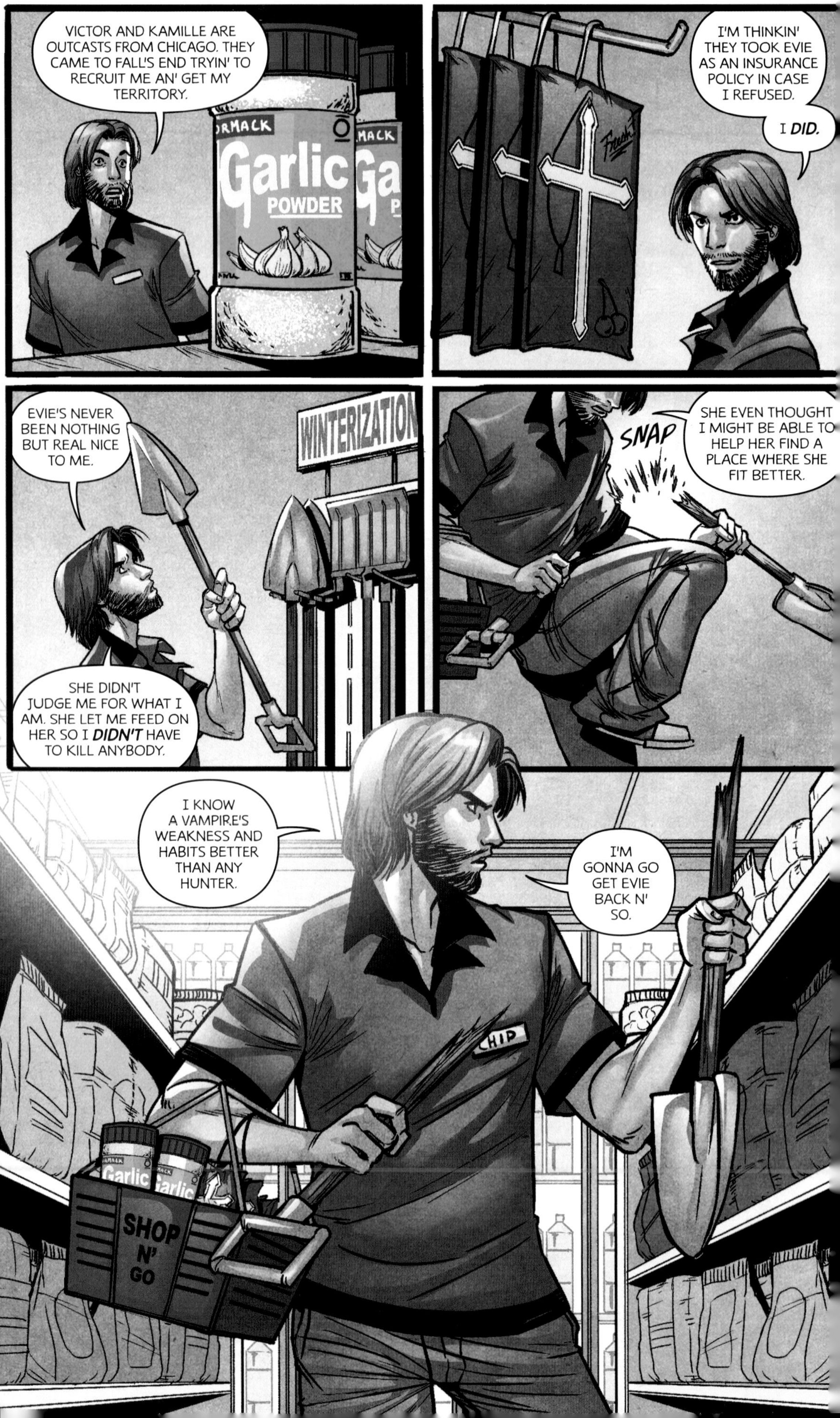
VICTOR AND KAMILLE ARE OUTCASTS FROM CHICAGO. THEY CAME TO FALL'S END TRYIN' TO RECRUIT ME AN' GET MY TERRITORY.
Garlic POWDER
I'M THINKIN' THEY TOOK EVIE AS AN INSURANCE POLICY IN CASE I REFUSED.
I ***DID.***
EVIE'S NEVER BEEN NOTHING BUT REAL NICE TO ME.
WINTERIZATION
SHE DIDN'T JUDGE ME FOR WHAT I AM. SHE LET ME FEED ON HER SO I ***DIDN'T*** HAVE TO KILL ANYBODY.
SNAP
SHE EVEN THOUGHT I MIGHT BE ABLE TO HELP HER FIND A PLACE WHERE SHE FIT BETTER.
I KNOW A VAMPIRE'S WEAKNESS AND HABITS BETTER THAN ANY HUNTER.
I'M GONNA GO GET EVIE BACK N' SO.
CHIP
SHOP N' GO

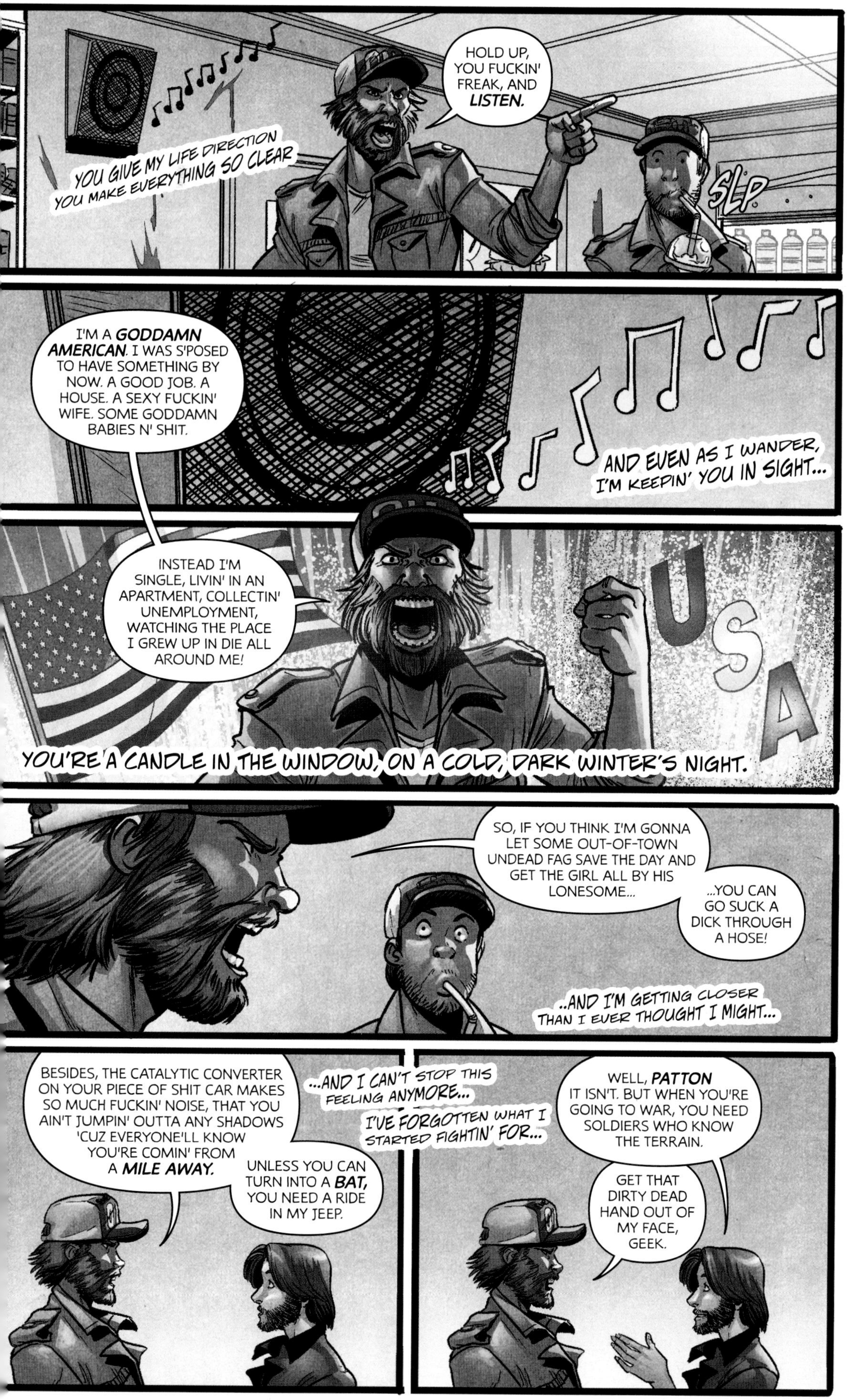
HOLD UP, YOU FUCKIN' FREAK, AND LISTEN.
YOU GIVE MY LIFE DIRECTION
YOU MAKE EVERYTHING SO CLEAR
SLP
I'M A GODDAMN AMERICAN. I WAS S'POSED TO HAVE SOMETHING BY NOW. A GOOD JOB. A HOUSE. A SEXY FUCKIN' WIFE. SOME GODDAMN BABIES N' SHIT.
AND EVEN AS I WANDER, I'M KEEPIN' YOU IN SIGHT...
INSTEAD I'M SINGLE, LIVIN' IN AN APARTMENT, COLLECTIN' UNEMPLOYMENT, WATCHING THE PLACE I GREW UP IN DIE ALL AROUND ME!
USA
YOU'RE A CANDLE IN THE WINDOW, ON A COLD, DARK WINTER'S NIGHT.
SO, IF YOU THINK I'M GONNA LET SOME OUT-OF-TOWN UNDEAD FAG SAVE THE DAY AND GET THE GIRL ALL BY HIS LONESOME...
...YOU CAN GO SUCK A DICK THROUGH A HOSE!
..AND I'M GETTING CLOSER THAN I EVER THOUGHT I MIGHT...
BESIDES, THE CATALYTIC CONVERTER ON YOUR PIECE OF SHIT CAR MAKES SO MUCH FUCKIN' NOISE, THAT YOU AIN'T JUMPIN' OUTTA ANY SHADOWS 'CUZ EVERYONE'LL KNOW YOU'RE COMIN' FROM A MILE AWAY.
UNLESS YOU CAN TURN INTO A BAT, YOU NEED A RIDE IN MY JEEP.
...AND I CAN'T STOP THIS FEELING ANYMORE...
I'VE FORGOTTEN WHAT I STARTED FIGHTIN' FOR...
WELL, PATTON IT ISN'T. BUT WHEN YOU'RE GOING TO WAR, YOU NEED SOLDIERS WHO KNOW THE TERRAIN.
GET THAT DIRTY DEAD HAND OUT OF MY FACE, GEEK.

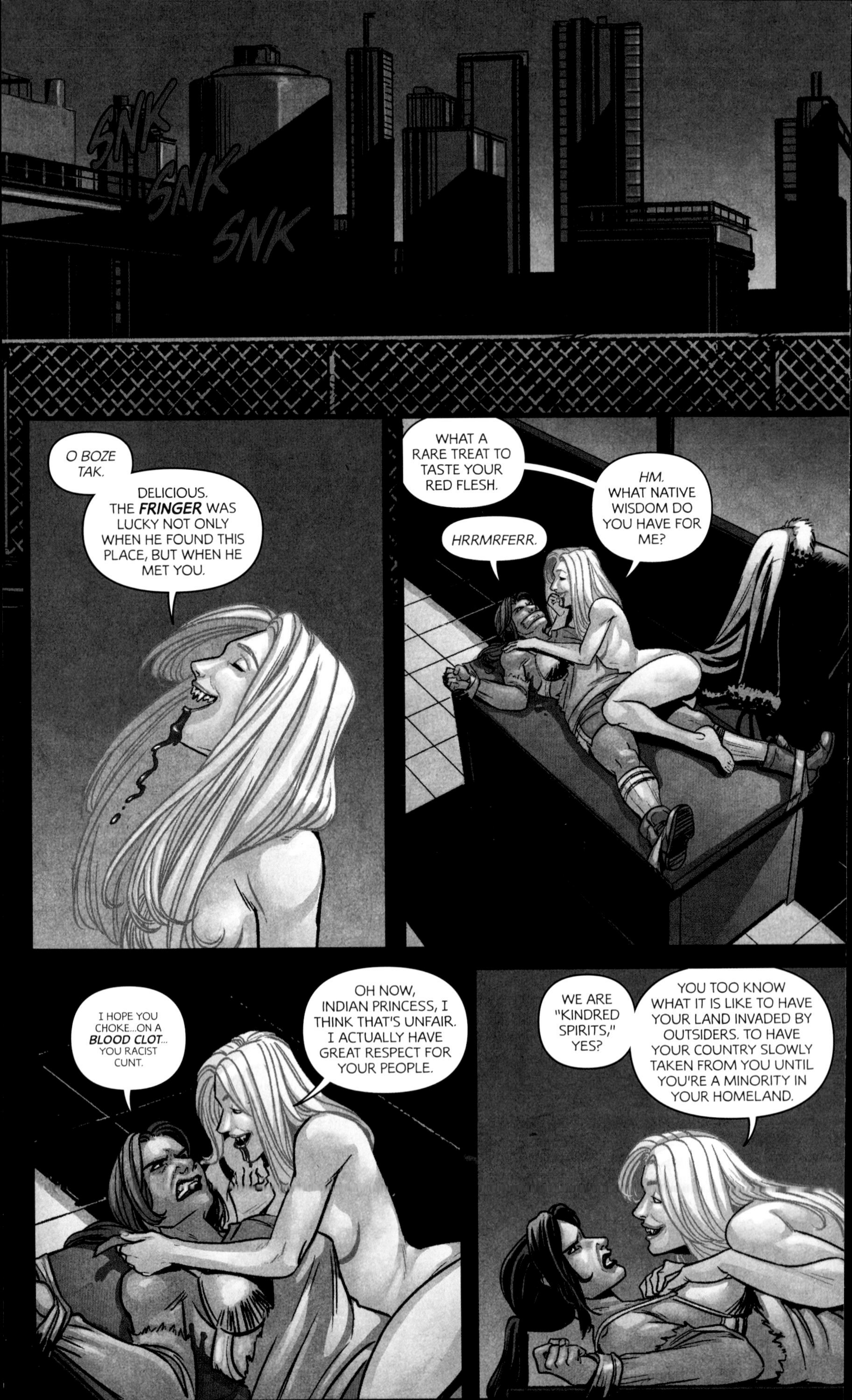
SNK
SNK
SNK
O BOZE TAK.
DELICIOUS. THE **FRINGER** WAS LUCKY NOT ONLY WHEN HE FOUND THIS PLACE, BUT WHEN HE MET YOU.
WHAT A RARE TREAT TO TASTE YOUR RED FLESH.
HM. WHAT NATIVE WISDOM DO YOU HAVE FOR ME?
HRRMRFERR.
I HOPE YOU CHOKE...ON A ***BLOOD CLOT***... YOU RACIST CUNT.
OH NOW, INDIAN PRINCESS, I THINK THAT'S UNFAIR. I ACTUALLY HAVE GREAT RESPECT FOR YOUR PEOPLE.
WE ARE "KINDRED SPIRITS," YES?
YOU TOO KNOW WHAT IT IS LIKE TO HAVE YOUR LAND INVADED BY OUTSIDERS. TO HAVE YOUR COUNTRY SLOWLY TAKEN FROM YOU UNTIL YOU'RE A MINORITY IN YOUR HOMELAND.

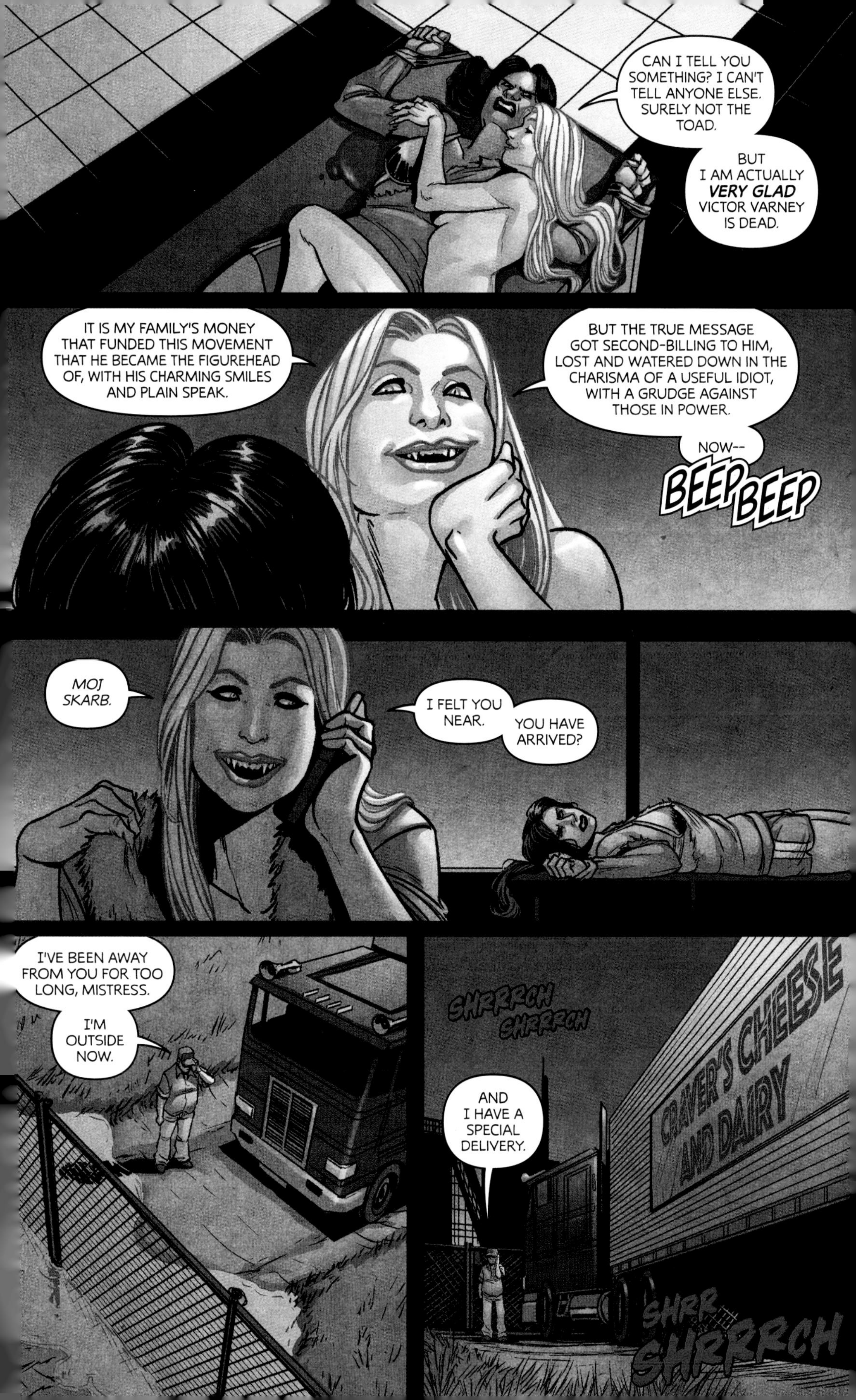
CAN I TELL YOU SOMETHING? I CAN'T TELL ANYONE ELSE. SURELY NOT THE TOAD.
BUT I AM ACTUALLY ***VERY GLAD*** VICTOR VARNEY IS DEAD.
IT IS MY FAMILY'S MONEY THAT FUNDED THIS MOVEMENT THAT HE BECAME THE FIGUREHEAD OF, WITH HIS CHARMING SMILES AND PLAIN SPEAK.
BUT THE TRUE MESSAGE GOT SECOND-BILLING TO HIM, LOST AND WATERED DOWN IN THE CHARISMA OF A USEFUL IDIOT, WITH A GRUDGE AGAINST THOSE IN POWER.
NOW--
BEEP BEEP
MOJ SKARB.
I FELT YOU NEAR.
YOU HAVE ARRIVED?
I'VE BEEN AWAY FROM YOU FOR TOO LONG, MISTRESS.
I'M OUTSIDE NOW.
SHRRRCH SHRRRCH
CRAVER'S CHEESE AND DAIRY
AND I HAVE A SPECIAL DELIVERY.
SHRR SHRRRCH

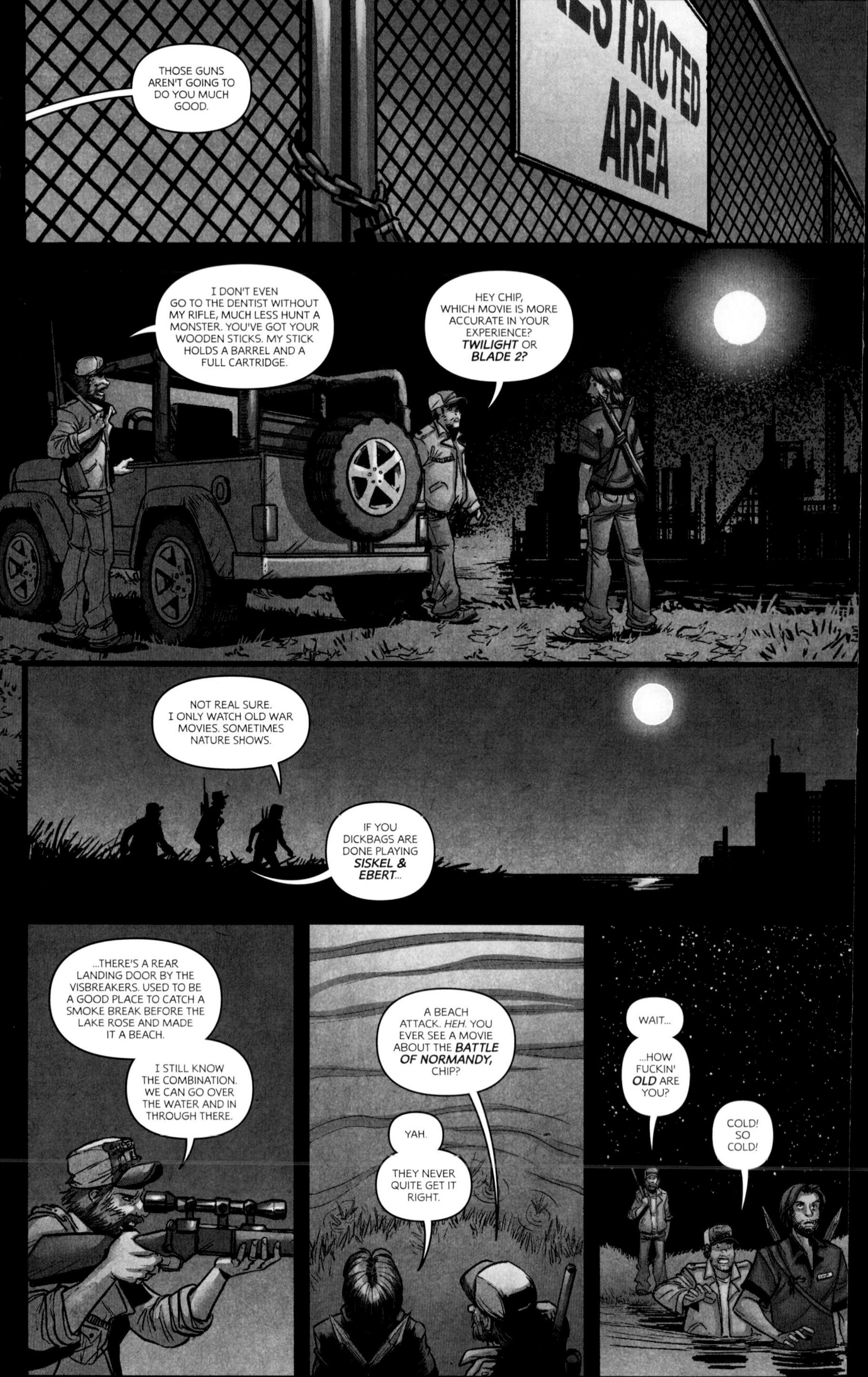
RESTRICTED AREA
THOSE GUNS AREN'T GOING TO DO YOU MUCH GOOD.
I DON'T EVEN GO TO THE DENTIST WITHOUT MY RIFLE, MUCH LESS HUNT A MONSTER. YOU'VE GOT YOUR WOODEN STICKS. MY STICK HOLDS A BARREL AND A FULL CARTRIDGE.
HEY CHIP, WHICH MOVIE IS MORE ACCURATE IN YOUR EXPERIENCE? TWILIGHT OR BLADE 2?
NOT REAL SURE. I ONLY WATCH OLD WAR MOVIES. SOMETIMES NATURE SHOWS.
IF YOU DICKBAGS ARE DONE PLAYING SISKEL & EBERT...
...THERE'S A REAR LANDING DOOR BY THE VISBREAKERS. USED TO BE A GOOD PLACE TO CATCH A SMOKE BREAK BEFORE THE LAKE ROSE AND MADE IT A BEACH.
I STILL KNOW THE COMBINATION. WE CAN GO OVER THE WATER AND IN THROUGH THERE.
A BEACH ATTACK. HEH. YOU EVER SEE A MOVIE ABOUT THE BATTLE OF NORMANDY, CHIP?
YAH.
THEY NEVER QUITE GET IT RIGHT.
WAIT...
...HOW FUCKIN' OLD ARE YOU?
COLD! SO COLD!

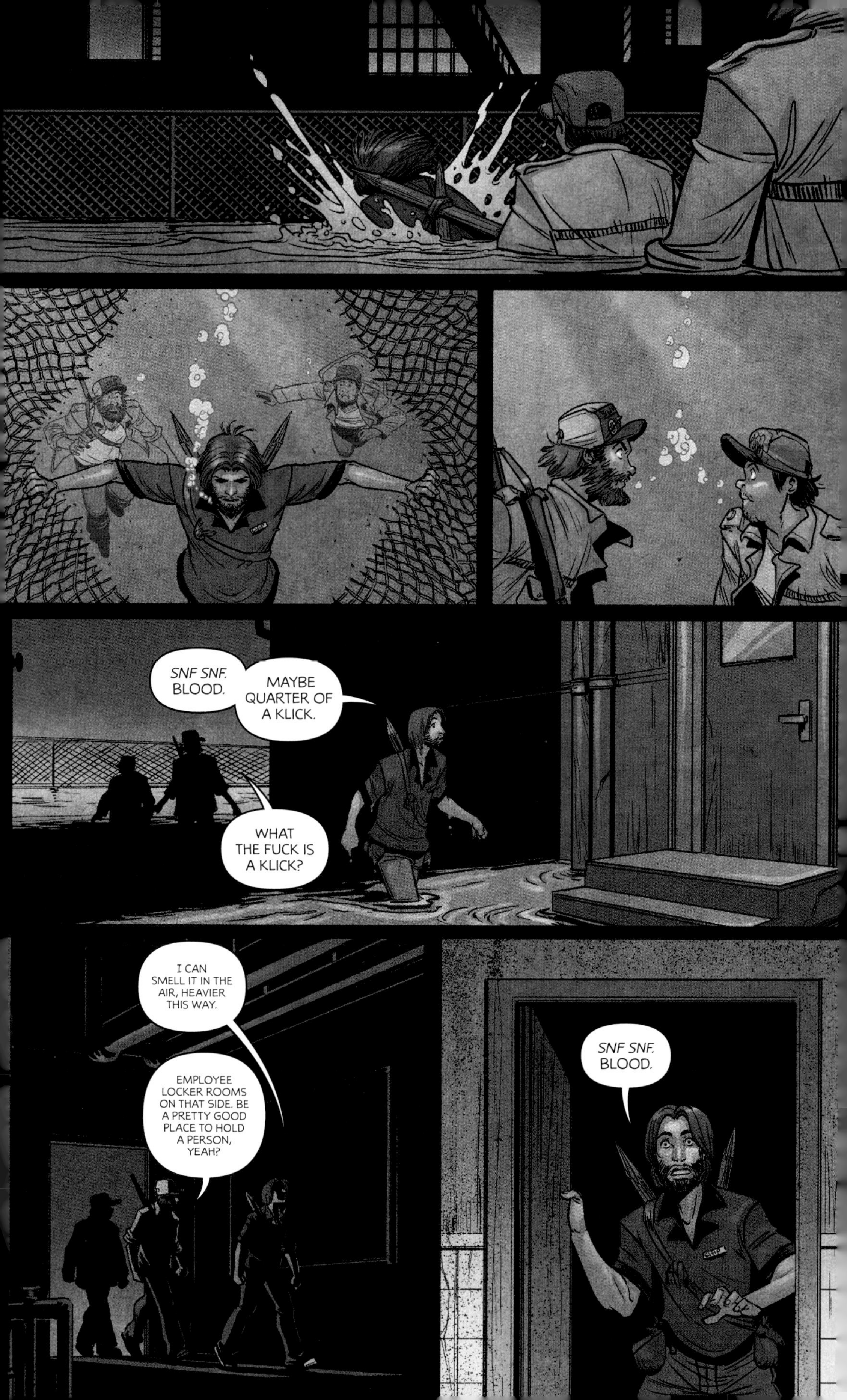
SNF SNF. BLOOD.
MAYBE QUARTER OF A KLICK.
WHAT THE FUCK IS A KLICK?
I CAN SMELL IT IN THE AIR, HEAVIER THIS WAY.
EMPLOYEE LOCKER ROOMS ON THAT SIDE. BE A PRETTY GOOD PLACE TO HOLD A PERSON, YEAH?
SNF SNF. BLOOD.

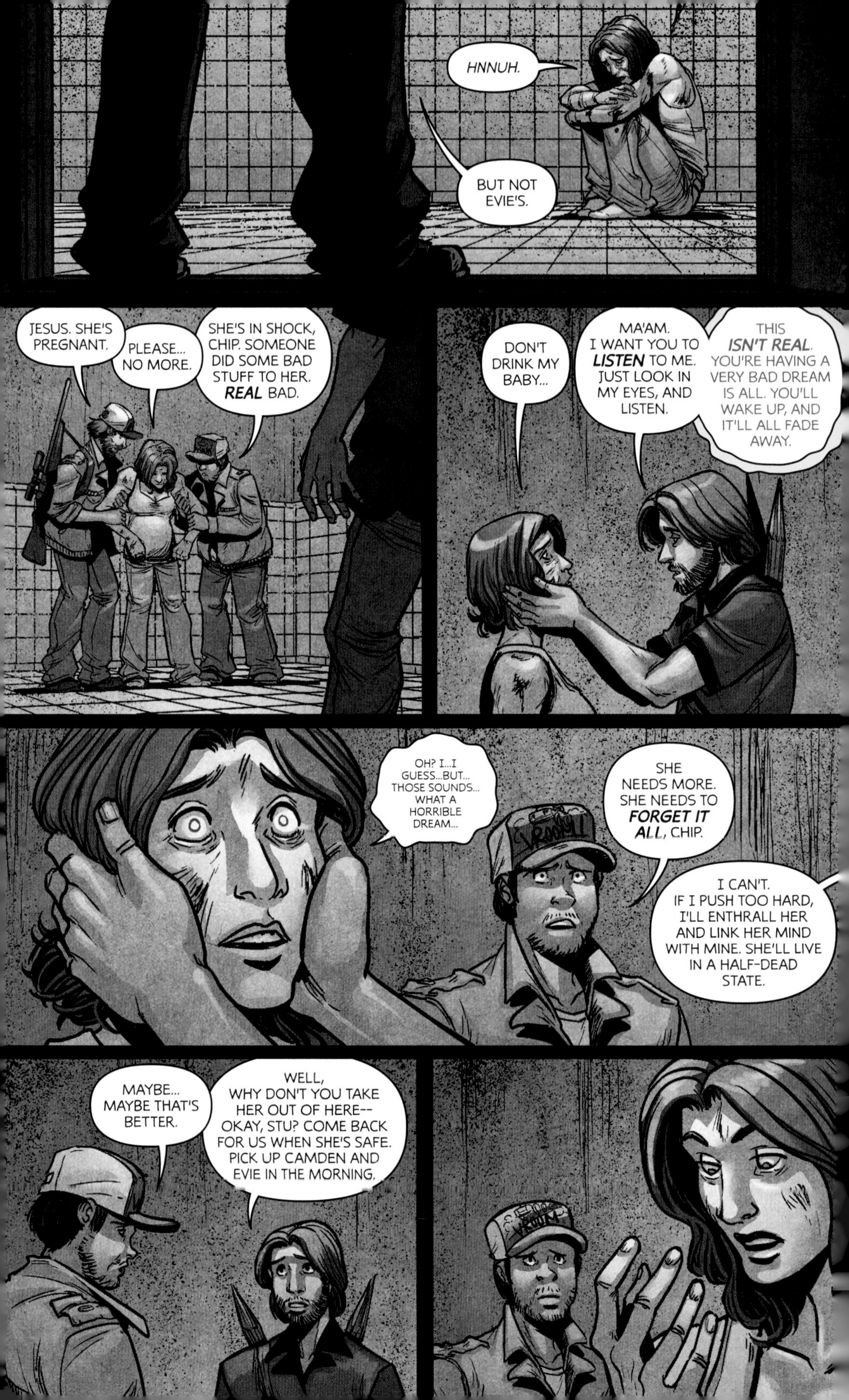
HNNUH.
BUT NOT EVIE'S.
JESUS. SHE'S PREGNANT.
PLEASE... NO MORE.
SHE'S IN SHOCK, CHIP. SOMEONE DID SOME BAD STUFF TO HER. REAL BAD.
DON'T DRINK MY BABY...
MA'AM. I WANT YOU TO LISTEN TO ME. JUST LOOK IN MY EYES, AND LISTEN.
THIS ISN'T REAL. YOU'RE HAVING A VERY BAD DREAM IS ALL. YOU'LL WAKE UP, AND IT'LL ALL FADE AWAY.
OH? I...I GUESS...BUT... THOSE SOUNDS... WHAT A HORRIBLE DREAM...
SHE NEEDS MORE. SHE NEEDS TO FORGET IT ALL, CHIP.
I CAN'T. IF I PUSH TOO HARD, I'LL ENTHRALL HER AND LINK HER MIND WITH MINE. SHE'LL LIVE IN A HALF-DEAD STATE.
MAYBE... MAYBE THAT'S BETTER.
WELL, WHY DON'T YOU TAKE HER OUT OF HERE-- OKAY, STU? COME BACK FOR US WHEN SHE'S SAFE. PICK UP CAMDEN AND EVIE IN THE MORNING.

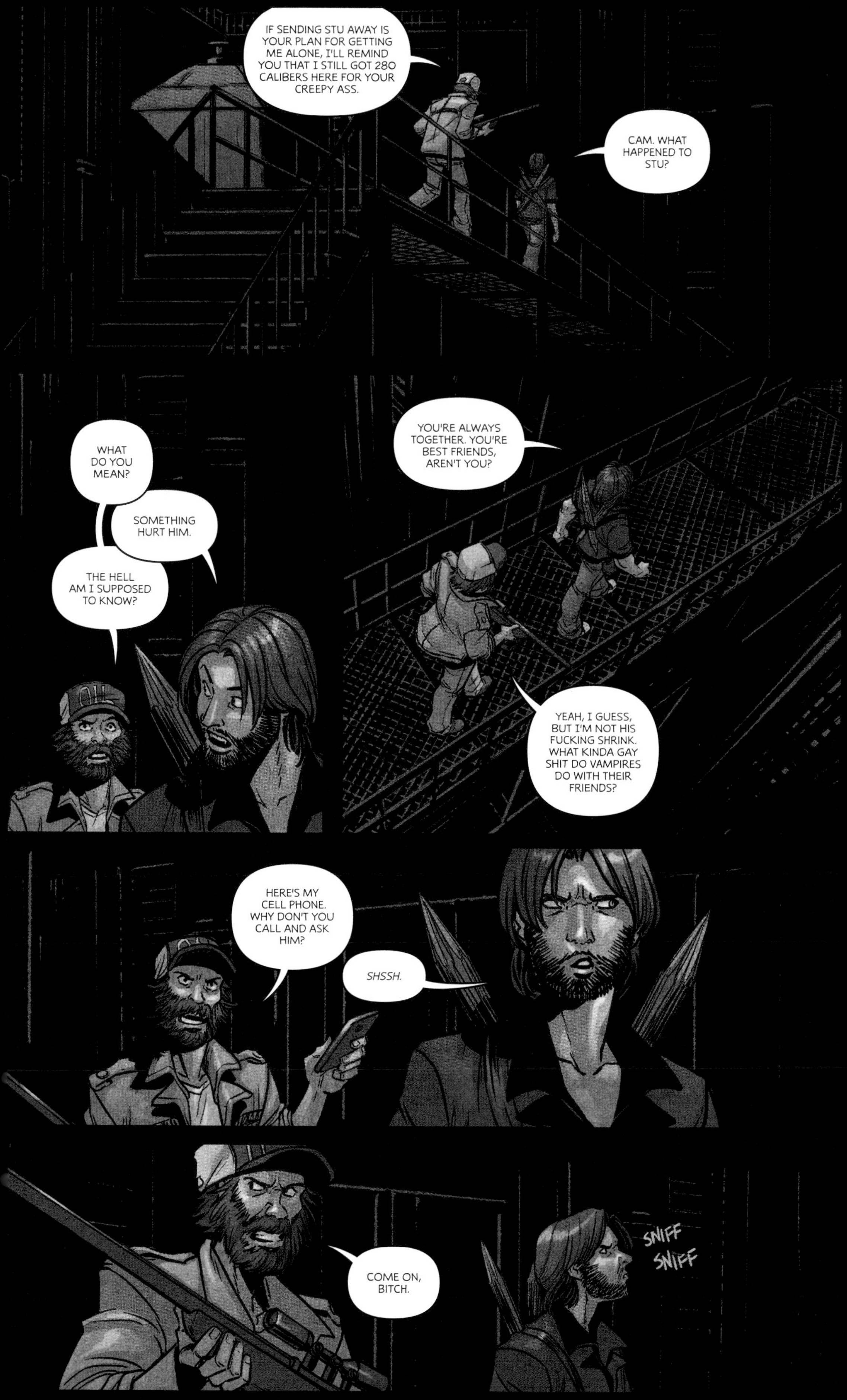
IF SENDING STU AWAY IS YOUR PLAN FOR GETTING ME ALONE, I'LL REMIND YOU THAT I STILL GOT 280 CALIBERS HERE FOR YOUR CREEPY ASS.
CAM. WHAT HAPPENED TO STU?
WHAT DO YOU MEAN?
SOMETHING HURT HIM.
THE HELL AM I SUPPOSED TO KNOW?
YOU'RE ALWAYS TOGETHER. YOU'RE BEST FRIENDS, AREN'T YOU?
YEAH, I GUESS, BUT I'M NOT HIS FUCKING SHRINK. WHAT KINDA GAY SHIT DO VAMPIRES DO WITH THEIR FRIENDS?
HERE'S MY CELL PHONE. WHY DON'T YOU CALL AND ASK HIM?
SHSSH.
COME ON, BITCH.
SNIFF
SNIFF

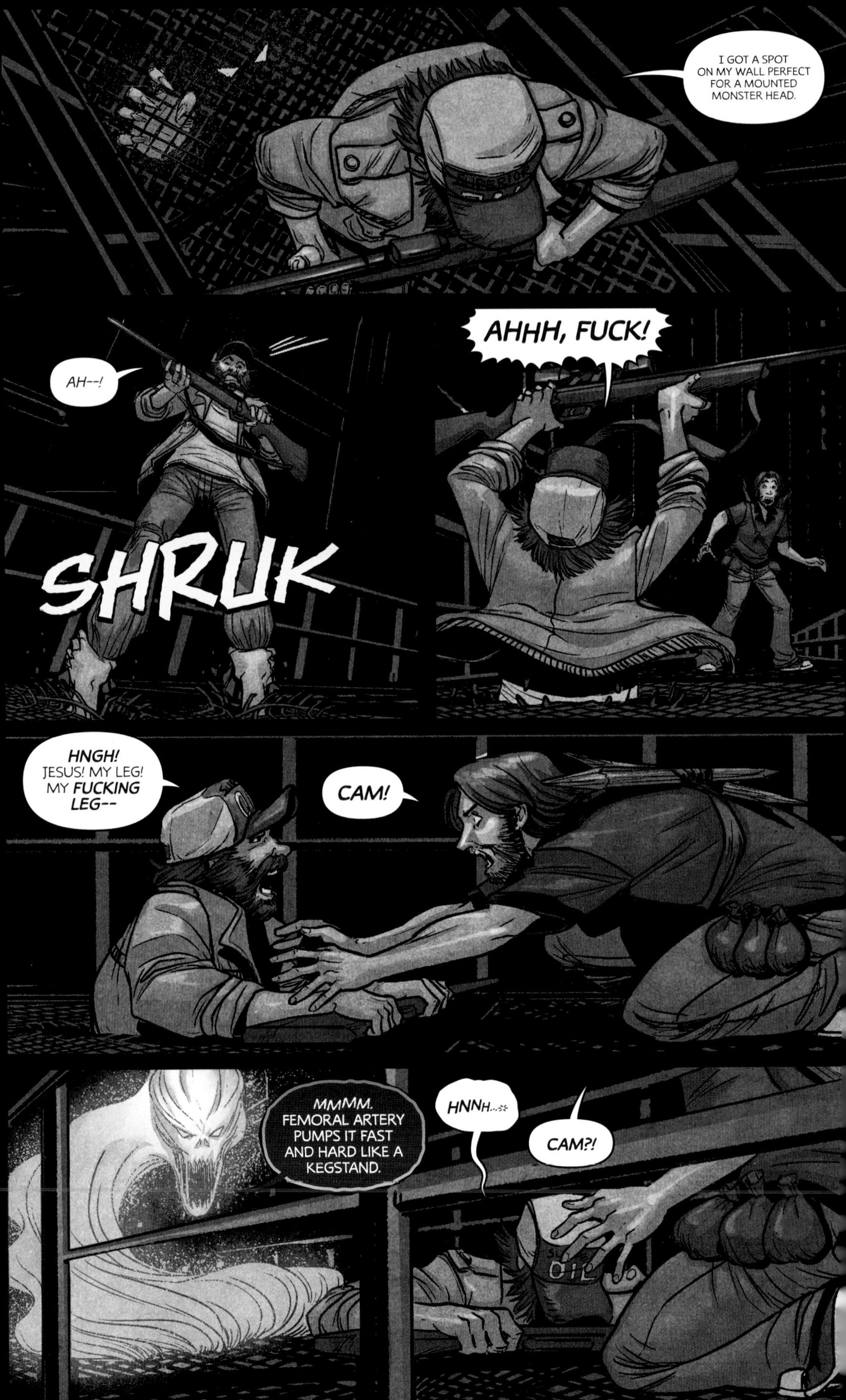
I GOT A SPOT ON MY WALL PERFECT FOR A MOUNTED MONSTER HEAD.
AH--!
SHRUK
AHHH, FUCK!
HNGH! JESUS! MY LEG! MY FUCKING LEG--
CAM!
MMMM. FEMORAL ARTERY PUMPS IT FAST AND HARD LIKE A KEGSTAND.
HNNH...
CAM?!

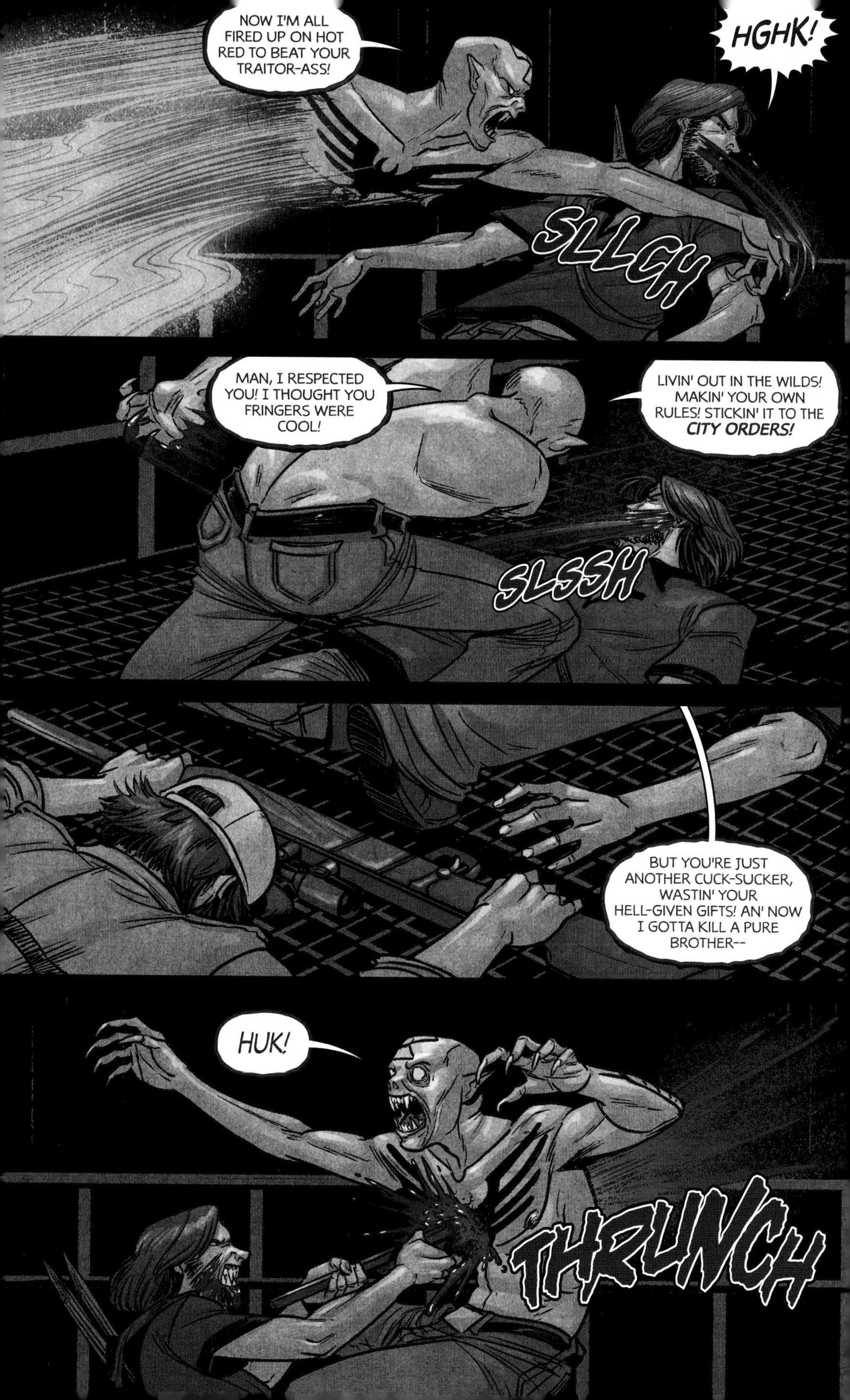
NOW I'M ALL FIRED UP ON HOT RED TO BEAT YOUR TRAITOR-ASS!
HGHK!
SLLCH
MAN, I RESPECTED YOU! I THOUGHT YOU FRINGERS WERE COOL!
LIVIN' OUT IN THE WILDS! MAKIN' YOUR OWN RULES! STICKIN' IT TO THE CITY ORDERS!
SLSSH
BUT YOU'RE JUST ANOTHER CUCK-SUCKER, WASTIN' YOUR HELL-GIVEN GIFTS! AN' NOW I GOTTA KILL A PURE BROTHER--
HUK!
THRUNCH

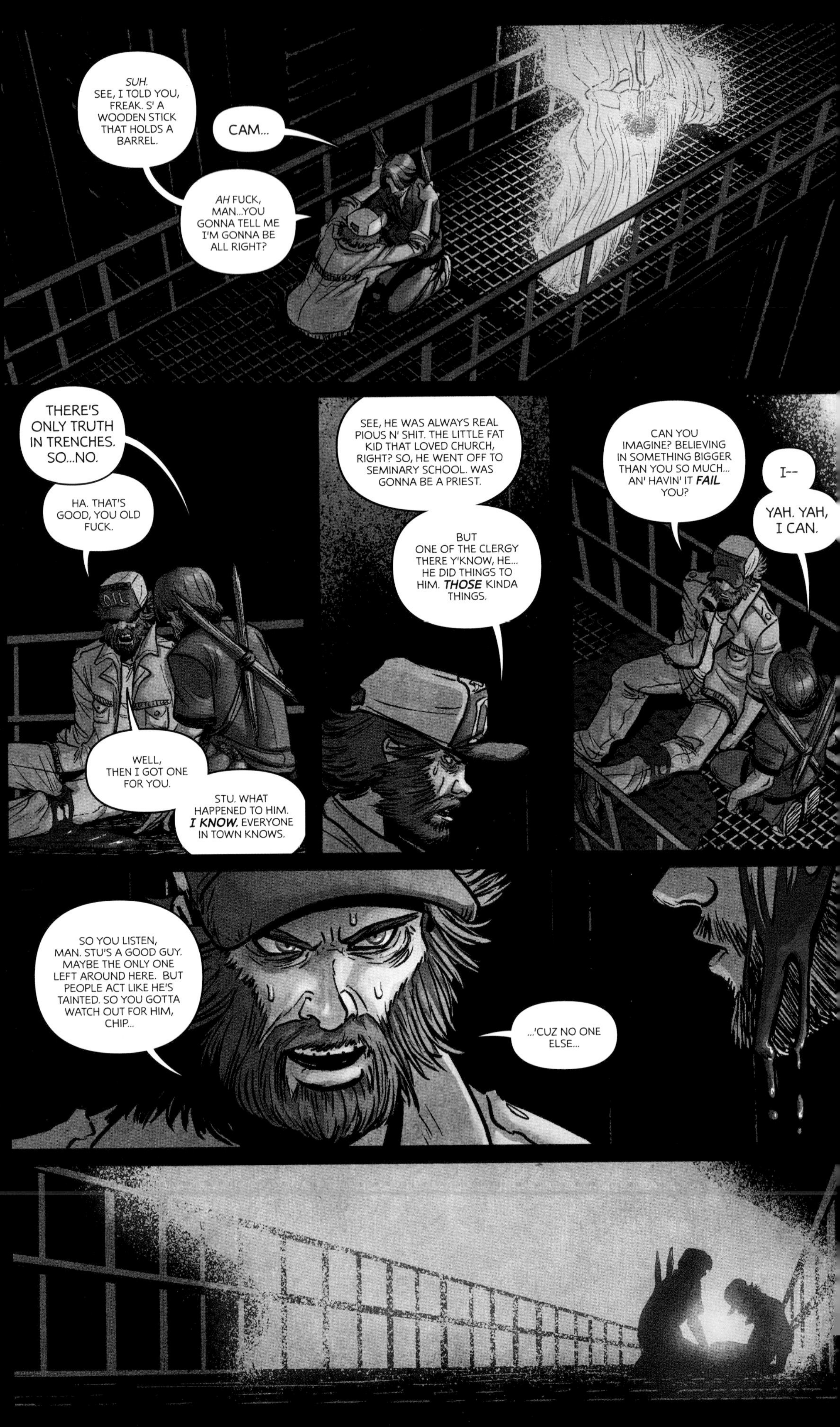
SUH.
SEE, I TOLD YOU, FREAK. S' A WOODEN STICK THAT HOLDS A BARREL.
CAM...
AH FUCK, MAN...YOU GONNA TELL ME I'M GONNA BE ALL RIGHT?
THERE'S ONLY TRUTH IN TRENCHES. SO...NO.
HA. THAT'S GOOD, YOU OLD FUCK.
WELL, THEN I GOT ONE FOR YOU.
STU. WHAT HAPPENED TO HIM. I KNOW. EVERYONE IN TOWN KNOWS.
SEE, HE WAS ALWAYS REAL PIOUS N' SHIT. THE LITTLE FAT KID THAT LOVED CHURCH, RIGHT? SO, HE WENT OFF TO SEMINARY SCHOOL. WAS GONNA BE A PRIEST.
BUT ONE OF THE CLERGY THERE Y'KNOW, HE... HE DID THINGS TO HIM. THOSE KINDA THINGS.
CAN YOU IMAGINE? BELIEVING IN SOMETHING BIGGER THAN YOU SO MUCH... AN' HAVIN' IT FAIL YOU?
I--
YAH. YAH, I CAN.
SO YOU LISTEN, MAN. STU'S A GOOD GUY. MAYBE THE ONLY ONE LEFT AROUND HERE. BUT PEOPLE ACT LIKE HE'S TAINTED. SO YOU GOTTA WATCH OUT FOR HIM, CHIP...
...'CUZ NO ONE ELSE...

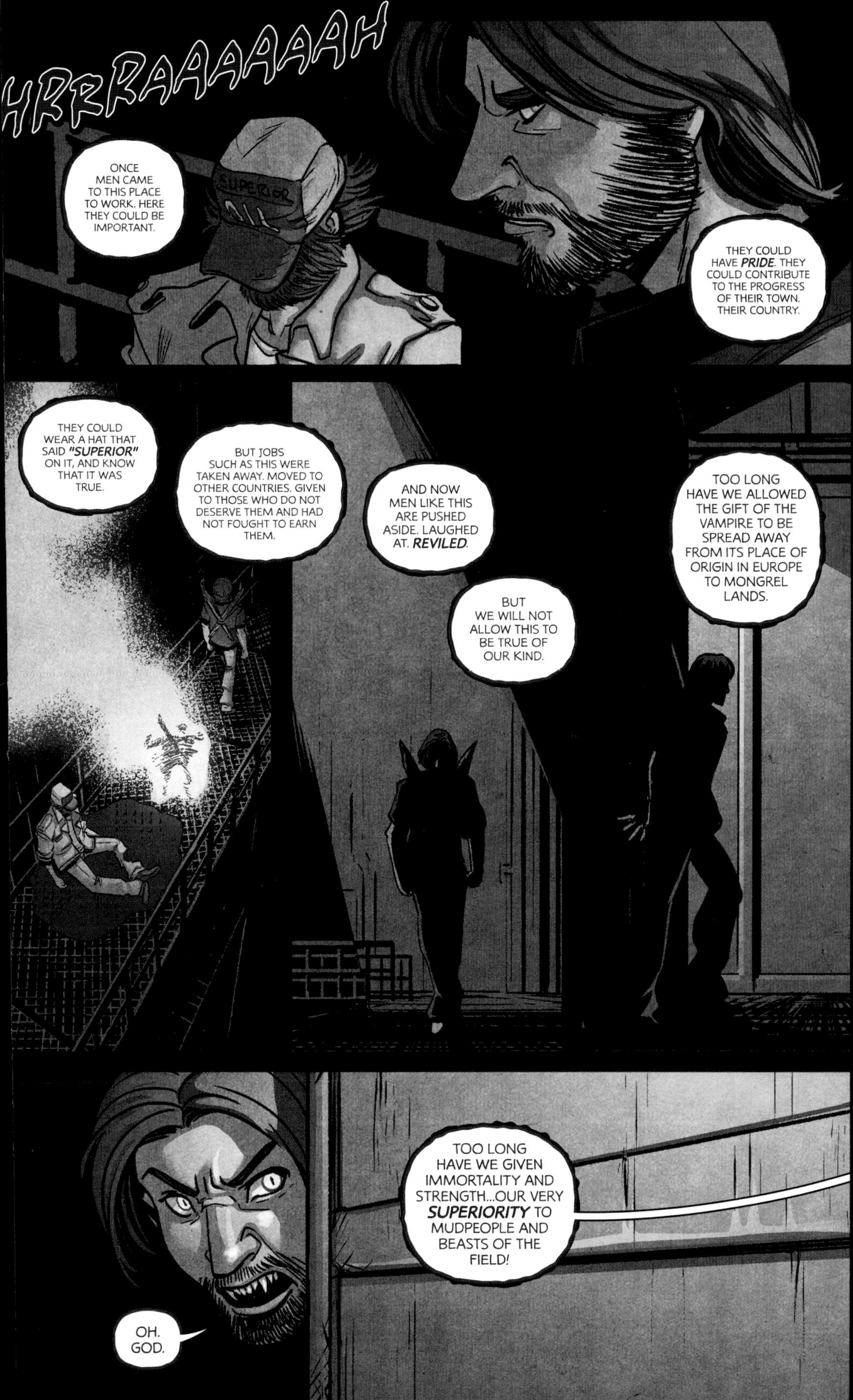
HRRRAAAAAAH
ONCE MEN CAME TO THIS PLACE TO WORK. HERE THEY COULD BE IMPORTANT.
SUPERIOR
THEY COULD HAVE PRIDE. THEY COULD CONTRIBUTE TO THE PROGRESS OF THEIR TOWN. THEIR COUNTRY.
THEY COULD WEAR A HAT THAT SAID "SUPERIOR" ON IT, AND KNOW THAT IT WAS TRUE.
BUT JOBS SUCH AS THIS WERE TAKEN AWAY. MOVED TO OTHER COUNTRIES. GIVEN TO THOSE WHO DO NOT DESERVE THEM AND HAD NOT FOUGHT TO EARN THEM.
AND NOW MEN LIKE THIS ARE PUSHED ASIDE. LAUGHED AT. REVILED.
BUT WE WILL NOT ALLOW THIS TO BE TRUE OF OUR KIND.
TOO LONG HAVE WE ALLOWED THE GIFT OF THE VAMPIRE TO BE SPREAD AWAY FROM ITS PLACE OF ORIGIN IN EUROPE TO MONGREL LANDS.
TOO LONG HAVE WE GIVEN IMMORTALITY AND STRENGTH...OUR VERY SUPERIORITY TO MUDPEOPLE AND BEASTS OF THE FIELD!
OH. GOD.

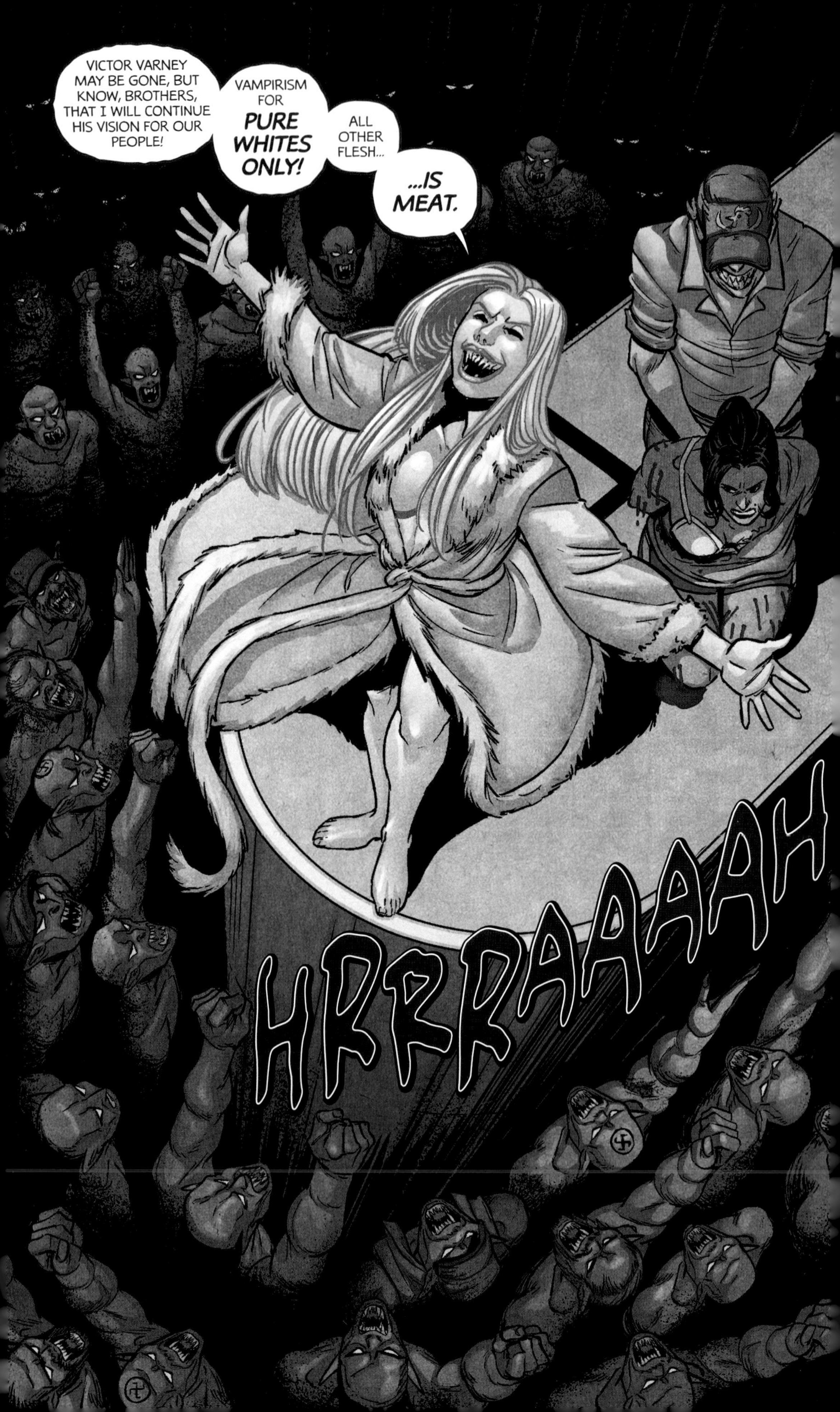
VICTOR VARNEY MAY BE GONE, BUT KNOW, BROTHERS, THAT I WILL CONTINUE HIS VISION FOR OUR PEOPLE!
VAMPIRISM FOR PURE WHITES ONLY!
ALL OTHER FLESH...
...IS MEAT.
HRRRAAAAAH

5

SALT

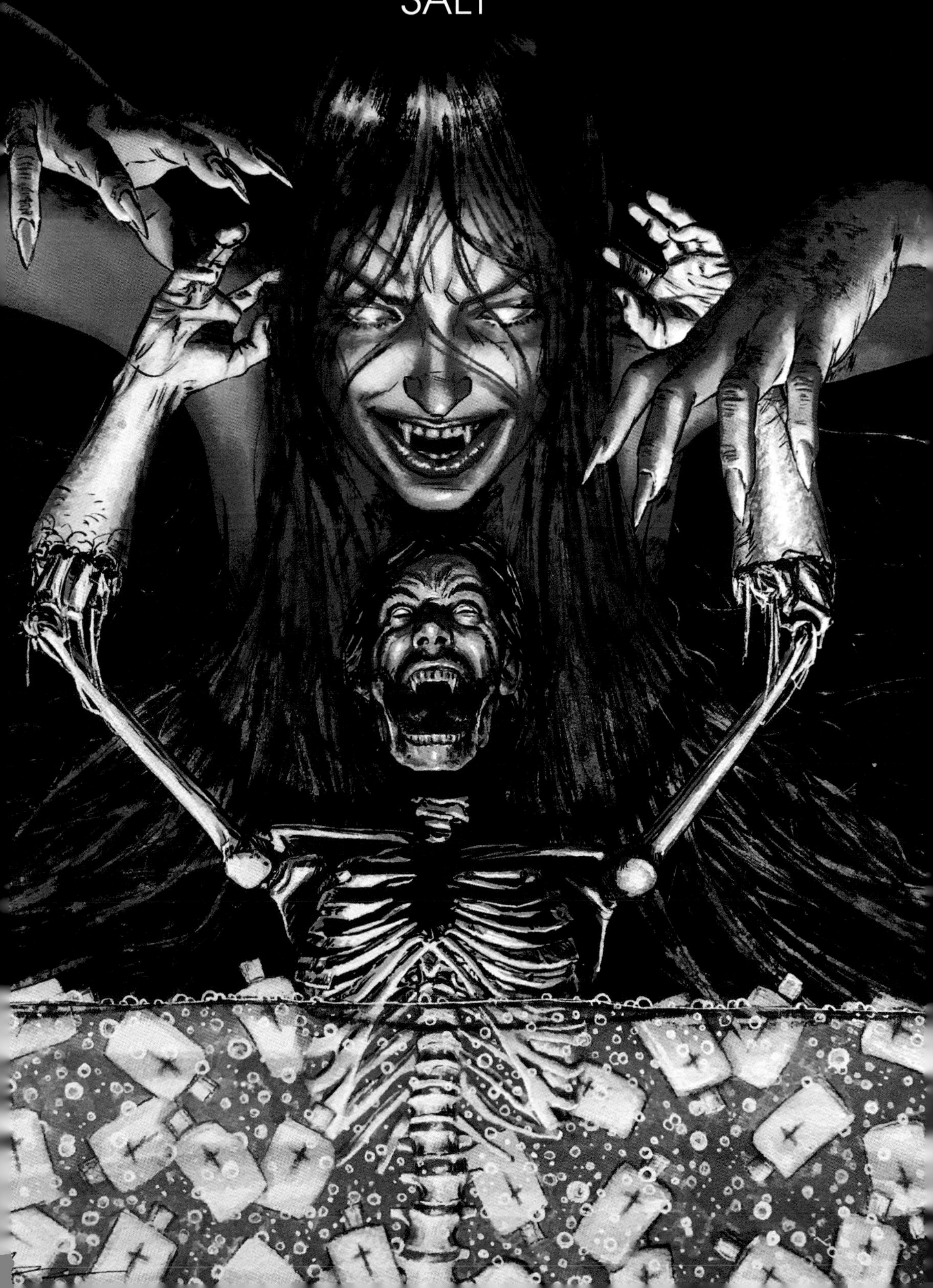

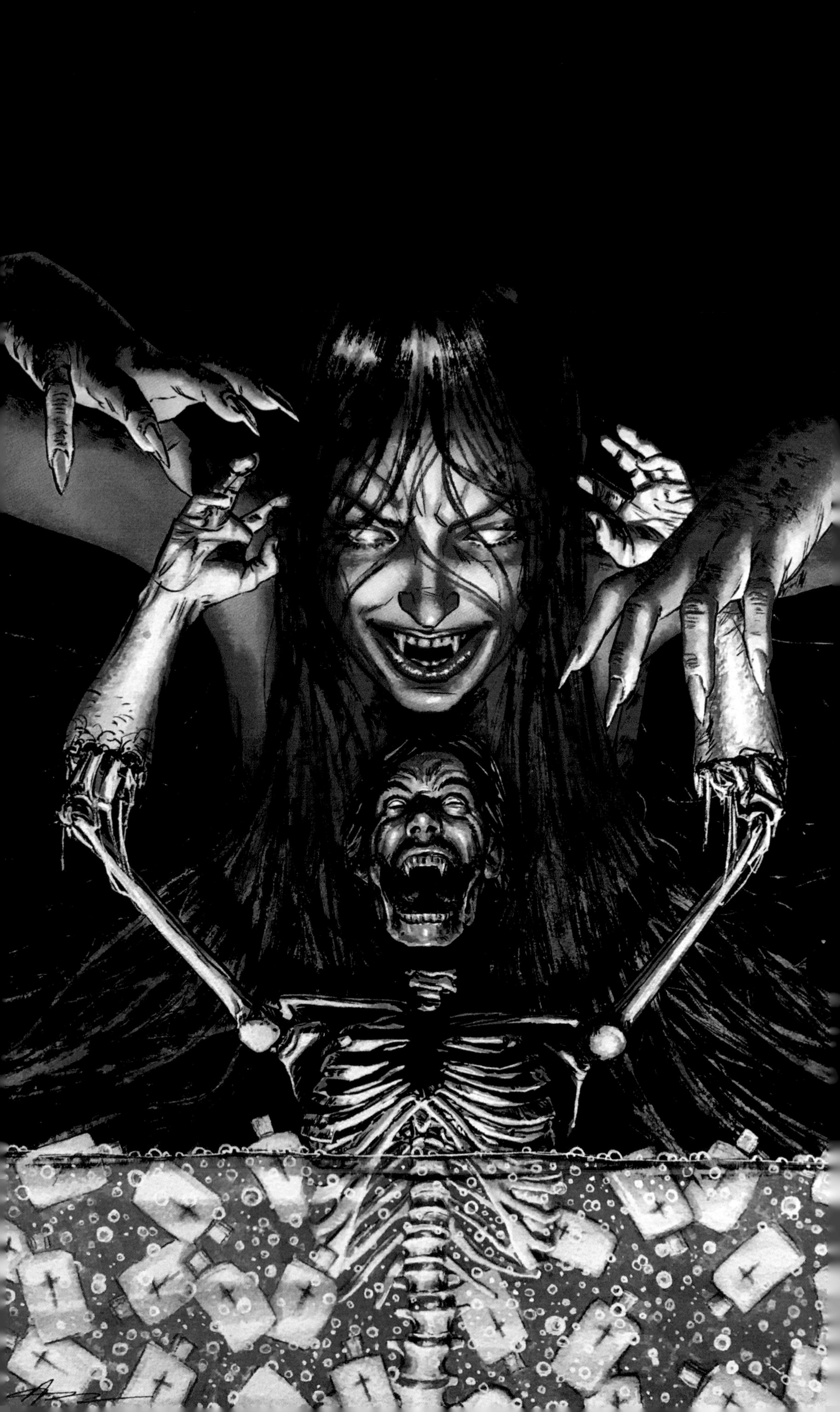

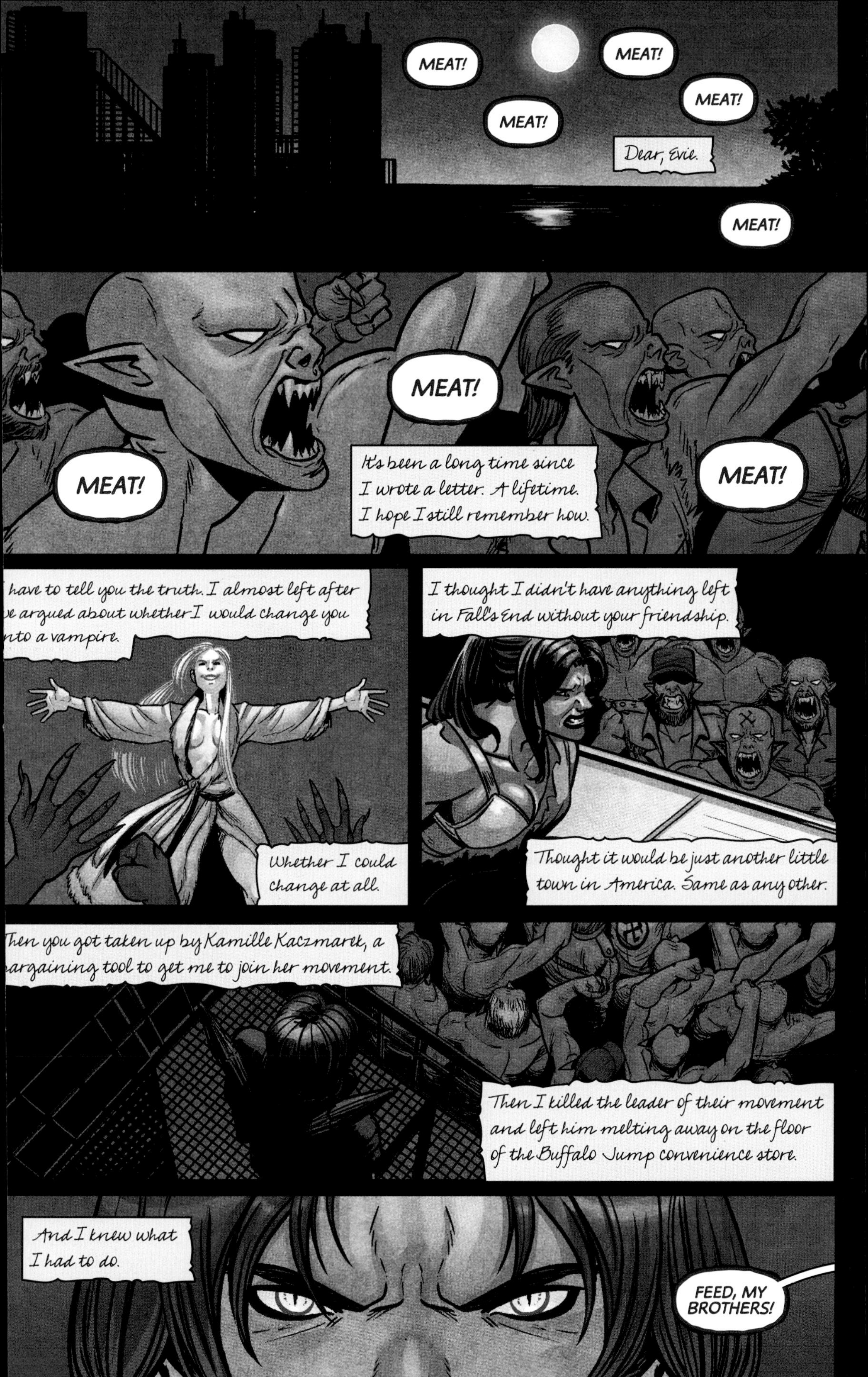
MEAT!
MEAT!
MEAT!
MEAT!
Dear, Evie.
MEAT!
MEAT!
MEAT!
It's been a long time since I wrote a letter. A lifetime. I hope I still remember how.
MEAT!
I have to tell you the truth. I almost left after we argued about whether I would change you into a vampire.
Whether I could change at all.
I thought I didn't have anything left in Fall's End without your friendship.
Thought it would be just another little town in America. Same as any other.
Then you got taken up by Kamille Kaczmarek, a bargaining tool to get me to join her movement.
Then I killed the leader of their movement and left him melting away on the floor of the Buffalo Jump convenience store.
And I knew what I had to do.
FEED, MY BROTHERS!

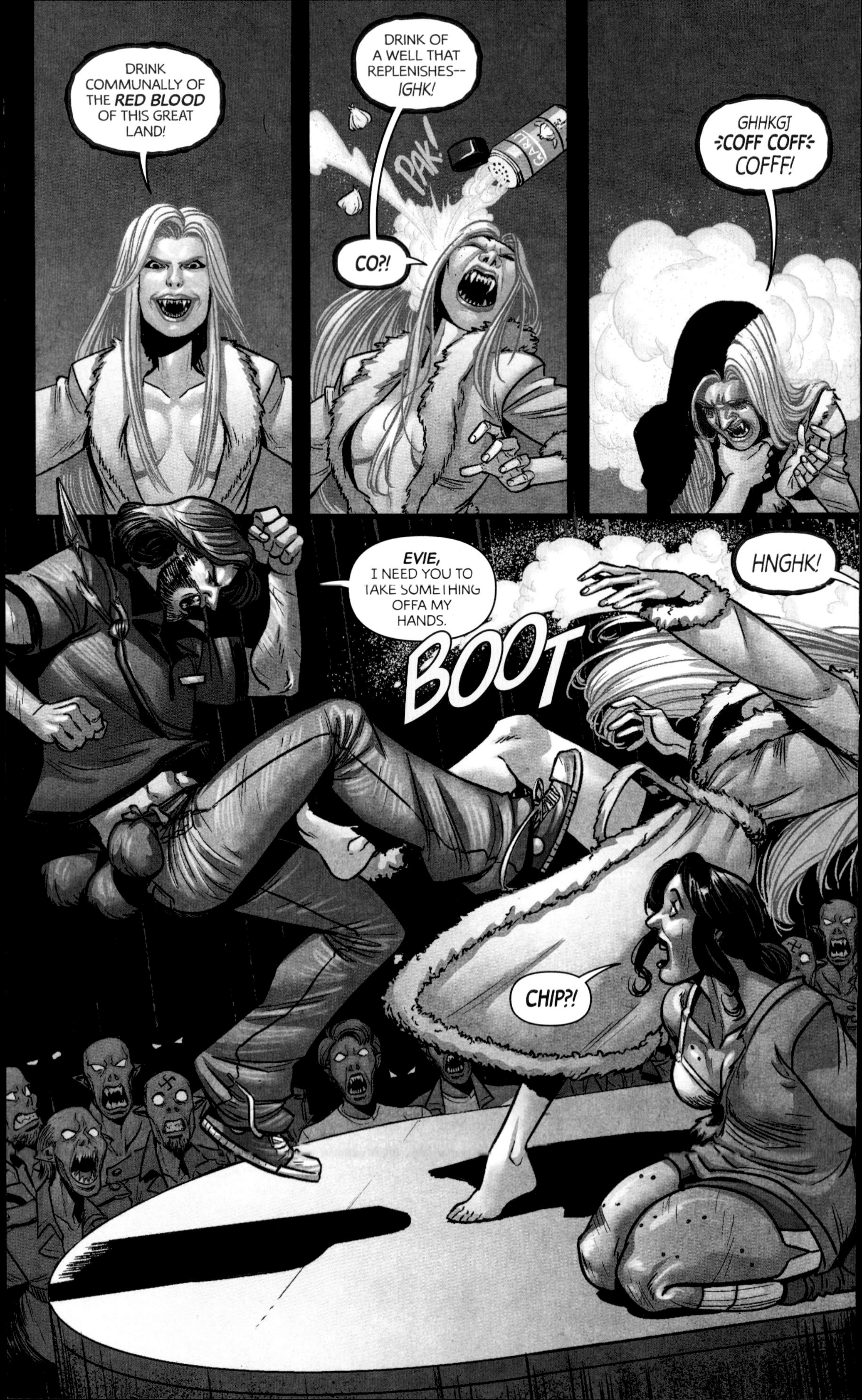
DRINK COMMUNALLY OF THE RED BLOOD OF THIS GREAT LAND!
DRINK OF A WELL THAT REPLENISHES-- IGHK!
PAK!
CO?!
GHHKGJ COFF COFF COFFF!
EVIE, I NEED YOU TO TAKE SOMETHING OFFA MY HANDS.
HNGHK!
BOOT
CHIP?!

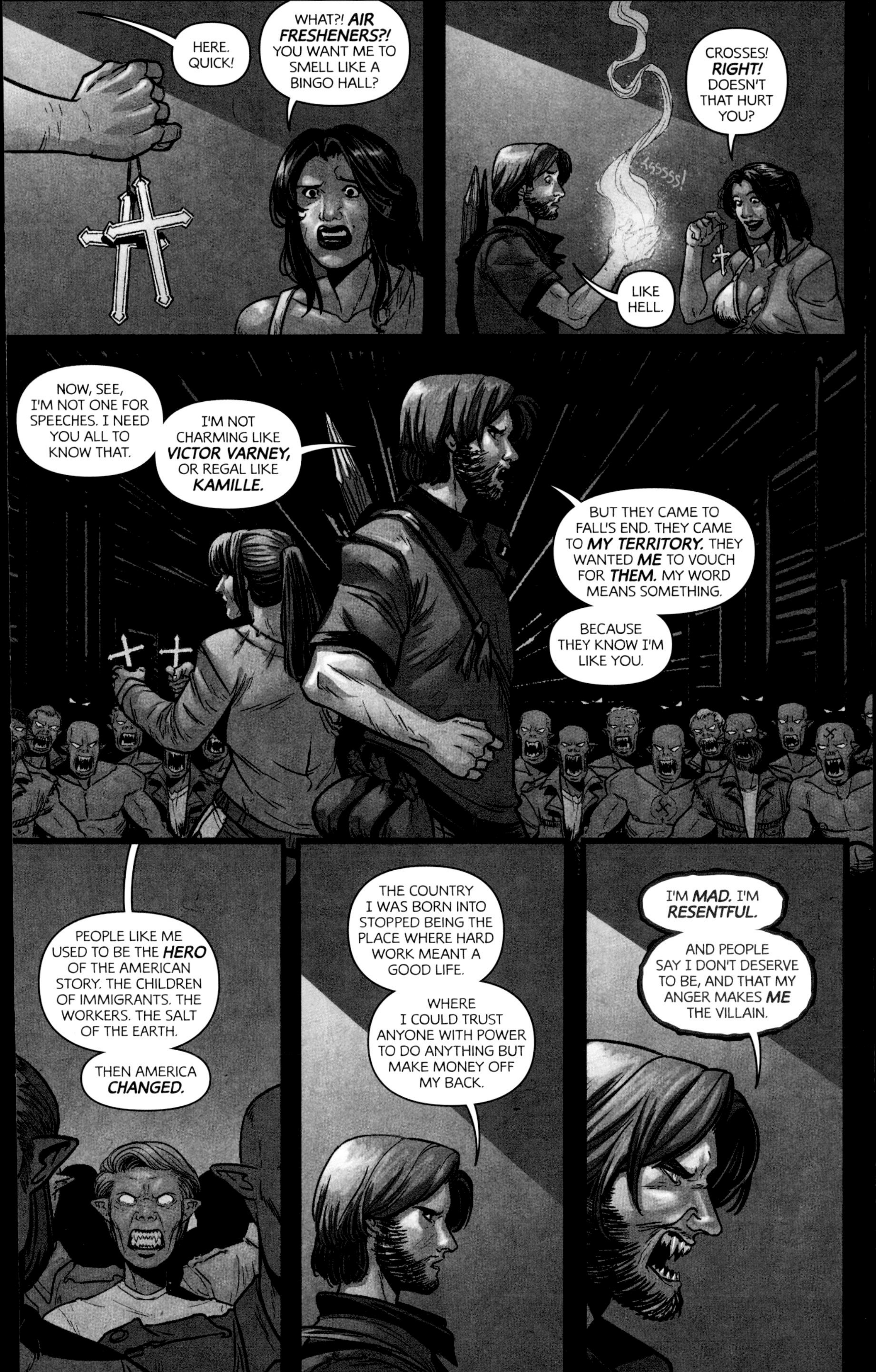
HERE. QUICK!
WHAT?! AIR FRESHENERS?! YOU WANT ME TO SMELL LIKE A BINGO HALL?
CROSSES! RIGHT! DOESN'T THAT HURT YOU?
SSSSSS!
LIKE HELL.
NOW, SEE, I'M NOT ONE FOR SPEECHES. I NEED YOU ALL TO KNOW THAT.
I'M NOT CHARMING LIKE VICTOR VARNEY, OR REGAL LIKE KAMILLE.
BUT THEY CAME TO FALL'S END. THEY CAME TO MY TERRITORY. THEY WANTED ME TO VOUCH FOR THEM. MY WORD MEANS SOMETHING.
BECAUSE THEY KNOW I'M LIKE YOU.
PEOPLE LIKE ME USED TO BE THE HERO OF THE AMERICAN STORY. THE CHILDREN OF IMMIGRANTS. THE WORKERS. THE SALT OF THE EARTH.
THEN AMERICA CHANGED.
THE COUNTRY I WAS BORN INTO STOPPED BEING THE PLACE WHERE HARD WORK MEANT A GOOD LIFE.
WHERE I COULD TRUST ANYONE WITH POWER TO DO ANYTHING BUT MAKE MONEY OFF MY BACK.
I'M MAD. I'M RESENTFUL.
AND PEOPLE SAY I DON'T DESERVE TO BE, AND THAT MY ANGER MAKES ME THE VILLAIN.

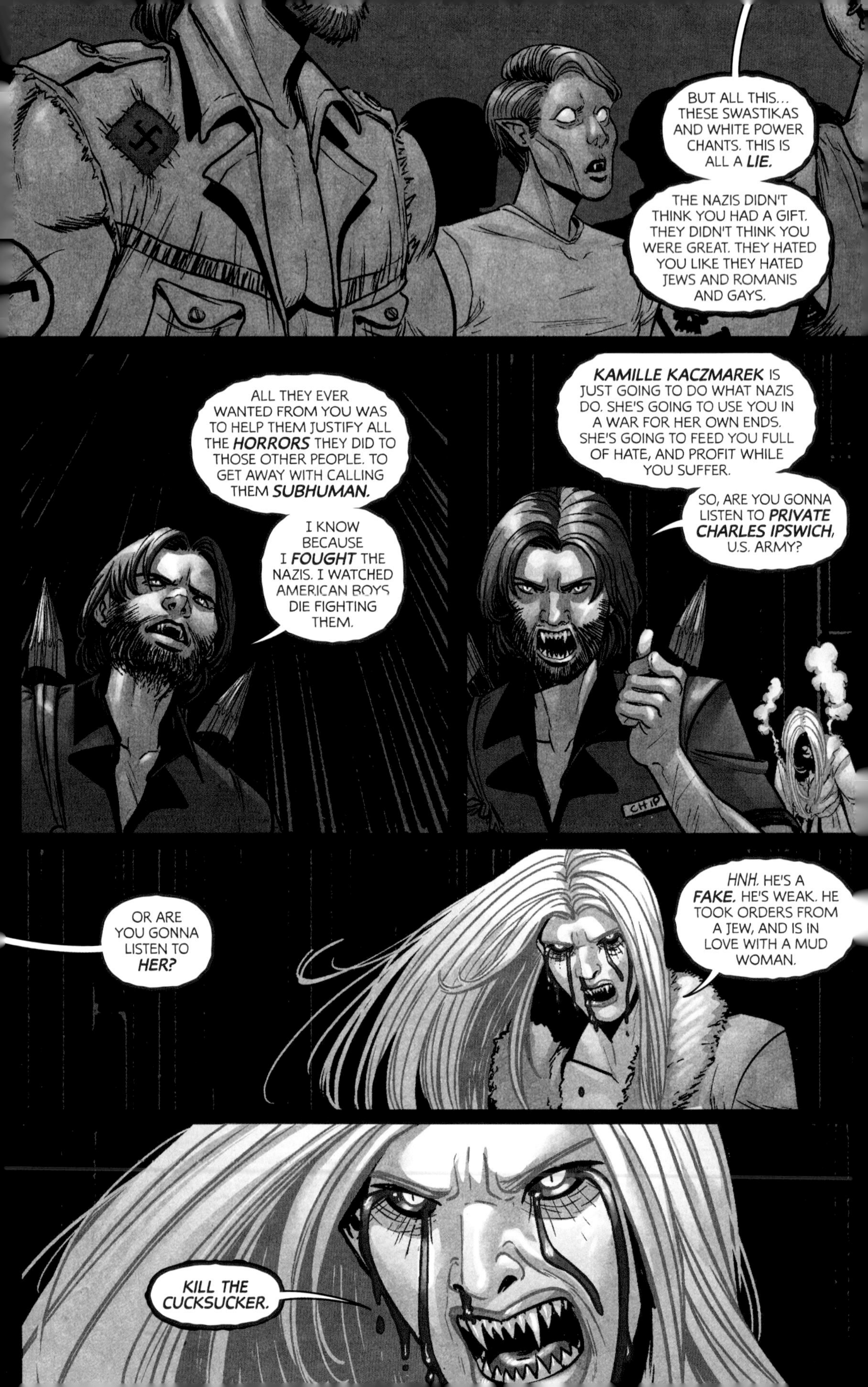

BUT ALL THIS... THESE SWASTIKAS AND WHITE POWER CHANTS. THIS IS ALL A LIE.
THE NAZIS DIDN'T THINK YOU HAD A GIFT. THEY DIDN'T THINK YOU WERE GREAT. THEY HATED YOU LIKE THEY HATED JEWS AND ROMANIS AND GAYS.
ALL THEY EVER WANTED FROM YOU WAS TO HELP THEM JUSTIFY ALL THE HORRORS THEY DID TO THOSE OTHER PEOPLE. TO GET AWAY WITH CALLING THEM SUBHUMAN.
I KNOW BECAUSE I FOUGHT THE NAZIS. I WATCHED AMERICAN BOYS DIE FIGHTING THEM.
KAMILLE KACZMAREK IS JUST GOING TO DO WHAT NAZIS DO. SHE'S GOING TO USE YOU IN A WAR FOR HER OWN ENDS. SHE'S GOING TO FEED YOU FULL OF HATE, AND PROFIT WHILE YOU SUFFER.
SO, ARE YOU GONNA LISTEN TO PRIVATE CHARLES IPSWICH, U.S. ARMY?
CHIP
OR ARE YOU GONNA LISTEN TO HER?
HNH. HE'S A FAKE. HE'S WEAK. HE TOOK ORDERS FROM A JEW, AND IS IN LOVE WITH A MUD WOMAN.
KILL THE CUCKSUCKER.

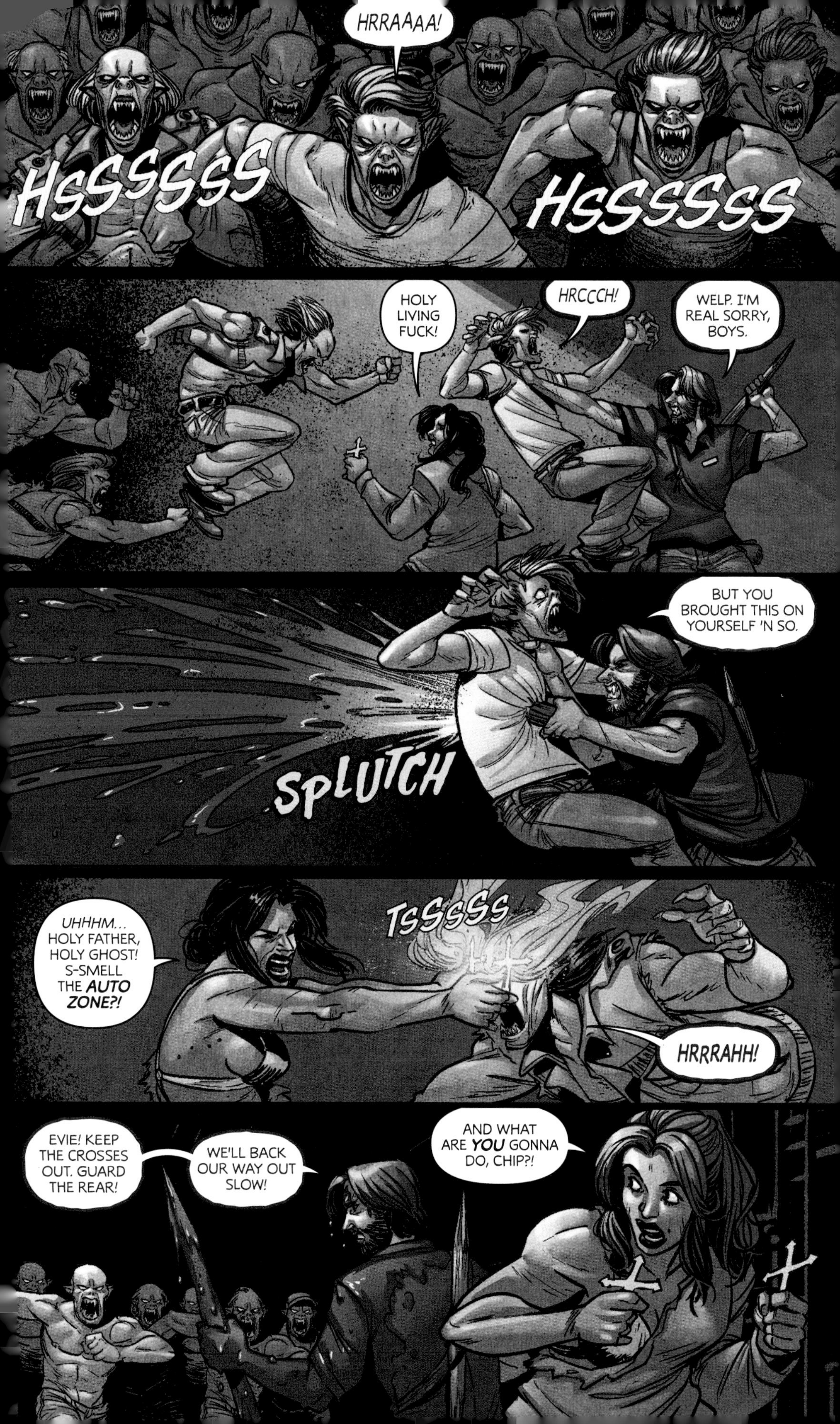
HRRAAAA!
HsSSSSS
HsSSSSS
HOLY LIVING FUCK!
HRCCCH!
WELP. I'M REAL SORRY, BOYS.
BUT YOU BROUGHT THIS ON YOURSELF 'N SO.
SPLUTCH
UHHHM... HOLY FATHER, HOLY GHOST! S-SMELL THE AUTO ZONE?!
TSSSSS
HRRRAHH!
EVIE! KEEP THE CROSSES OUT. GUARD THE REAR!
WE'LL BACK OUR WAY OUT SLOW!
AND WHAT ARE YOU GONNA DO, CHIP?!

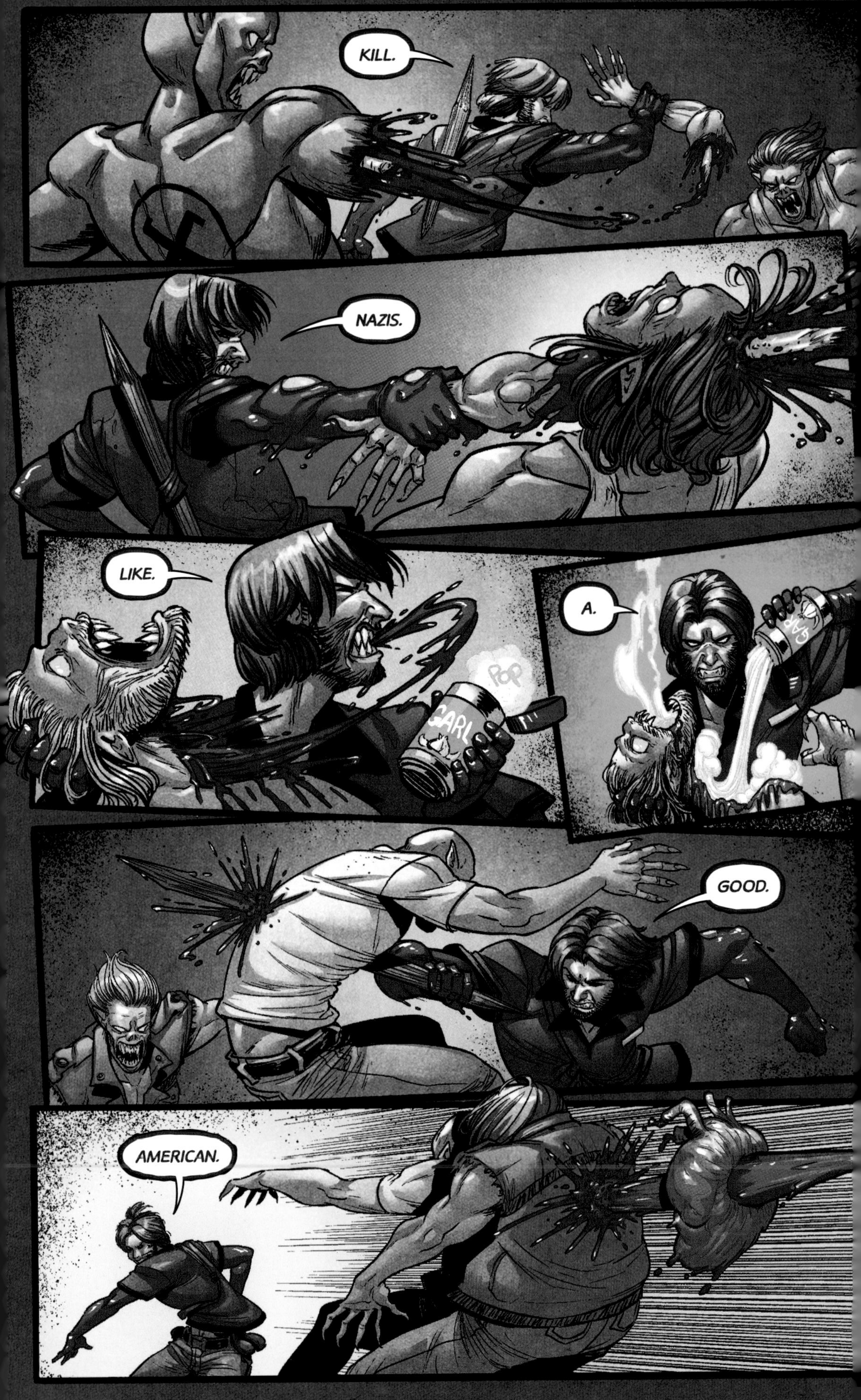
KILL.
NAZIS.
LIKE.
POP
GARL
A.
GOOD.
AMERICAN.

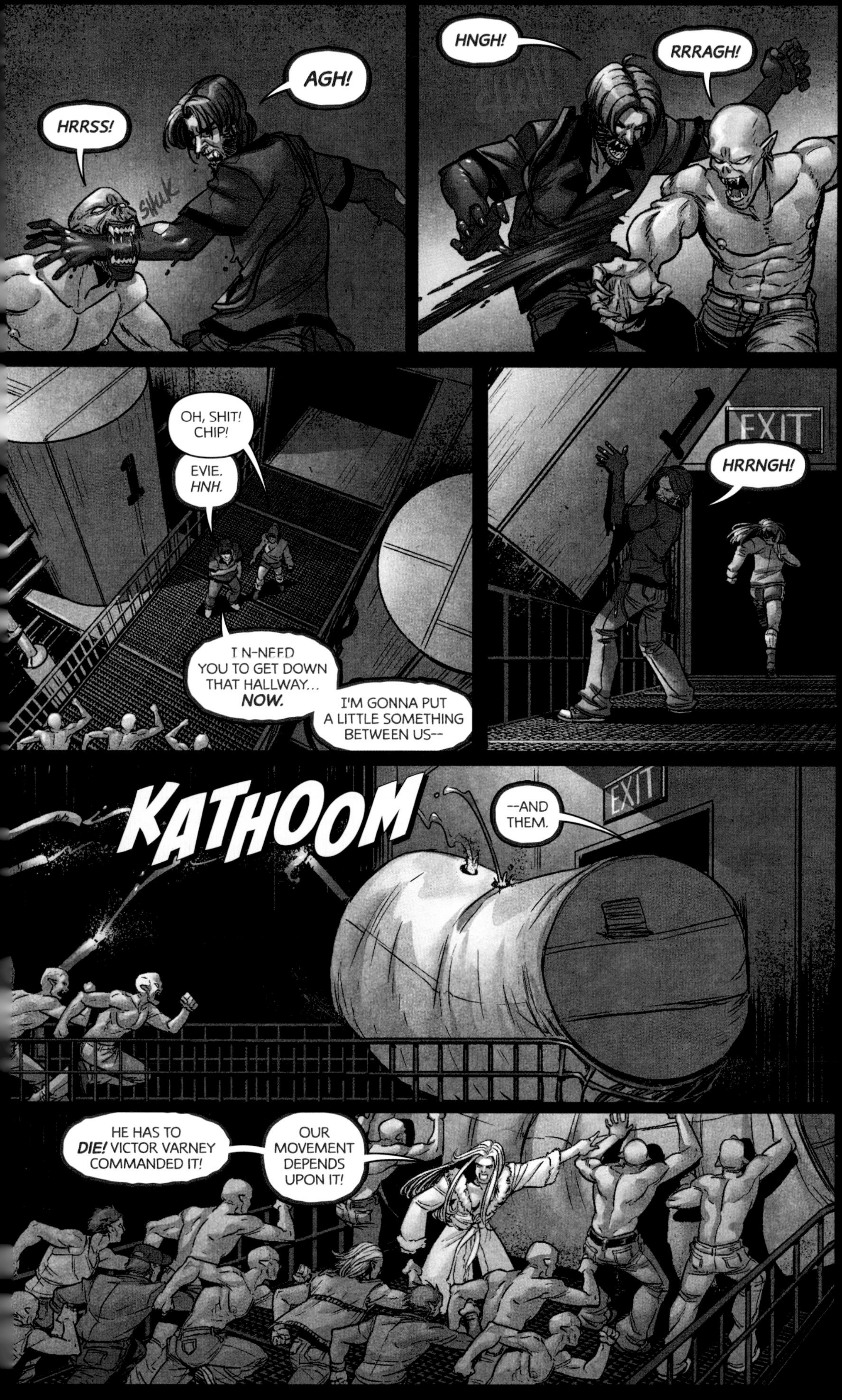

HRRSS!
AGH!
SHLUK
HNGH!
RRRAGH!
OH, SHIT! CHIP!
EVIE. *HNH.*
I N-NEED YOU TO GET DOWN THAT HALLWAY... **NOW.**
I'M GONNA PUT A LITTLE SOMETHING BETWEEN US--
EXIT
HRRNGH!
KATHOOM
EXIT
--AND THEM.
HE HAS TO ***DIE!*** VICTOR VARNEY COMMANDED IT!
OUR MOVEMENT DEPENDS UPON IT!

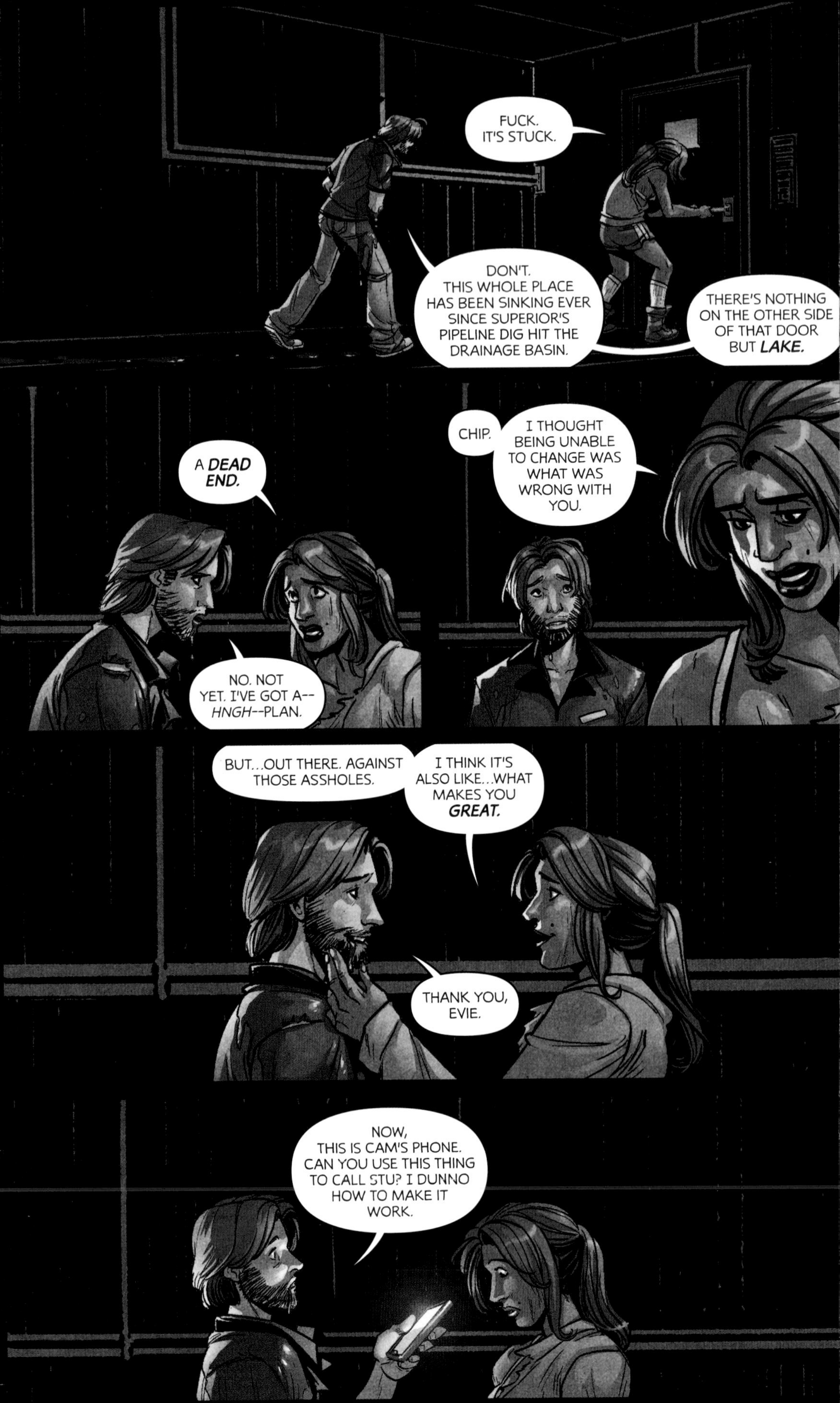
FUCK. IT'S STUCK.
DON'T. THIS WHOLE PLACE HAS BEEN SINKING EVER SINCE SUPERIOR'S PIPELINE DIG HIT THE DRAINAGE BASIN.
THERE'S NOTHING ON THE OTHER SIDE OF THAT DOOR BUT *LAKE.*
A *DEAD END.*
NO. NOT YET. I'VE GOT A-- *HNGH*--PLAN.
CHIP.
I THOUGHT BEING UNABLE TO CHANGE WAS WHAT WAS WRONG WITH YOU.
BUT...OUT THERE. AGAINST THOSE ASSHOLES.
I THINK IT'S ALSO LIKE...WHAT MAKES YOU *GREAT.*
THANK YOU, EVIE.
NOW, THIS IS CAM'S PHONE. CAN YOU USE THIS THING TO CALL STU? I DUNNO HOW TO MAKE IT WORK.

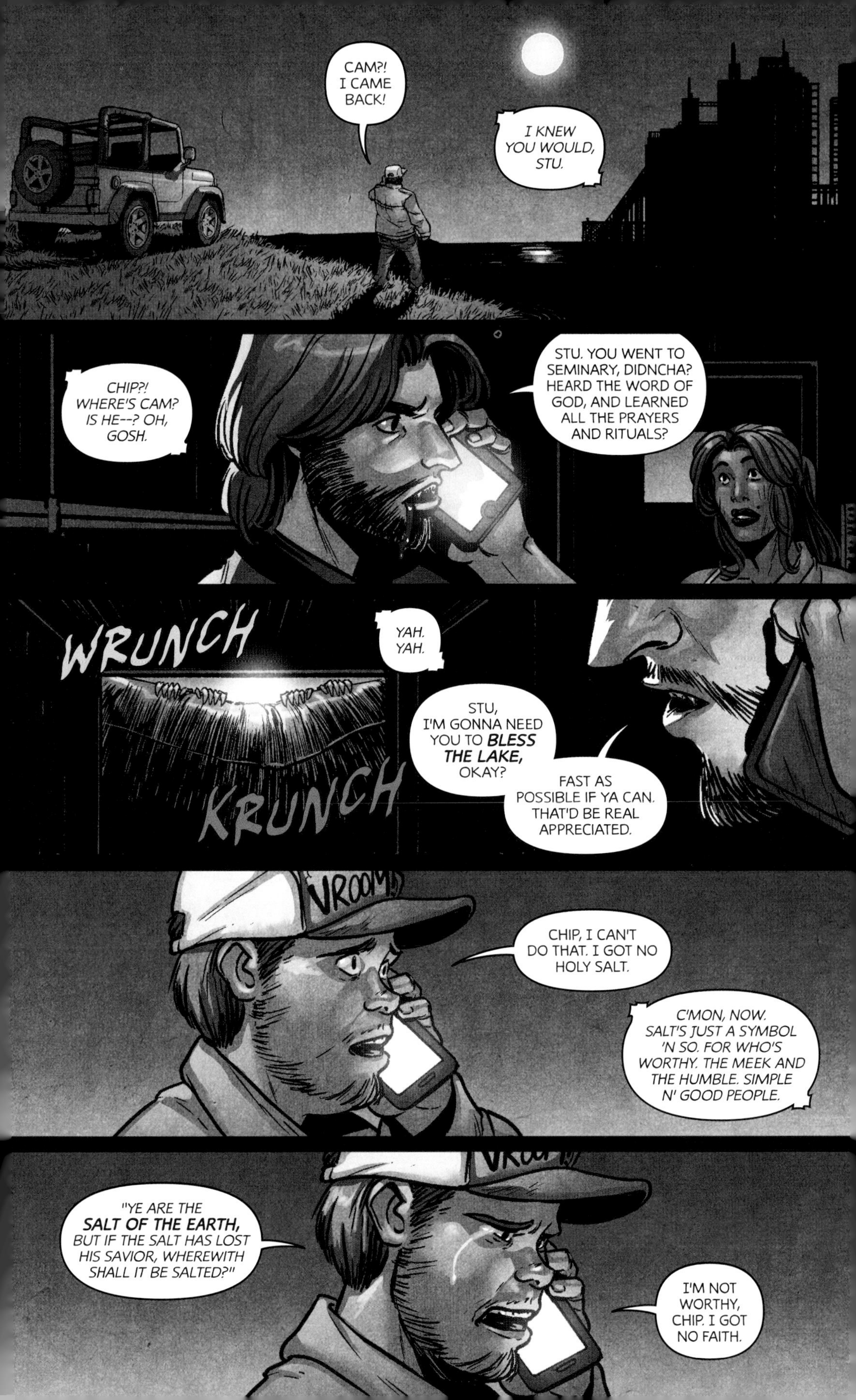
CAM?! I CAME BACK!
I KNEW YOU WOULD, STU.
CHIP?! WHERE'S CAM? IS HE--? OH, GOSH.
STU. YOU WENT TO SEMINARY, DIDNCHA? HEARD THE WORD OF GOD, AND LEARNED ALL THE PRAYERS AND RITUALS?
WRUNCH
YAH. YAH.
STU, I'M GONNA NEED YOU TO ***BLESS THE LAKE,*** OKAY?
KRUNCH
FAST AS POSSIBLE IF YA CAN. THAT'D BE REAL APPRECIATED.
VROOM
CHIP, I CAN'T DO THAT. I GOT NO HOLY SALT.
C'MON, NOW. SALT'S JUST A SYMBOL 'N SO. FOR WHO'S WORTHY. THE MEEK AND THE HUMBLE. SIMPLE N' GOOD PEOPLE.
"YE ARE THE ***SALT OF THE EARTH,*** BUT IF THE SALT HAS LOST HIS SAVIOR, WHEREWITH SHALL IT BE SALTED?"
I'M NOT WORTHY, CHIP. I GOT NO FAITH.

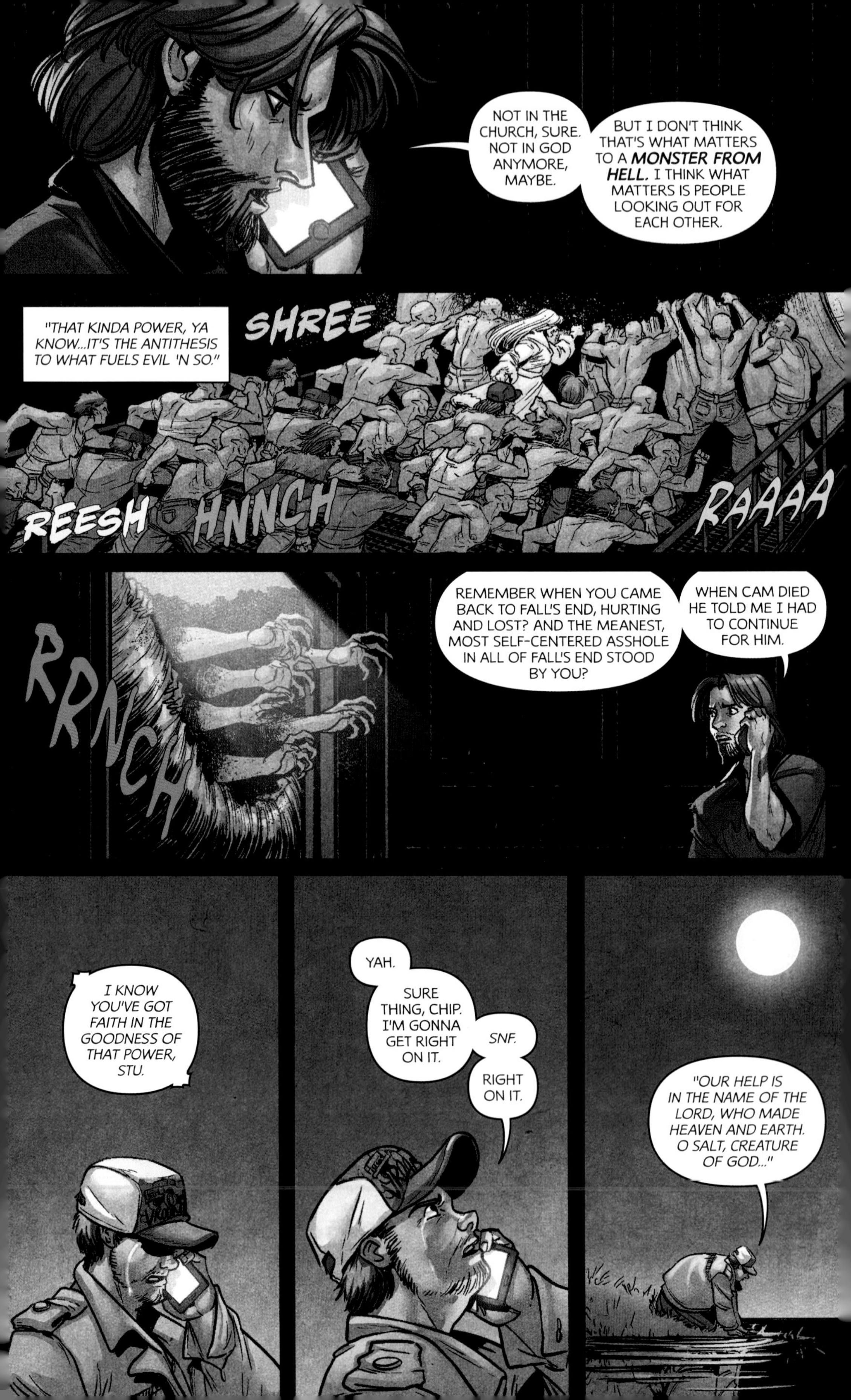

NOT IN THE CHURCH, SURE. NOT IN GOD ANYMORE, MAYBE.
BUT I DON'T THINK THAT'S WHAT MATTERS TO A MONSTER FROM HELL. I THINK WHAT MATTERS IS PEOPLE LOOKING OUT FOR EACH OTHER.
"THAT KINDA POWER, YA KNOW...IT'S THE ANTITHESIS TO WHAT FUELS EVIL 'N SO."
SHREE
REESH
HNNCH
RAAAA
RRNCH
REMEMBER WHEN YOU CAME BACK TO FALL'S END, HURTING AND LOST? AND THE MEANEST, MOST SELF-CENTERED ASSHOLE IN ALL OF FALL'S END STOOD BY YOU?
WHEN CAM DIED HE TOLD ME I HAD TO CONTINUE FOR HIM.
I KNOW YOU'VE GOT FAITH IN THE GOODNESS OF THAT POWER, STU.
YAH.
SURE THING, CHIP. I'M GONNA GET RIGHT ON IT.
SNF.
RIGHT ON IT.
"OUR HELP IS IN THE NAME OF THE LORD, WHO MADE HEAVEN AND EARTH. O SALT, CREATURE OF GOD..."

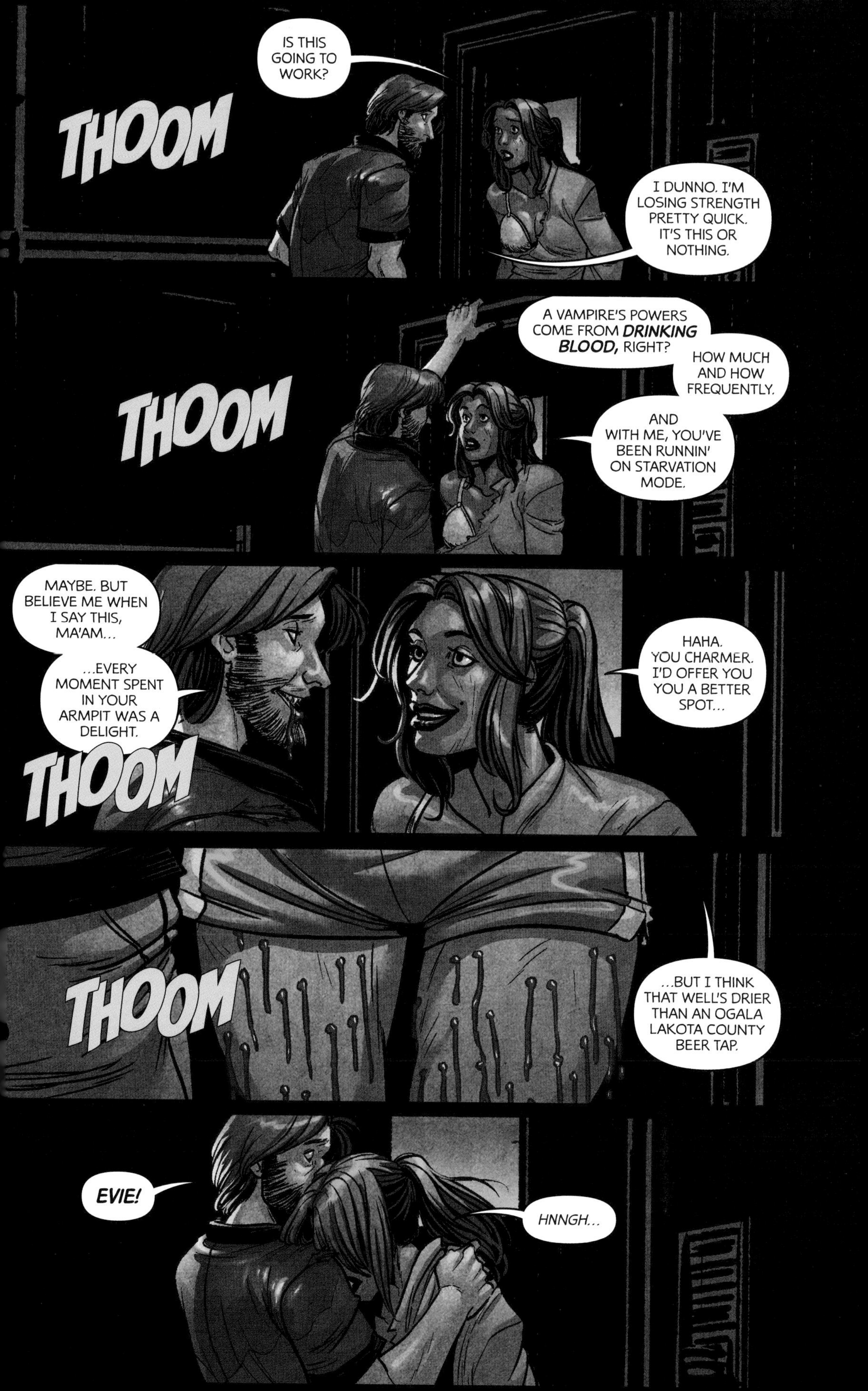
IS THIS GOING TO WORK?
THOOM
I DUNNO. I'M LOSING STRENGTH PRETTY QUICK. IT'S THIS OR NOTHING.
THOOM
A VAMPIRE'S POWERS COME FROM DRINKING BLOOD, RIGHT?
HOW MUCH AND HOW FREQUENTLY.
AND WITH ME, YOU'VE BEEN RUNNIN' ON STARVATION MODE.
MAYBE. BUT BELIEVE ME WHEN I SAY THIS, MA'AM...
...EVERY MOMENT SPENT IN YOUR ARMPIT WAS A DELIGHT.
THOOM
HAHA. YOU CHARMER. I'D OFFER YOU YOU A BETTER SPOT...
THOOM
...BUT I THINK THAT WELL'S DRIER THAN AN OGALA LAKOTA COUNTY BEER TAP.
EVIE!
HNNGH...

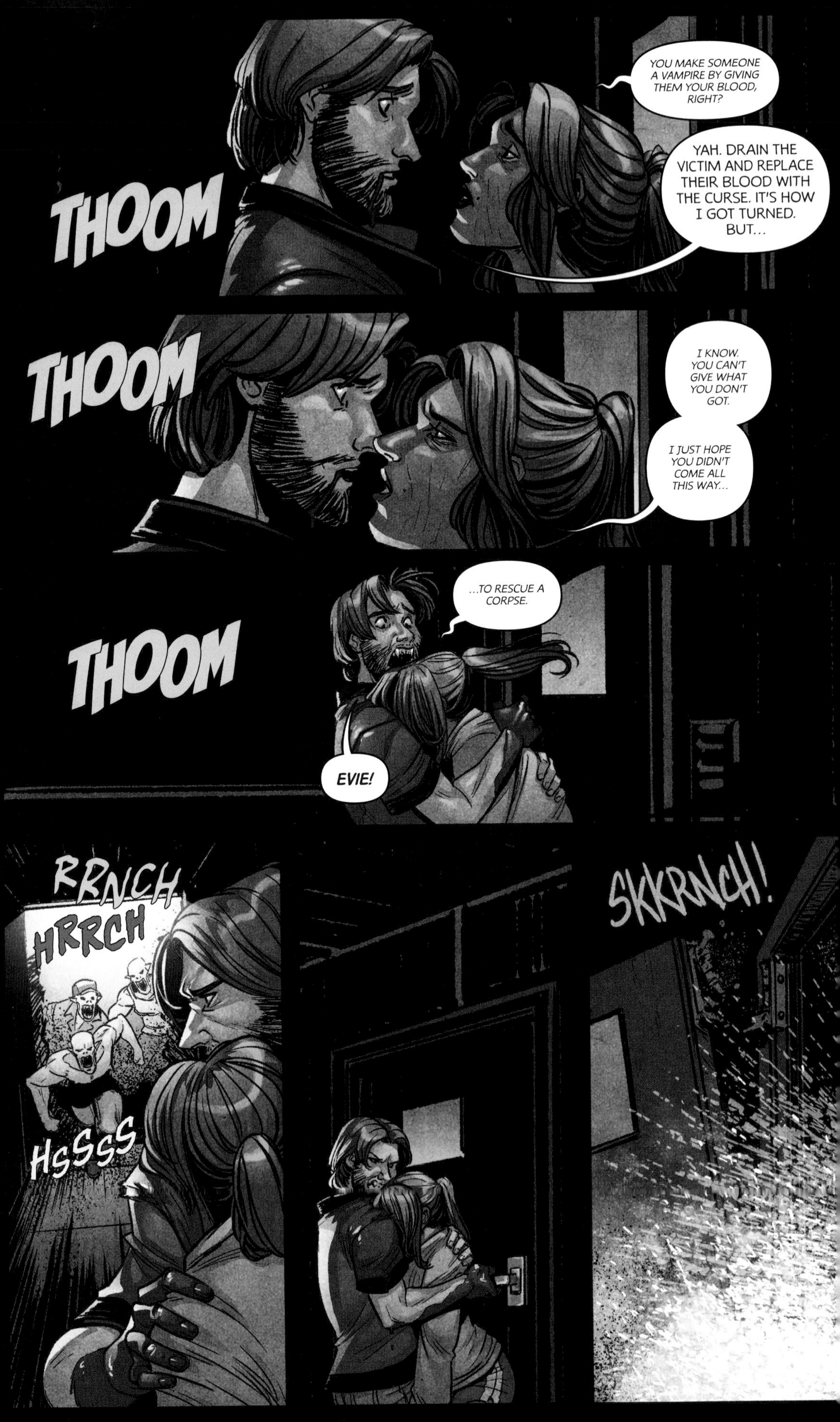
YOU MAKE SOMEONE A VAMPIRE BY GIVING THEM YOUR BLOOD, RIGHT?
THOOM
YAH. DRAIN THE VICTIM AND REPLACE THEIR BLOOD WITH THE CURSE. IT'S HOW I GOT TURNED. BUT…
THOOM
I KNOW. YOU CAN'T GIVE WHAT YOU DON'T GOT.
I JUST HOPE YOU DIDN'T COME ALL THIS WAY…
THOOM
…TO RESCUE A CORPSE.
EVIE!
RRNCH
HRRCH
HsSSS
SKRNCH!

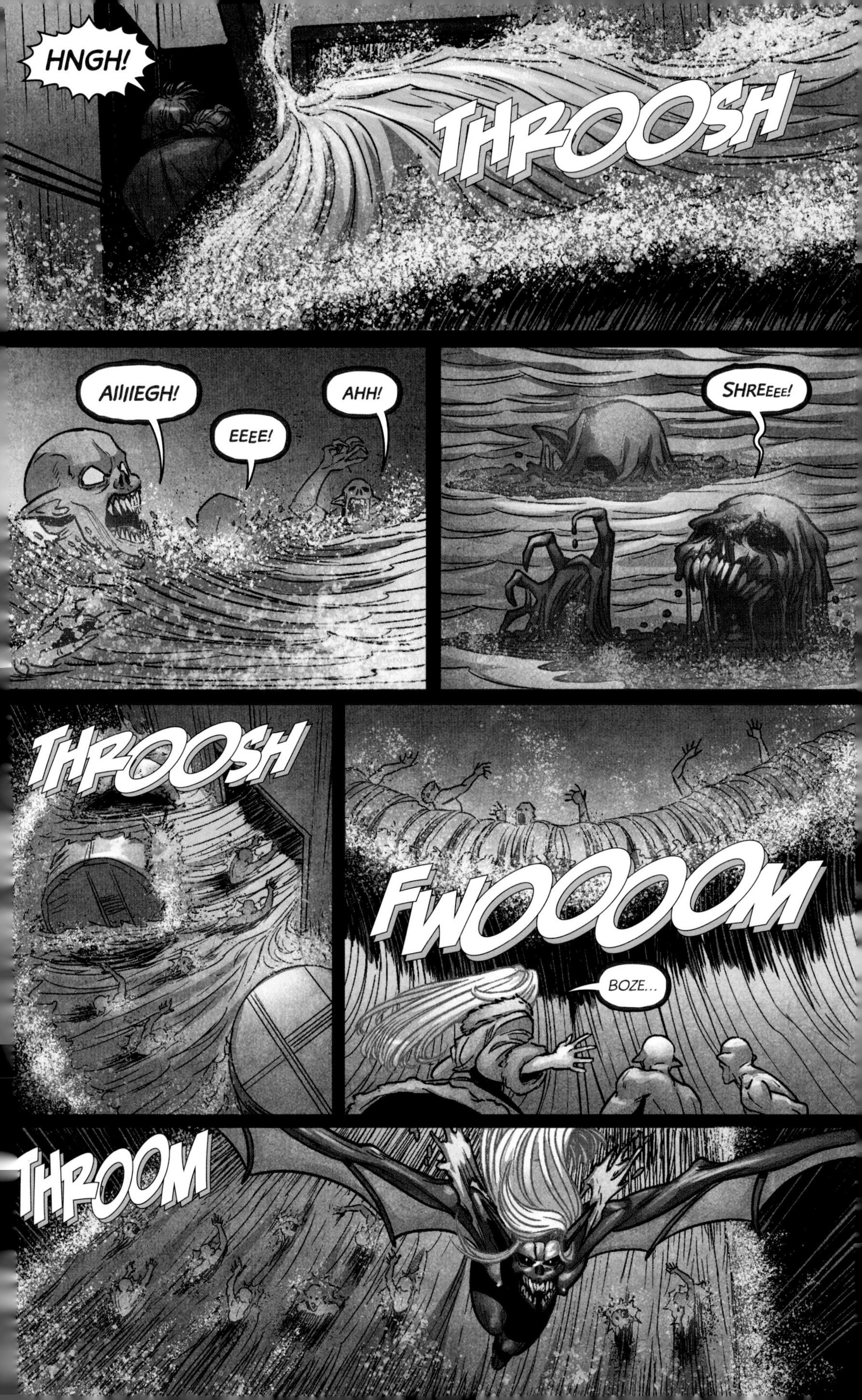
HNGH!
THROOSH
AIIIIEGH!
EEEE!
AHH!
SHREEEE!
THROOSH
FWOOOOOM
BOZE...
THROOM

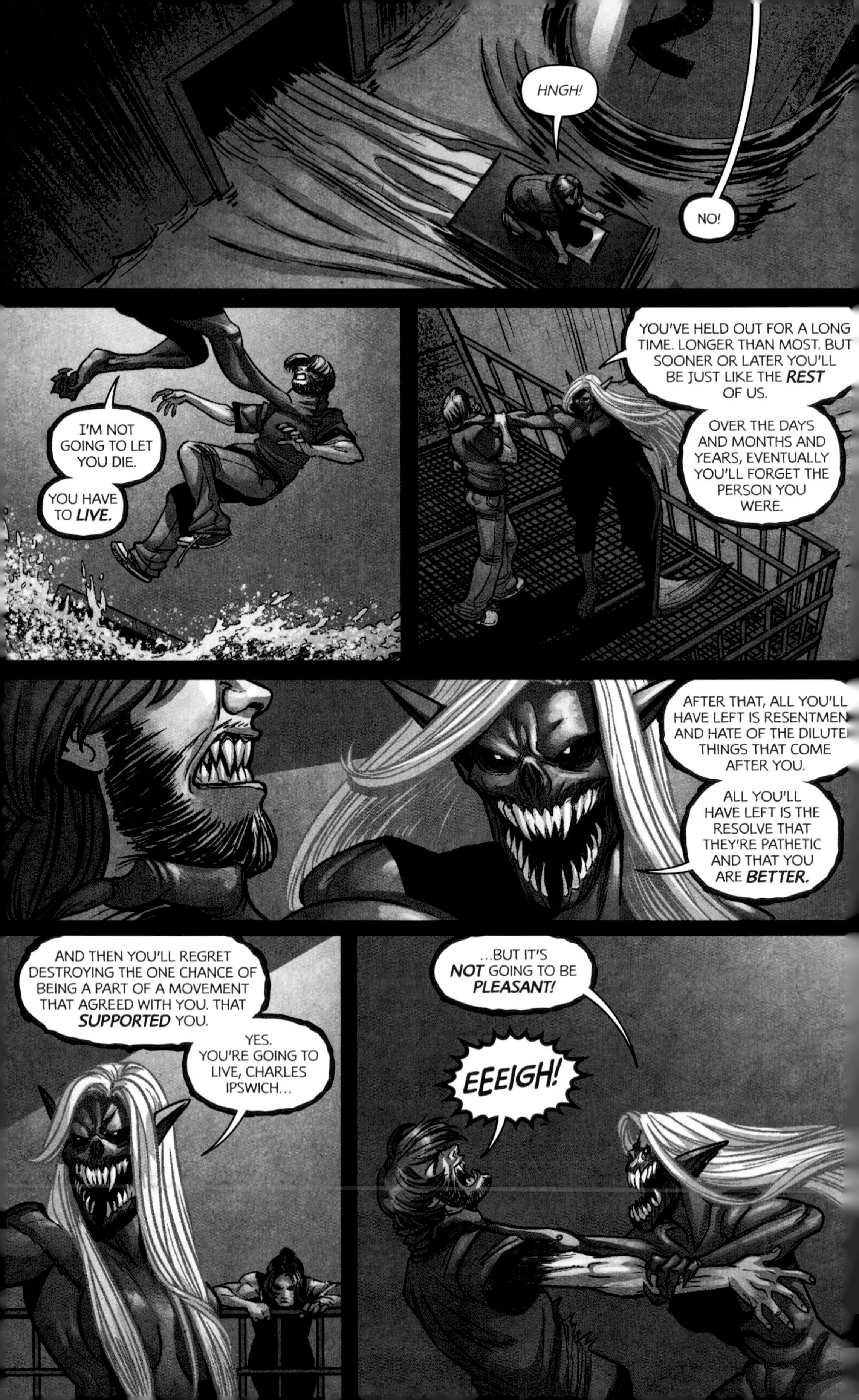
HNGH!
NO!
I'M NOT GOING TO LET YOU DIE.
YOU HAVE TO **LIVE.**
YOU'VE HELD OUT FOR A LONG TIME. LONGER THAN MOST. BUT SOONER OR LATER YOU'LL BE JUST LIKE THE **REST** OF US.
OVER THE DAYS AND MONTHS AND YEARS, EVENTUALLY YOU'LL FORGET THE PERSON YOU WERE.
AFTER THAT, ALL YOU'LL HAVE LEFT IS RESENTMEN AND HATE OF THE DILUTE THINGS THAT COME AFTER YOU.
ALL YOU'LL HAVE LEFT IS THE RESOLVE THAT THEY'RE PATHETIC AND THAT YOU ARE **BETTER.**
AND THEN YOU'LL REGRET DESTROYING THE ONE CHANCE OF BEING A PART OF A MOVEMENT THAT AGREED WITH YOU. THAT **SUPPORTED** YOU.
YES. YOU'RE GOING TO LIVE, CHARLES IPSWICH...
...BUT IT'S **NOT** GOING TO BE **PLEASANT!**
EEEIGH!

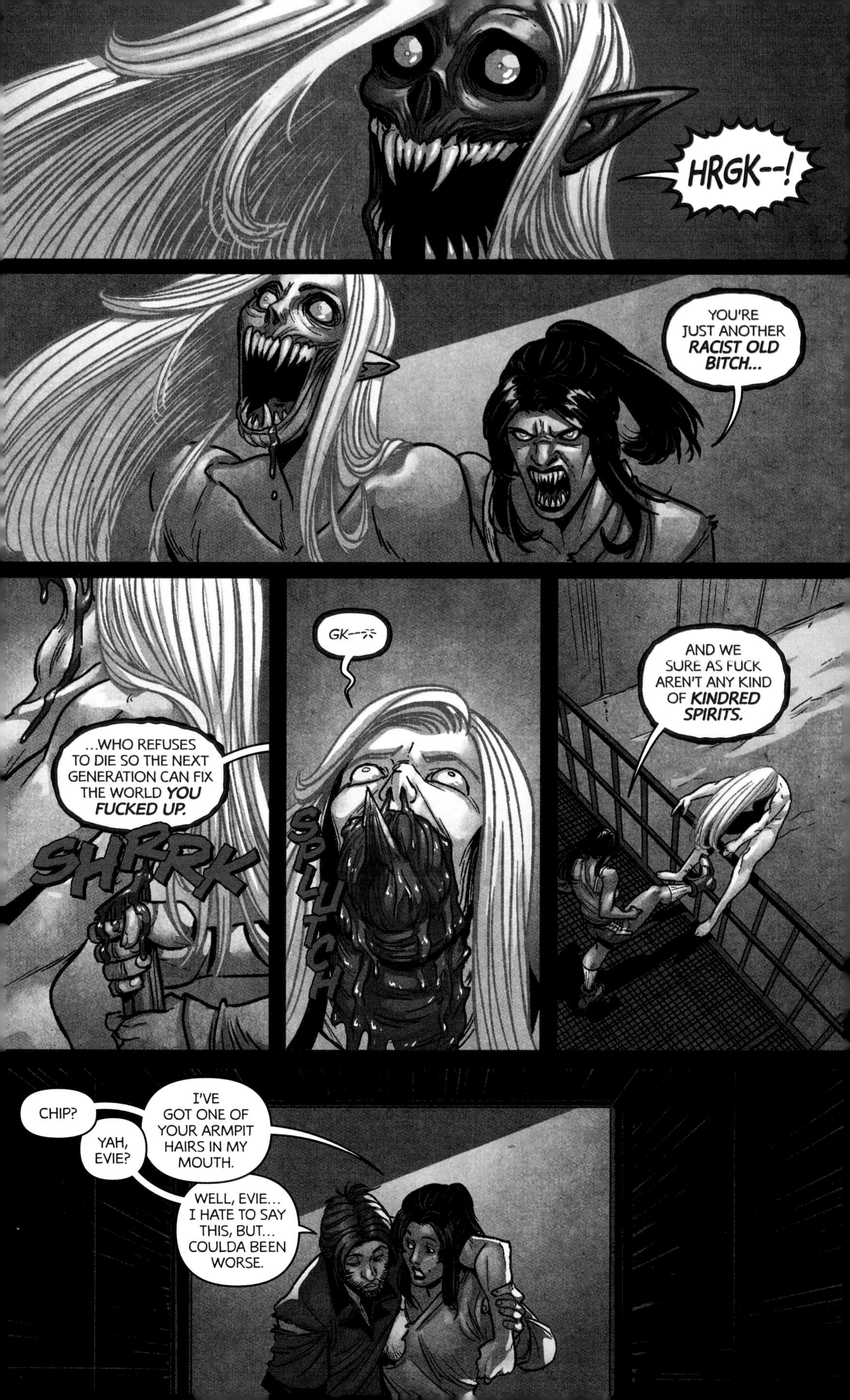
HRGK--!
YOU'RE JUST ANOTHER RACIST OLD BITCH...
...WHO REFUSES TO DIE SO THE NEXT GENERATION CAN FIX THE WORLD YOU FUCKED UP.
SHRRK
GK--
SPLUTCH
AND WE SURE AS FUCK AREN'T ANY KIND OF KINDRED SPIRITS.
CHIP?
YAH, EVIE?
I'VE GOT ONE OF YOUR ARMPIT HAIRS IN MY MOUTH.
WELL, EVIE... I HATE TO SAY THIS, BUT... COULDA BEEN WORSE.

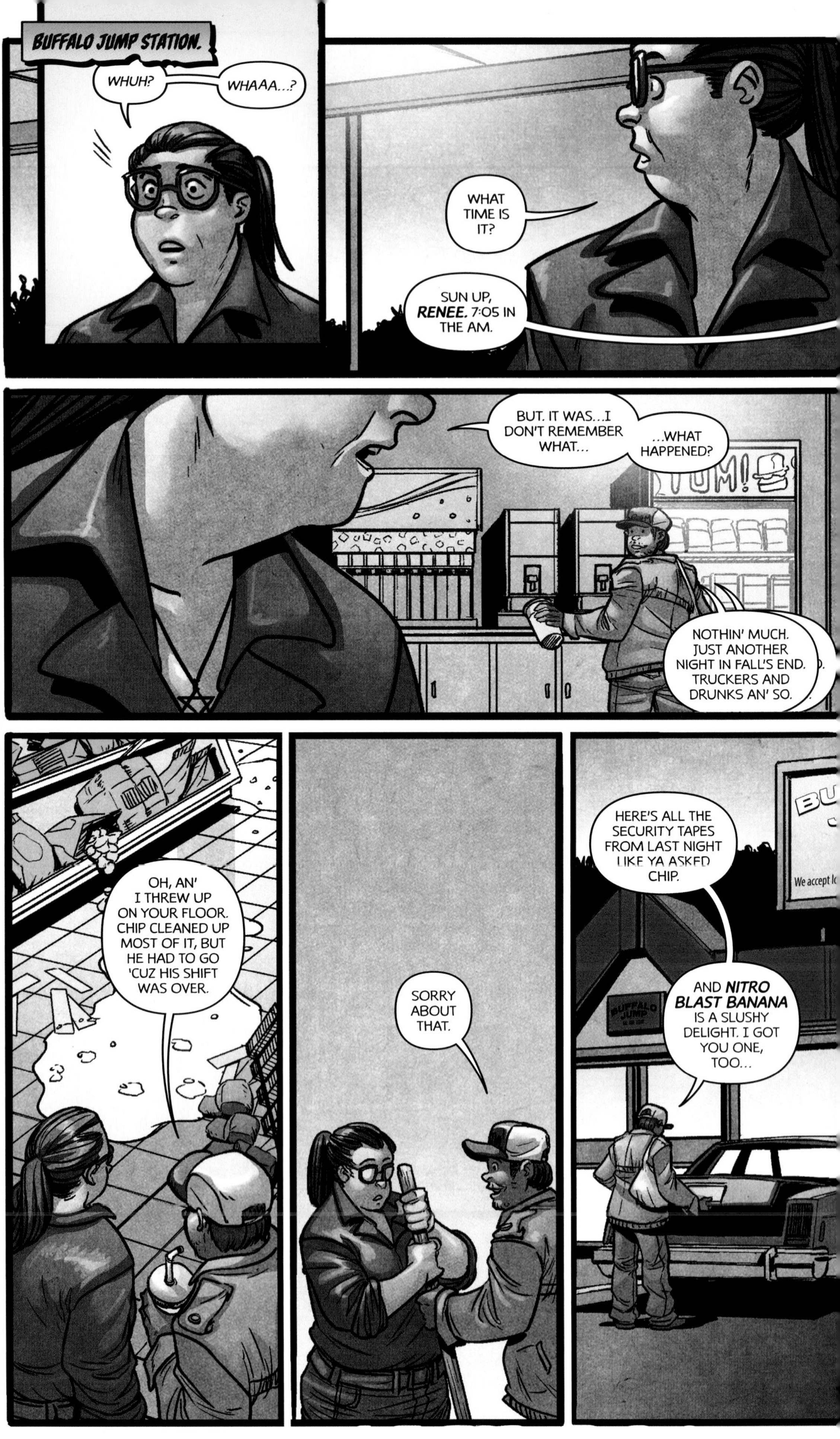
BUFFALO JUMP STATION.
WHUH?
WHAAA...?
WHAT TIME IS IT?
SUN UP, **RENEE.** 7:05 IN THE AM.
BUT. IT WAS...I DON'T REMEMBER WHAT...
...WHAT HAPPENED?
NOTHIN' MUCH. JUST ANOTHER NIGHT IN FALL'S END. TRUCKERS AND DRUNKS AN' SO.
OH, AN' I THREW UP ON YOUR FLOOR. CHIP CLEANED UP MOST OF IT, BUT HE HAD TO GO 'CUZ HIS SHIFT WAS OVER.
SORRY ABOUT THAT.
HERE'S ALL THE SECURITY TAPES FROM LAST NIGHT LIKE YA ASKED CHIP.
AND ***NITRO BLAST BANANA*** IS A SLUSHY DELIGHT. I GOT YOU ONE, TOO...

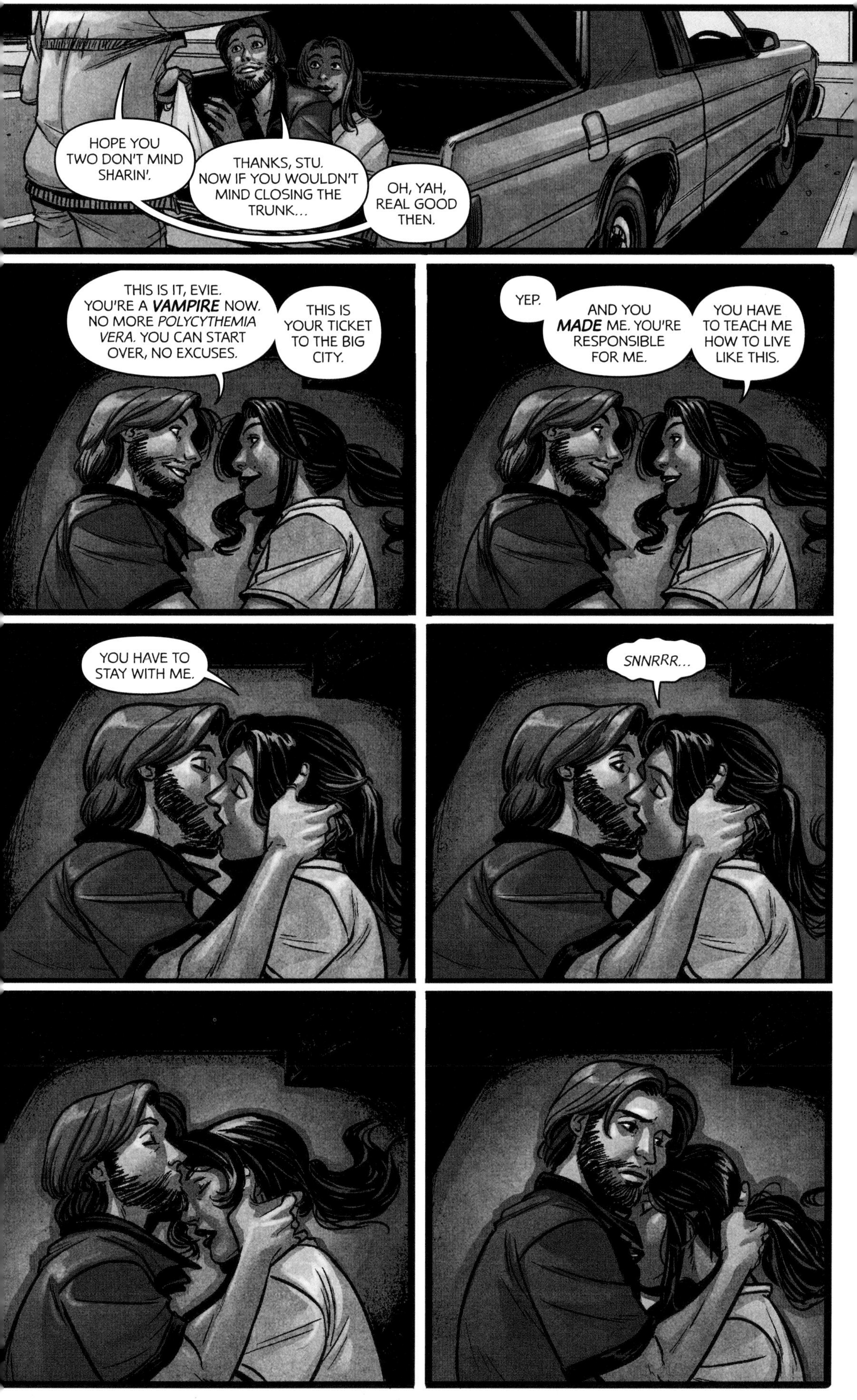
HOPE YOU TWO DON'T MIND SHARIN'.
THANKS, STU. NOW IF YOU WOULDN'T MIND CLOSING THE TRUNK...
OH, YAH, REAL GOOD THEN.
THIS IS IT, EVIE. YOU'RE A ***VAMPIRE*** NOW. NO MORE *POLYCYTHEMIA VERA*. YOU CAN START OVER, NO EXCUSES.
THIS IS YOUR TICKET TO THE BIG CITY.
YEP.
AND YOU ***MADE*** ME. YOU'RE RESPONSIBLE FOR ME.
YOU HAVE TO TEACH ME HOW TO LIVE LIKE THIS.
YOU HAVE TO STAY WITH ME.
SNNRRR...

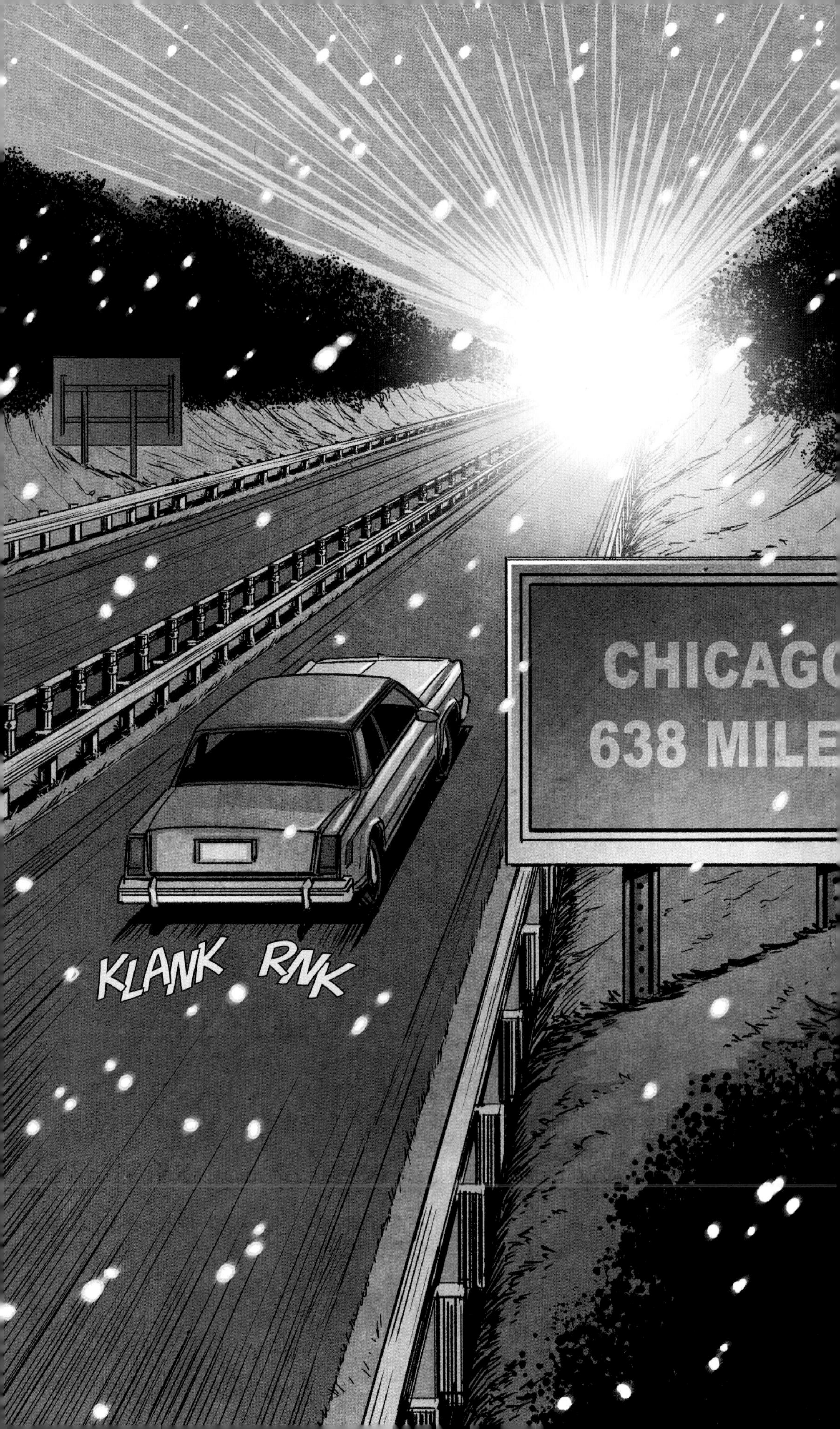
CHICAGO
638 MILE
KLANK RNK

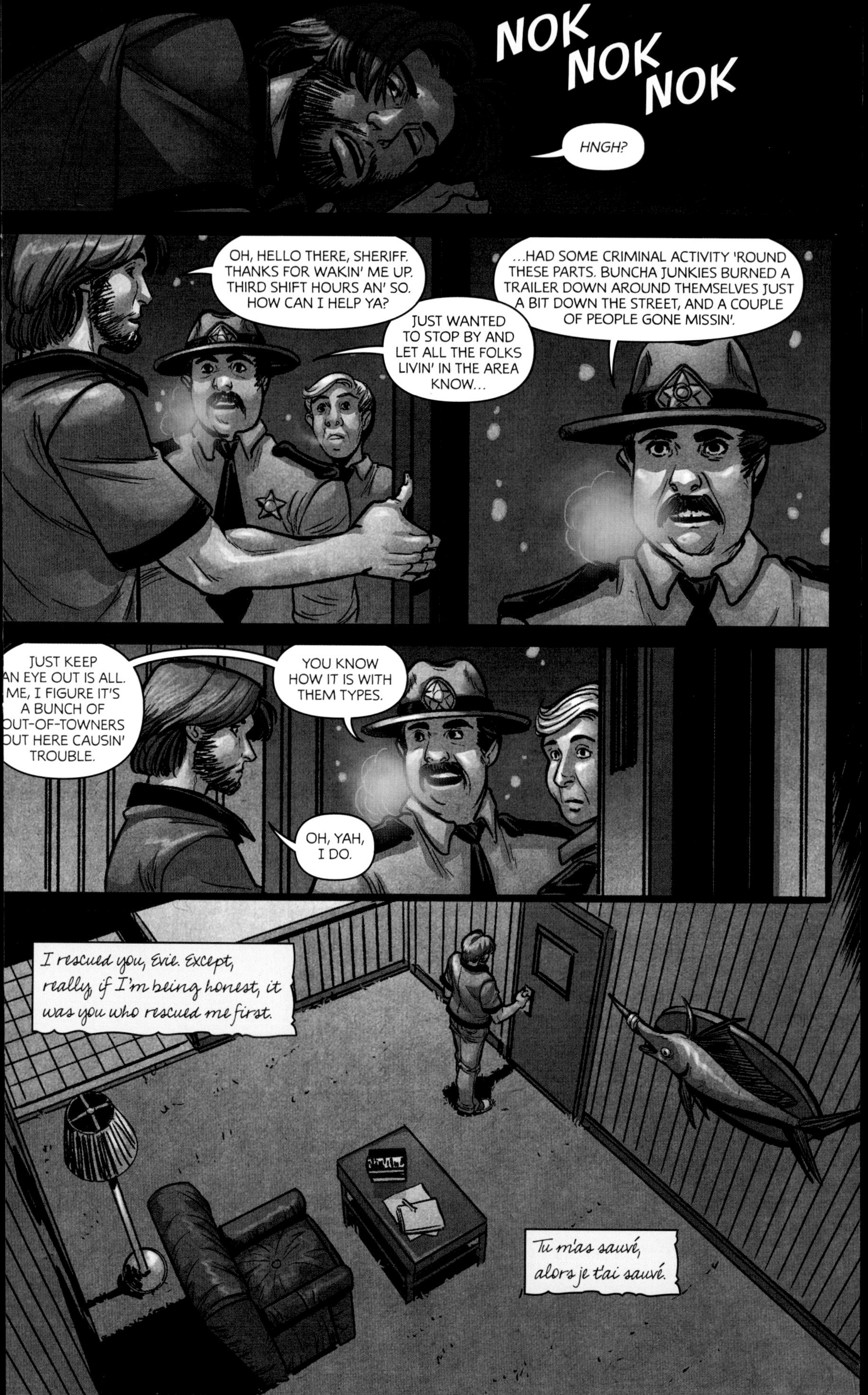
NOK NOK NOK
HNGH?
OH, HELLO THERE, SHERIFF. THANKS FOR WAKIN' ME UP. THIRD SHIFT HOURS AN' SO. HOW CAN I HELP YA?
JUST WANTED TO STOP BY AND LET ALL THE FOLKS LIVIN' IN THE AREA KNOW...
...HAD SOME CRIMINAL ACTIVITY 'ROUND THESE PARTS. BUNCHA JUNKIES BURNED A TRAILER DOWN AROUND THEMSELVES JUST A BIT DOWN THE STREET, AND A COUPLE OF PEOPLE GONE MISSIN'.
JUST KEEP AN EYE OUT IS ALL. ME, I FIGURE IT'S A BUNCH OF OUT-OF-TOWNERS OUT HERE CAUSIN' TROUBLE.
YOU KNOW HOW IT IS WITH THEM TYPES.
OH, YAH, I DO.
I rescued you, Evie. Except, really, if I'm being honest, it was you who rescued me first.
Tu m'as sauvé, alors je t'ai sauvé.

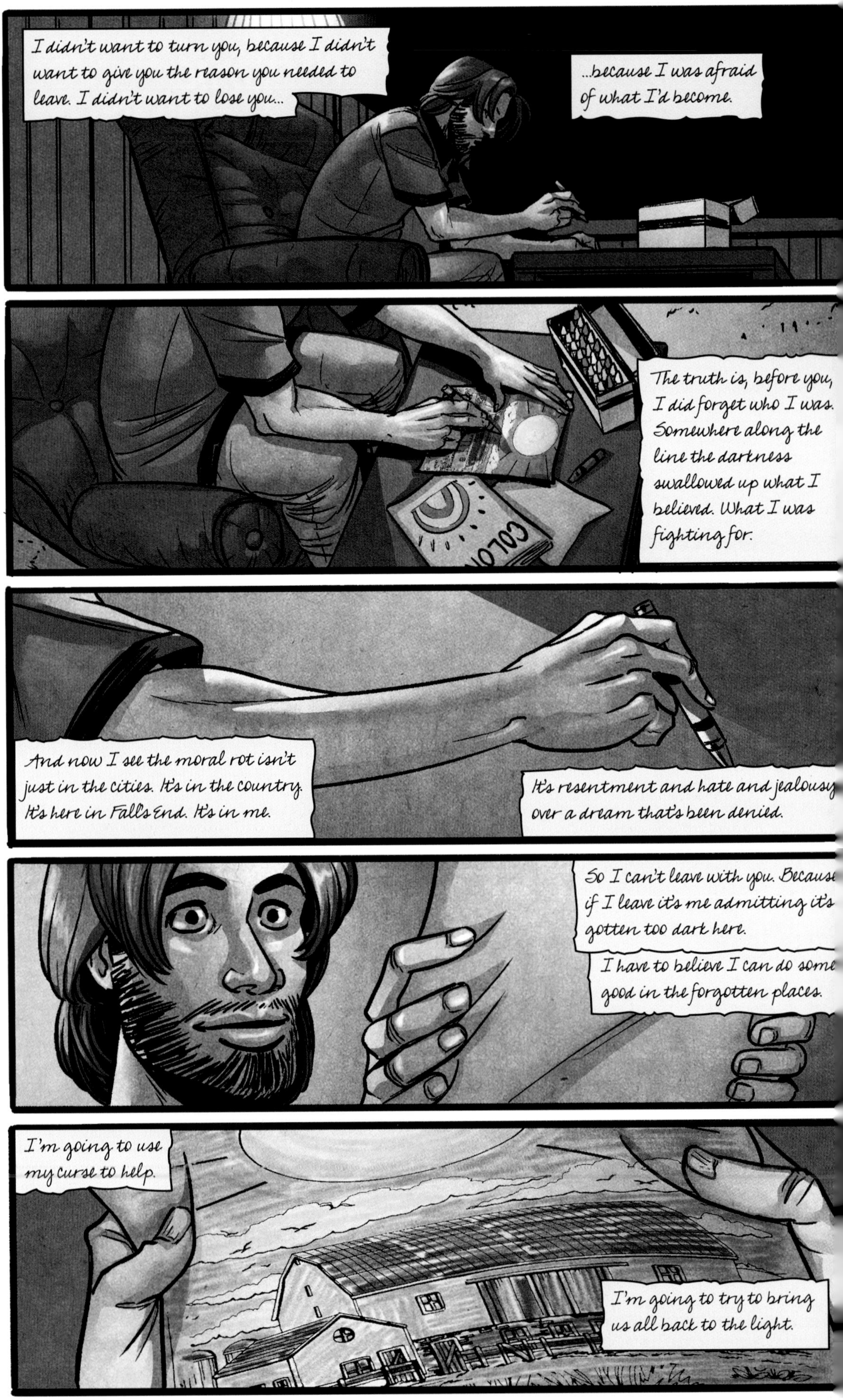
I didn't want to turn you, because I didn't want to give you the reason you needed to leave. I didn't want to lose you...
...because I was afraid of what I'd become.
The truth is, before you, I did forget who I was. Somewhere along the line the darkness swallowed up what I believed. What I was fighting for.
COLO
And now I see the moral rot isn't just in the cities. It's in the country. It's here in Fall's End. It's in me.
It's resentment and hate and jealousy over a dream that's been denied.
So I can't leave with you. Because if I leave it's me admitting it's gotten too dark here.
I have to believe I can do some good in the forgotten places.
I'm going to use my curse to help.
I'm going to try to bring us all back to the light.

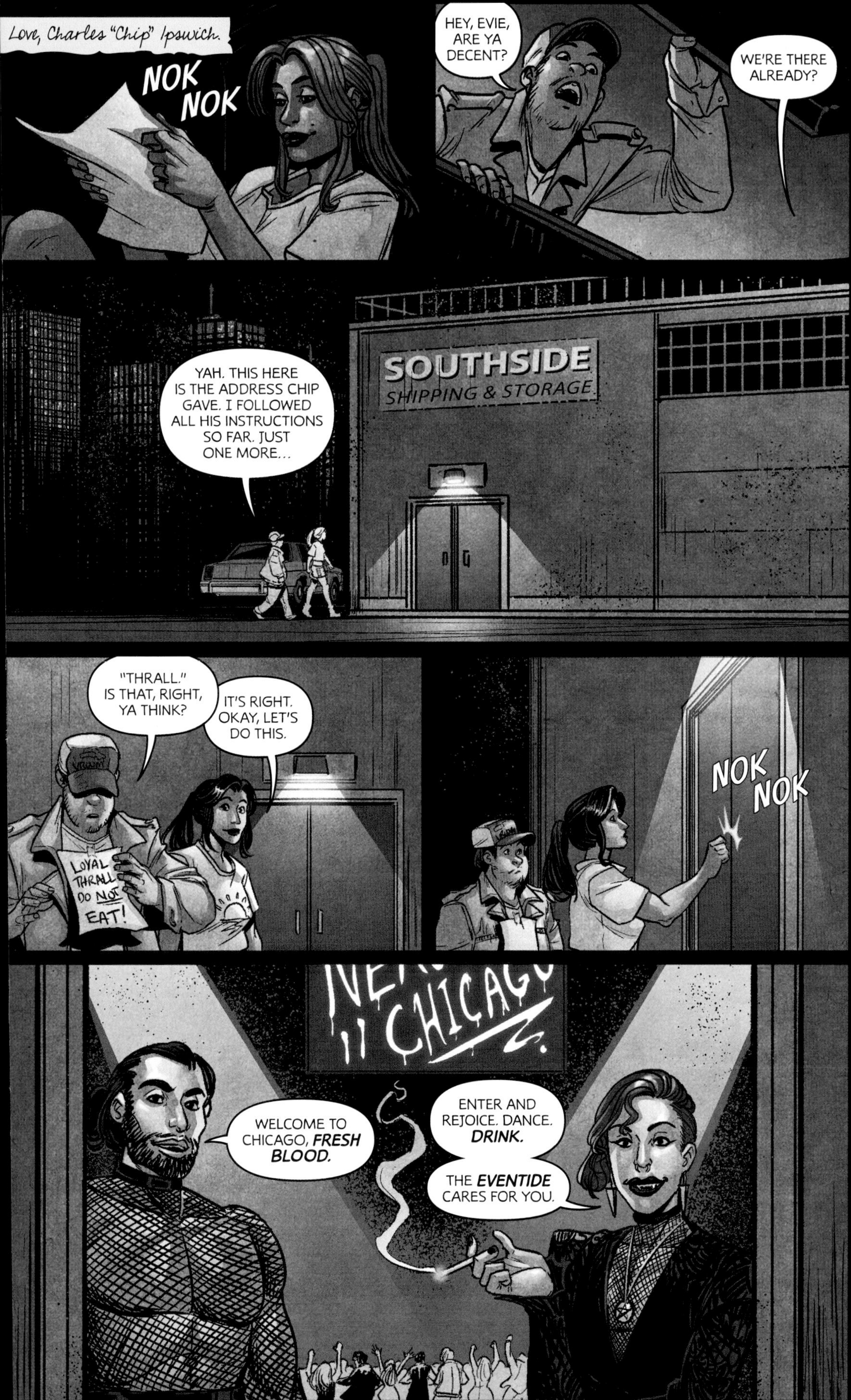
Love, Charles "Chip" Ipswich.
NOK NOK
HEY, EVIE, ARE YA DECENT?
WE'RE THERE ALREADY?
SOUTHSIDE SHIPPING & STORAGE
YAH. THIS HERE IS THE ADDRESS CHIP GAVE. I FOLLOWED ALL HIS INSTRUCTIONS SO FAR. JUST ONE MORE...
"THRALL." IS THAT, RIGHT, YA THINK?
IT'S RIGHT. OKAY, LET'S DO THIS.
LOYAL THRALL DO NOT EAT!
NOK NOK
CHICAGO
WELCOME TO CHICAGO, FRESH BLOOD.
ENTER AND REJOICE. DANCE. DRINK.
THE EVENTIDE CARES FOR YOU.

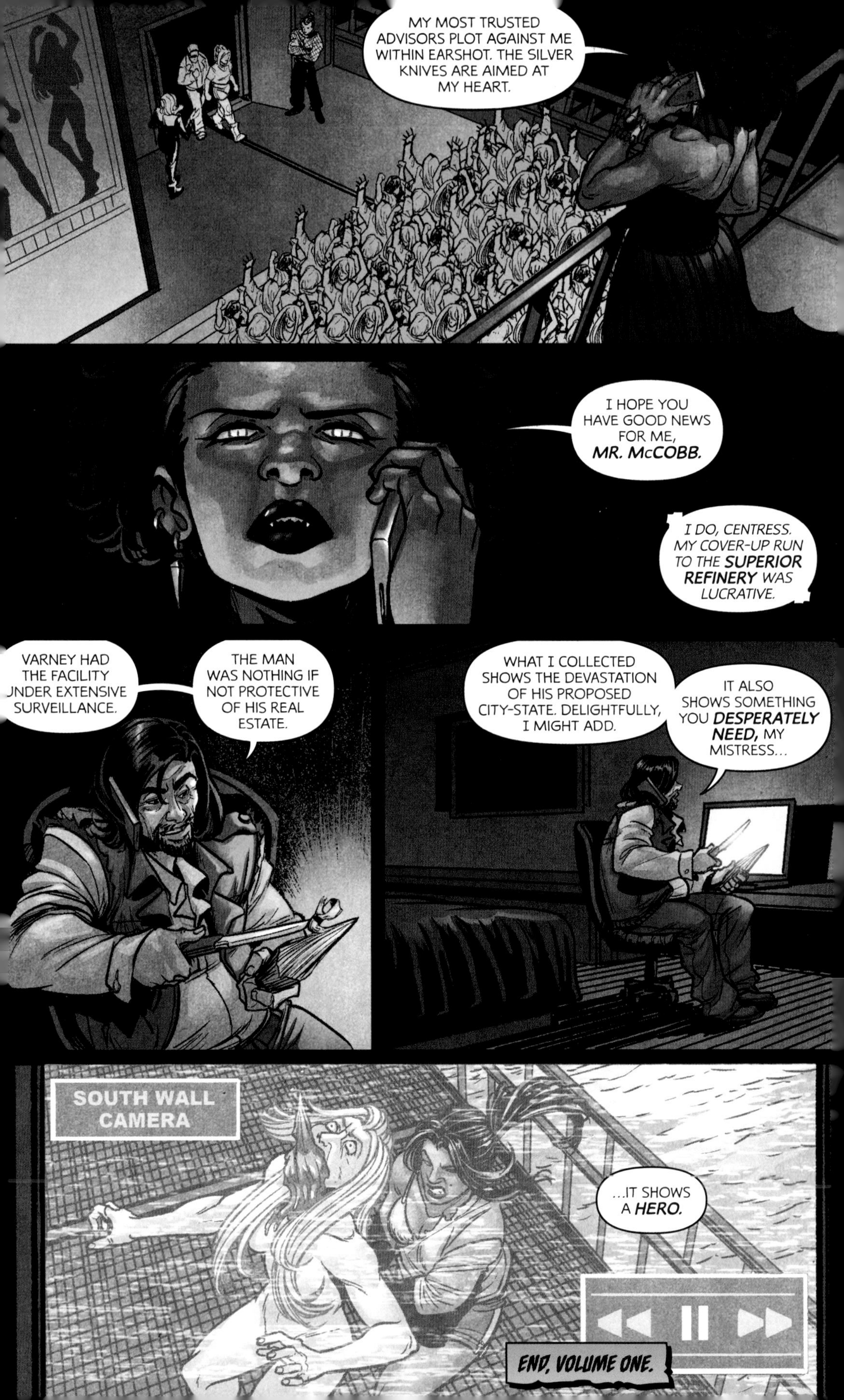
MY MOST TRUSTED ADVISORS PLOT AGAINST ME WITHIN EARSHOT. THE SILVER KNIVES ARE AIMED AT MY HEART.
I HOPE YOU HAVE GOOD NEWS FOR ME, **MR. McCOBB.**
*I DO, CENTRESS. MY COVER-UP RUN TO THE **SUPERIOR REFINERY** WAS LUCRATIVE.*
VARNEY HAD THE FACILITY UNDER EXTENSIVE SURVEILLANCE.
THE MAN WAS NOTHING IF NOT PROTECTIVE OF HIS REAL ESTATE.
WHAT I COLLECTED SHOWS THE DEVASTATION OF HIS PROPOSED CITY-STATE. DELIGHTFULLY, I MIGHT ADD.
IT ALSO SHOWS SOMETHING YOU ***DESPERATELY NEED,*** MY MISTRESS...
SOUTH WALL CAMERA
...IT SHOWS A ***HERO.***
END, VOLUME ONE.

DARK RED™

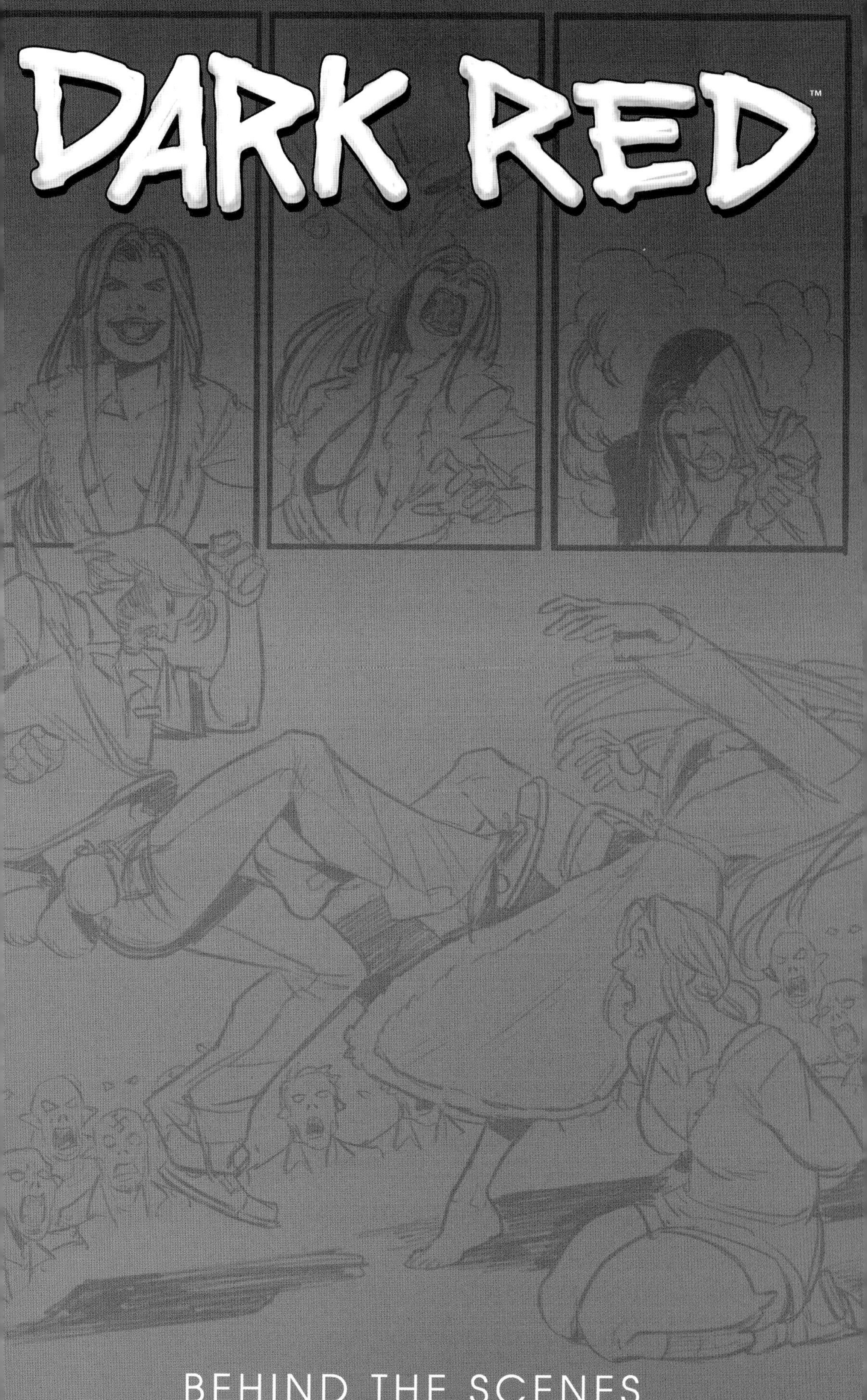

BEHIND THE SCENES

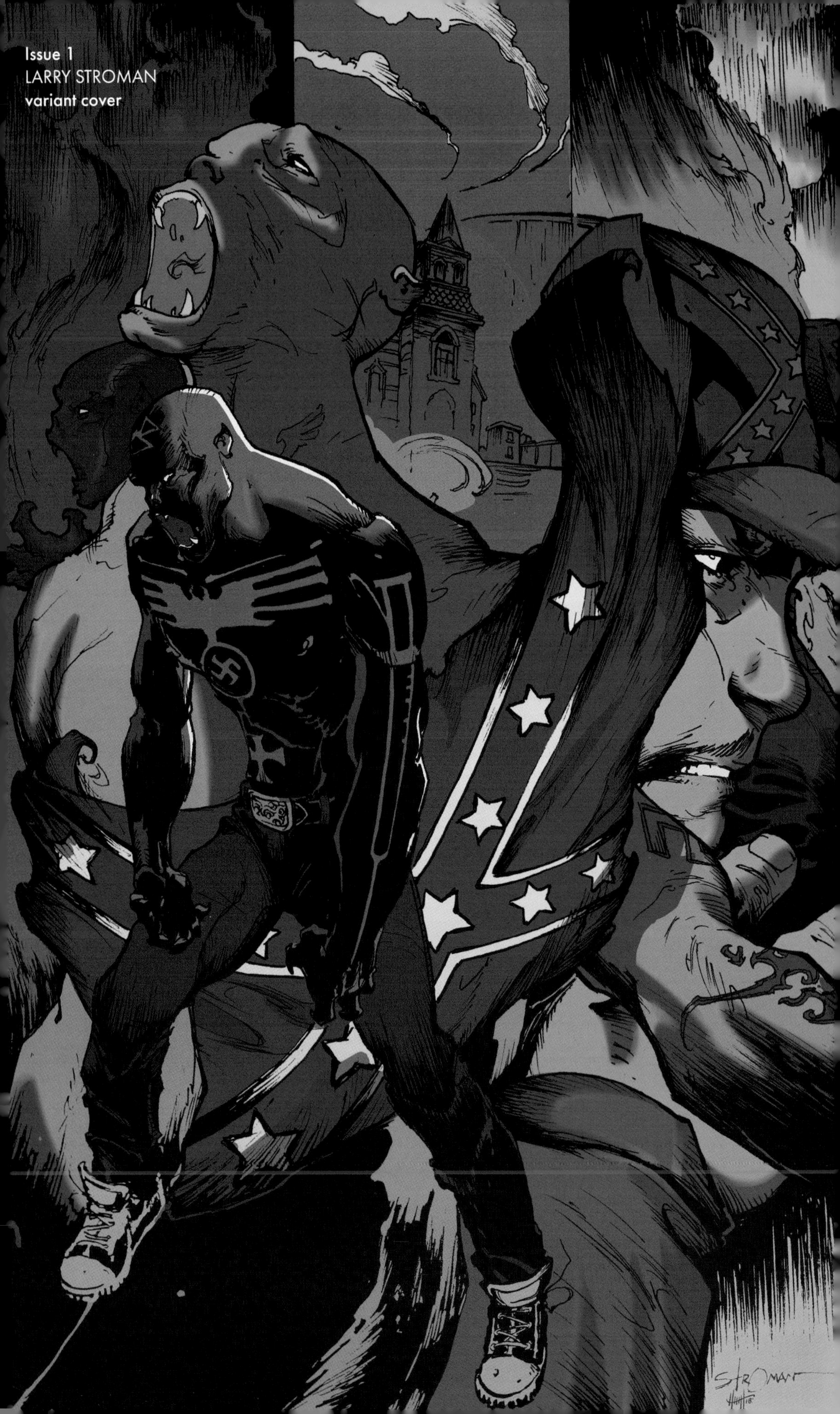

Issue 1
LARRY STROMAN
variant cover

Issue 1
TIM SEELEY w/ MARK ENGLERT
C2E2 exclusive variant cover

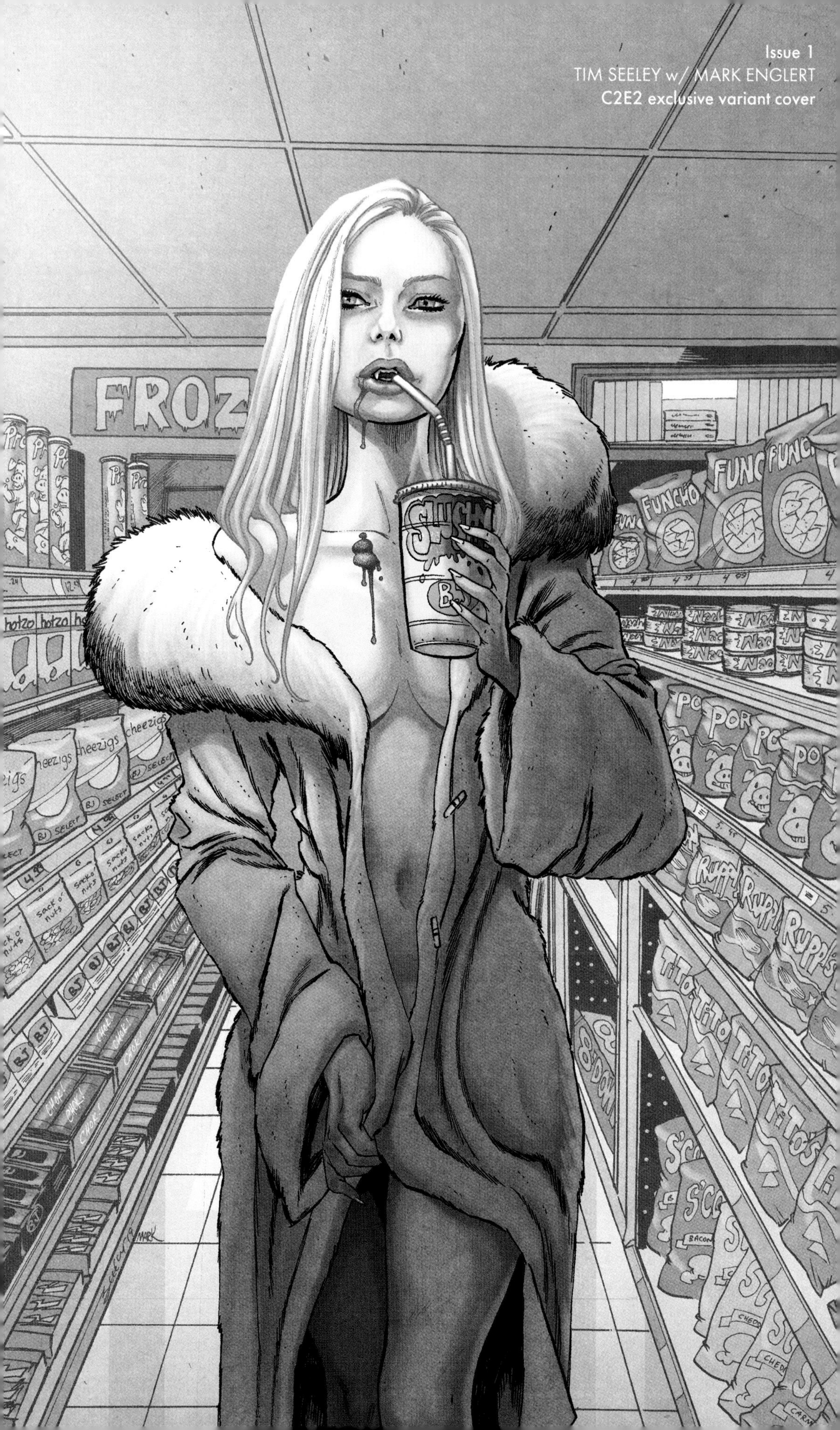
FROZ
FUNCHO
hotzo
cheezigs
MARK

Issue 1
SHANNON MAER
The Comic Mint variant cover

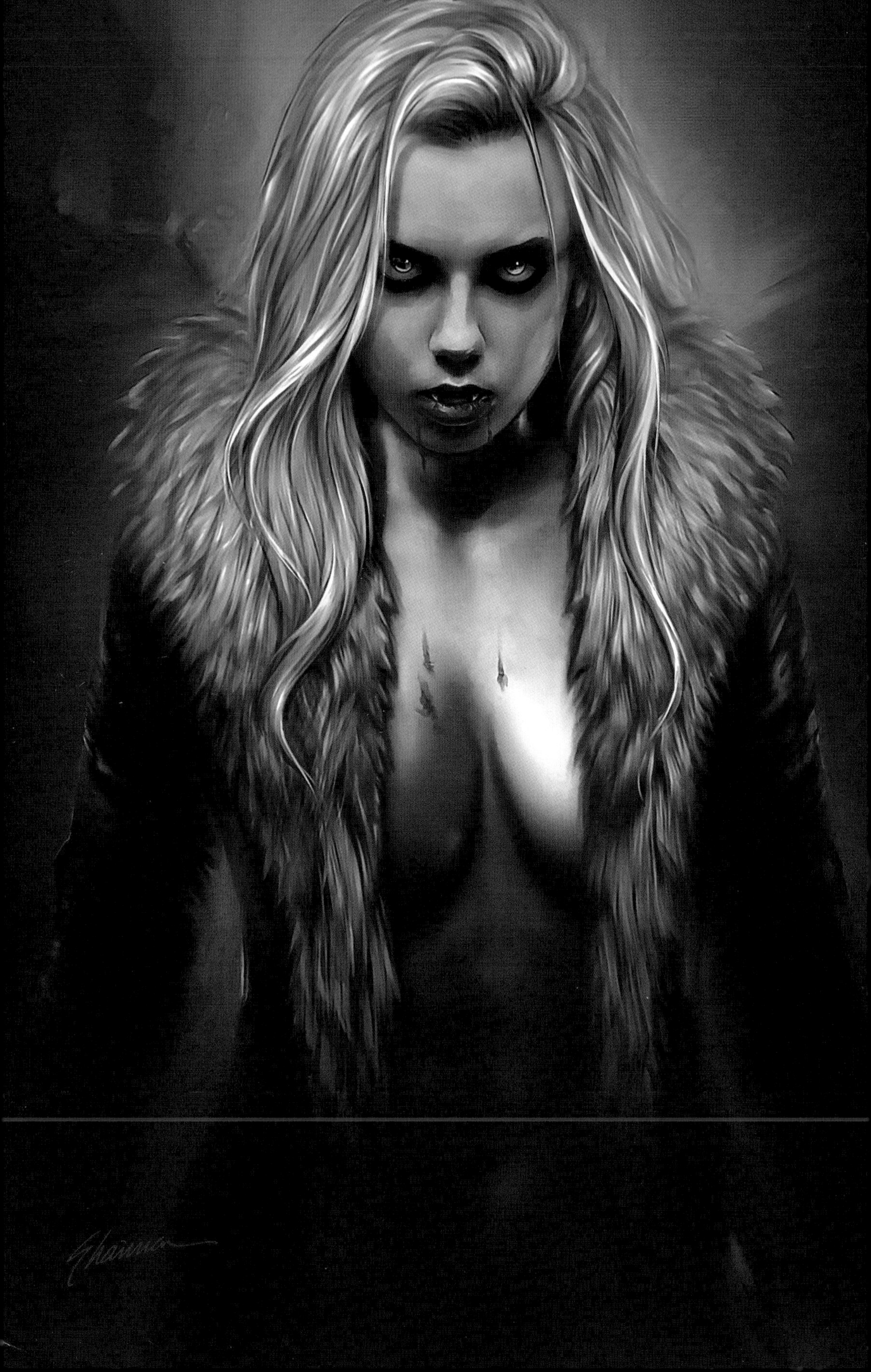

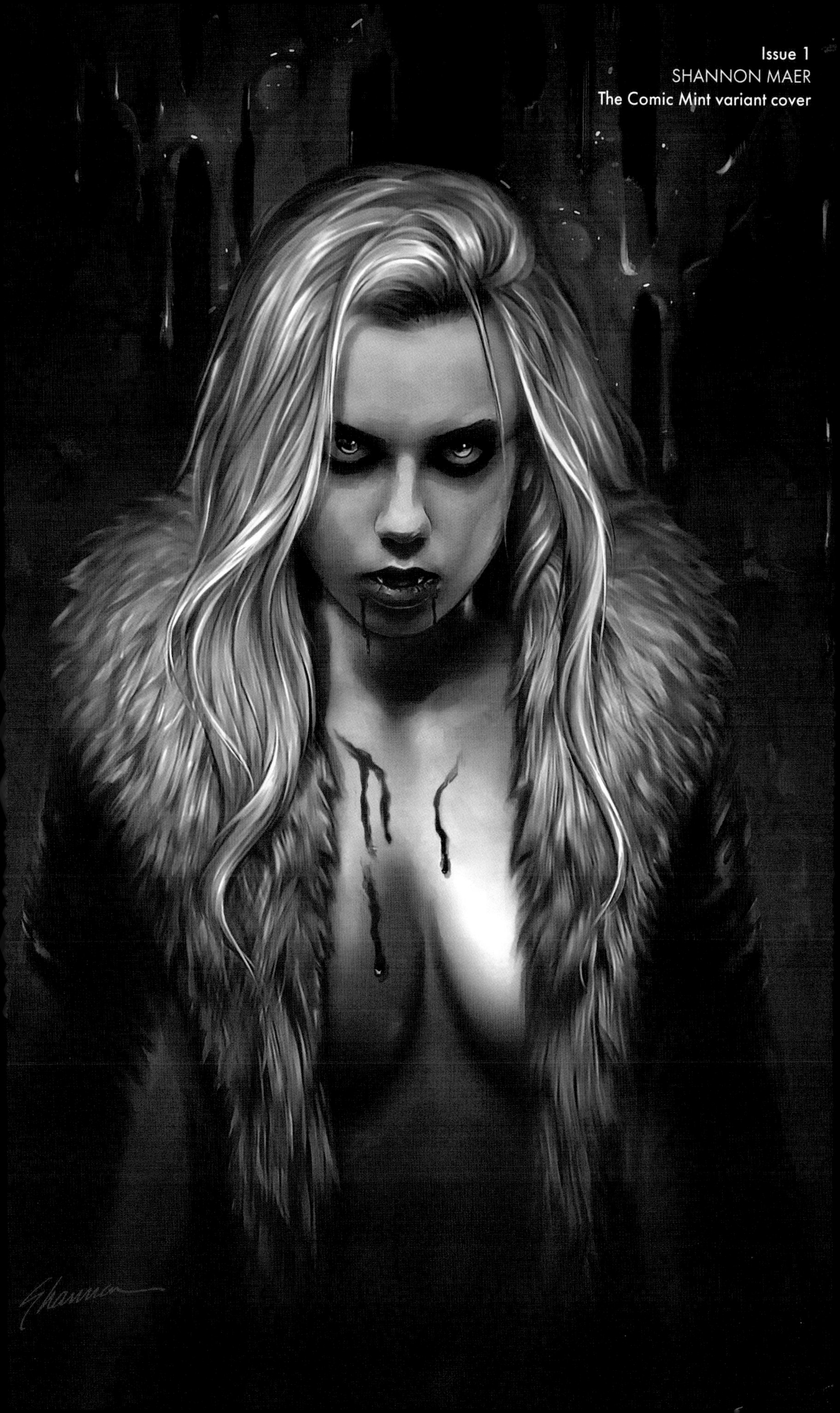

Issue 1
SHANNON MAER
The Comic Mint variant cover

Issue 1
BRIAN LEBLANC
Port City Comics variant cover

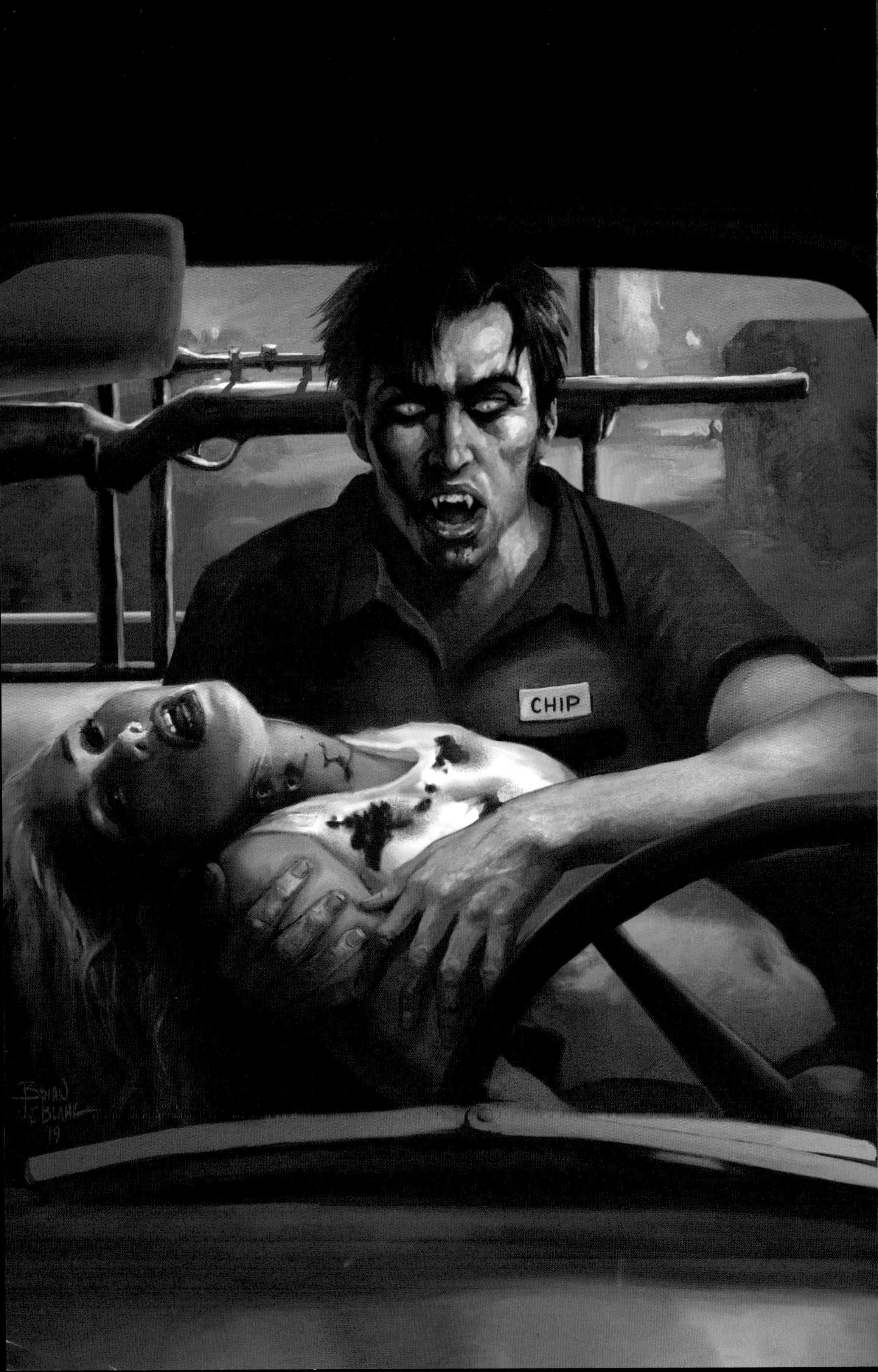
CHIP

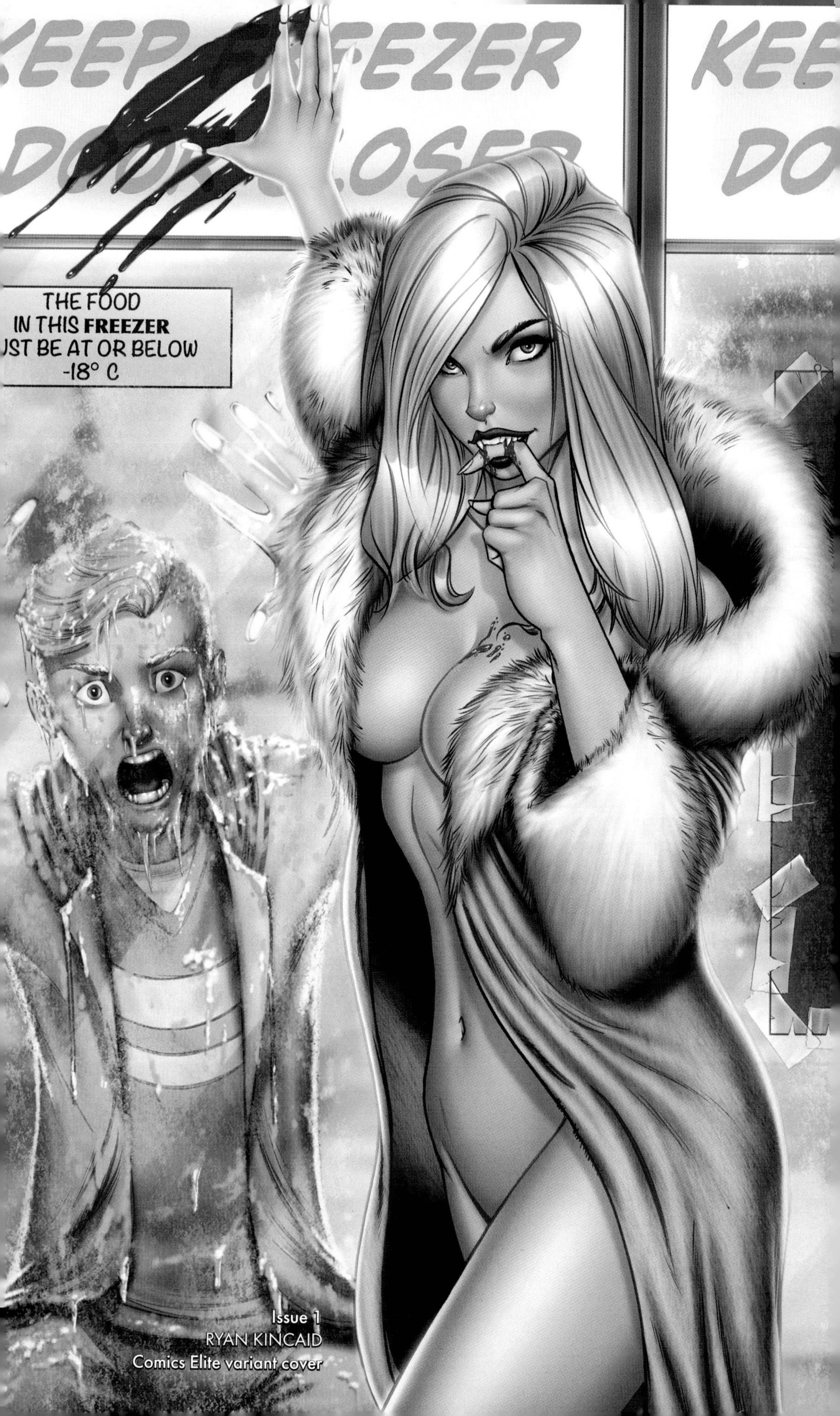
THE FOOD
IN THIS FREEZER
UST BE AT OR BELOW
-18° C

Issue 1
RYAN KINCAID
Comics Elite variant cover

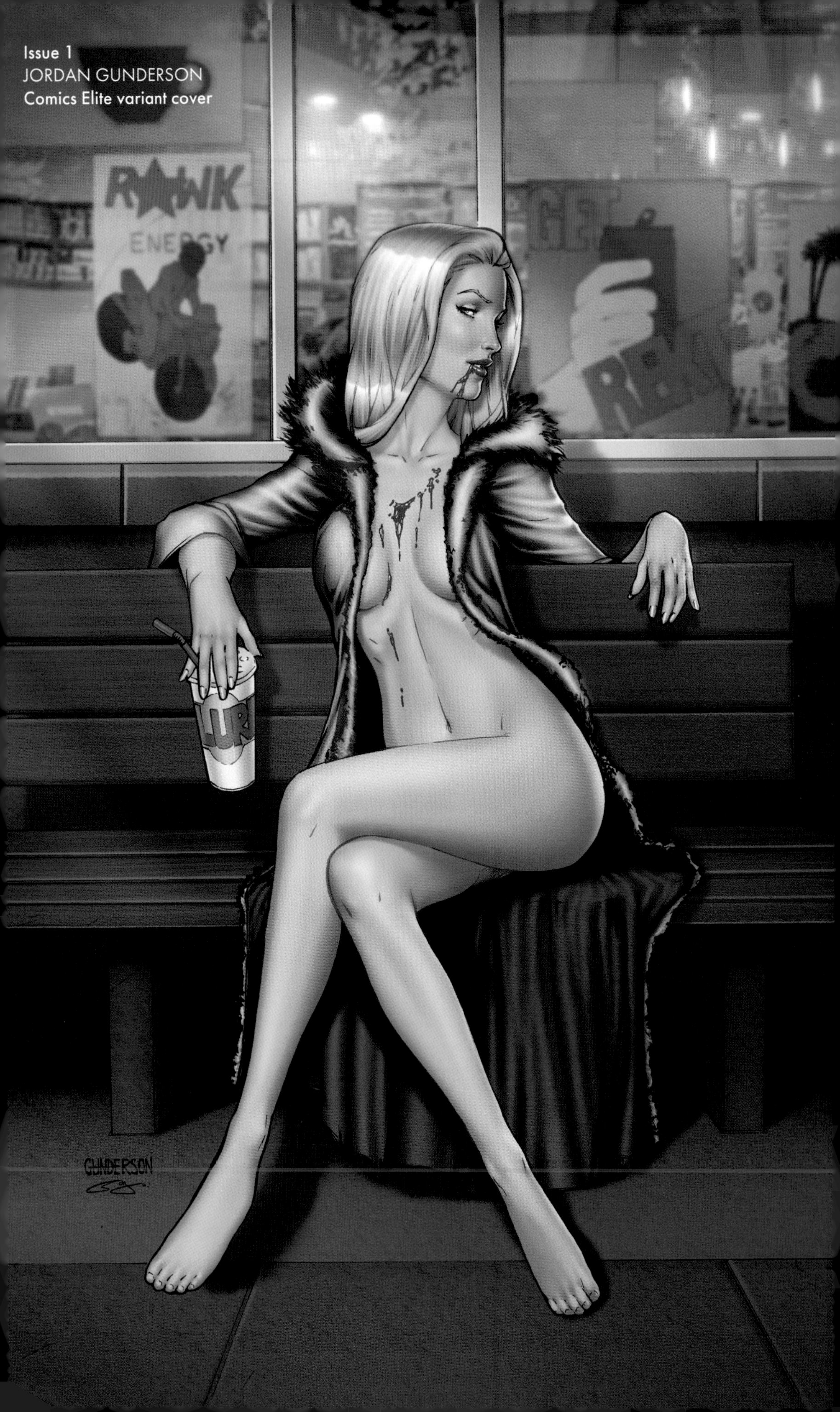
RAWK
ENERGY
GUNDERSON

Issue 1
JORDAN GUNDERSON
Comics Elite variant cover

Issue 1
NAT JONES
Gotham Central Comics & Collectibles variant cover

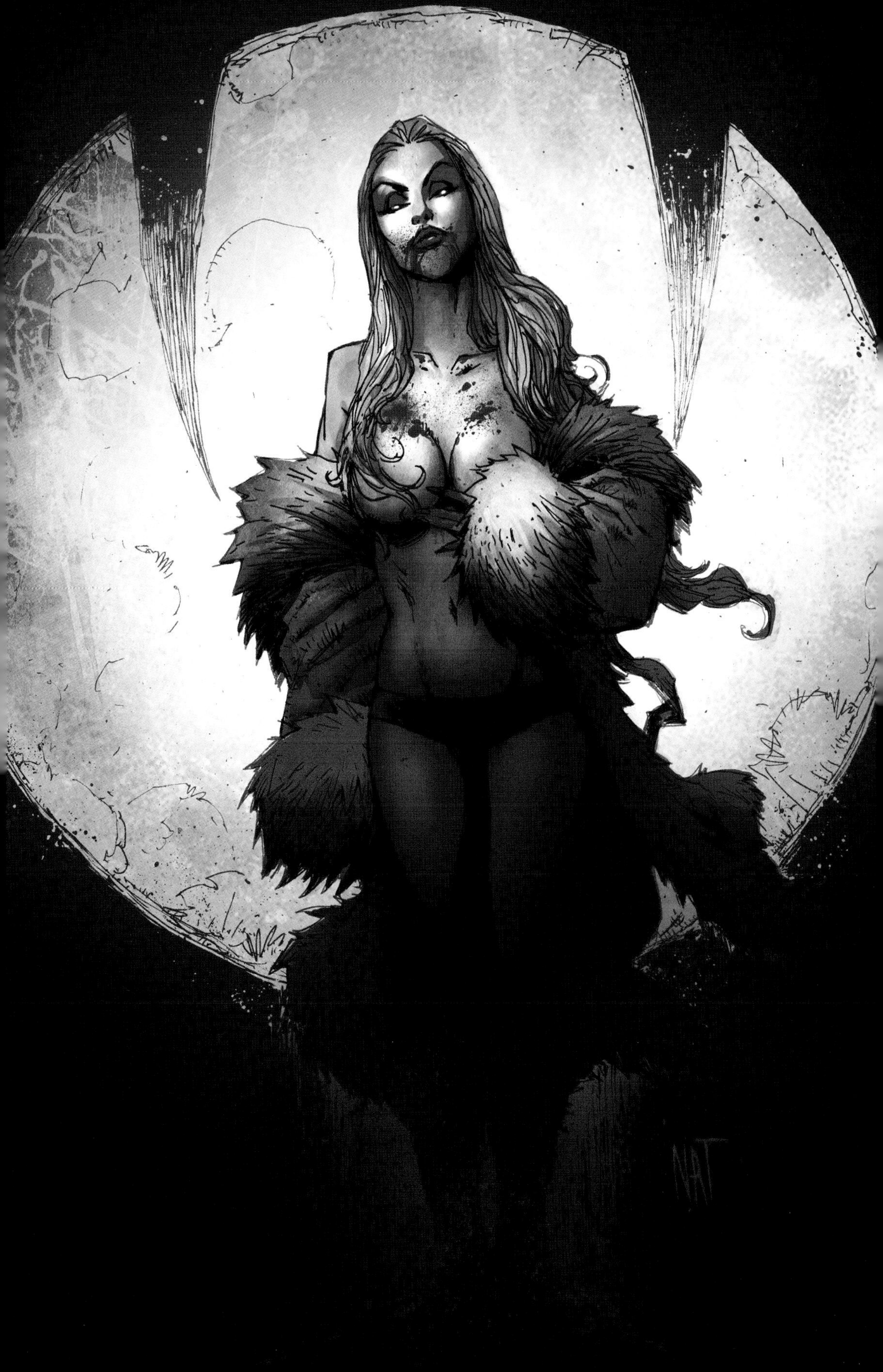

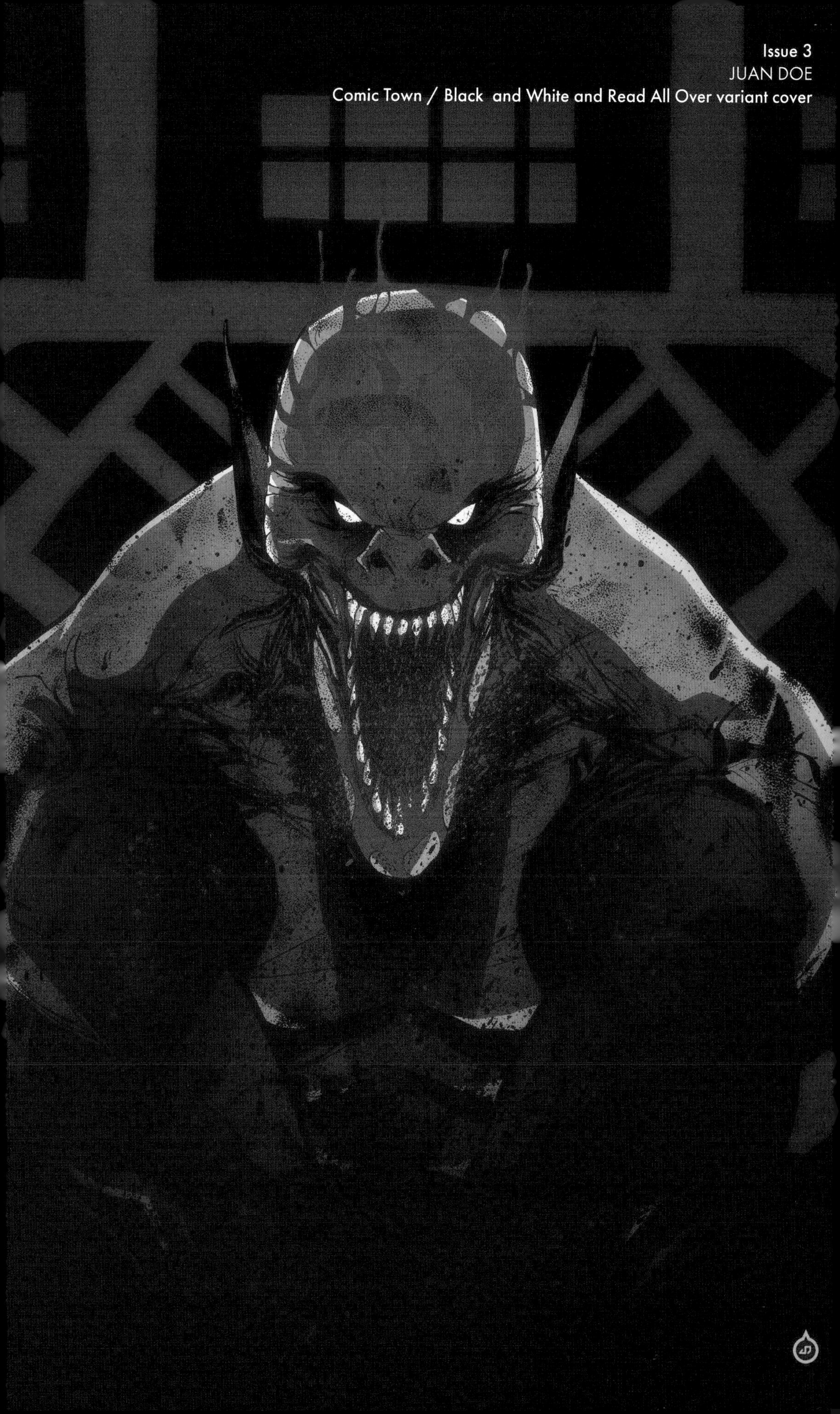

Issue 3
JUAN DOE
Comic Town / Black and White and Read All Over variant cover

Issue 3
RYAN KINCAID
Comics Elite variant cover

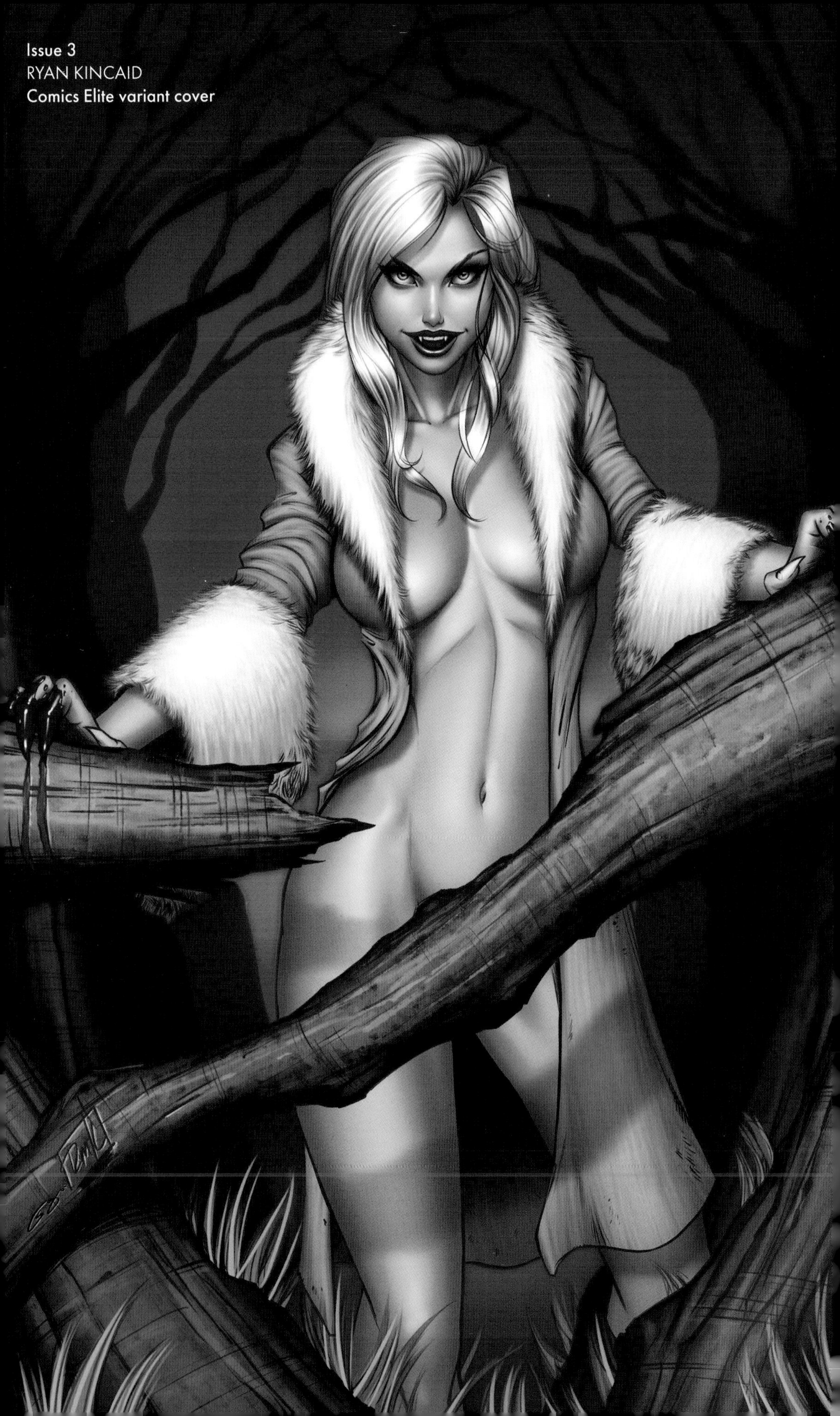

Issue 3
ANNA ZHOU
Sanctuary of Heroes variant cover

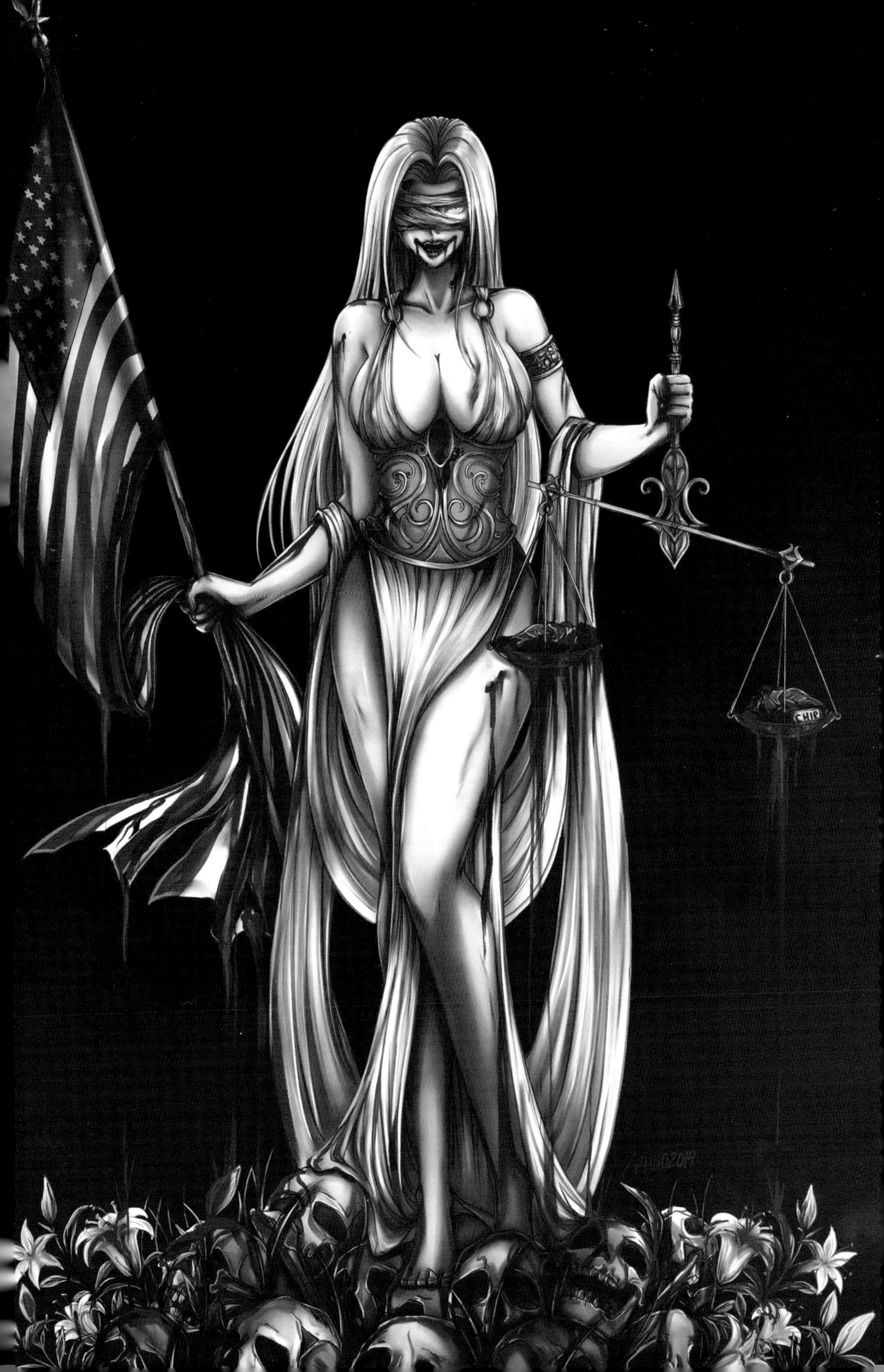
CHIP

Issue 3
ANNA ZHOU
Sanctuary of Heroes variant cover

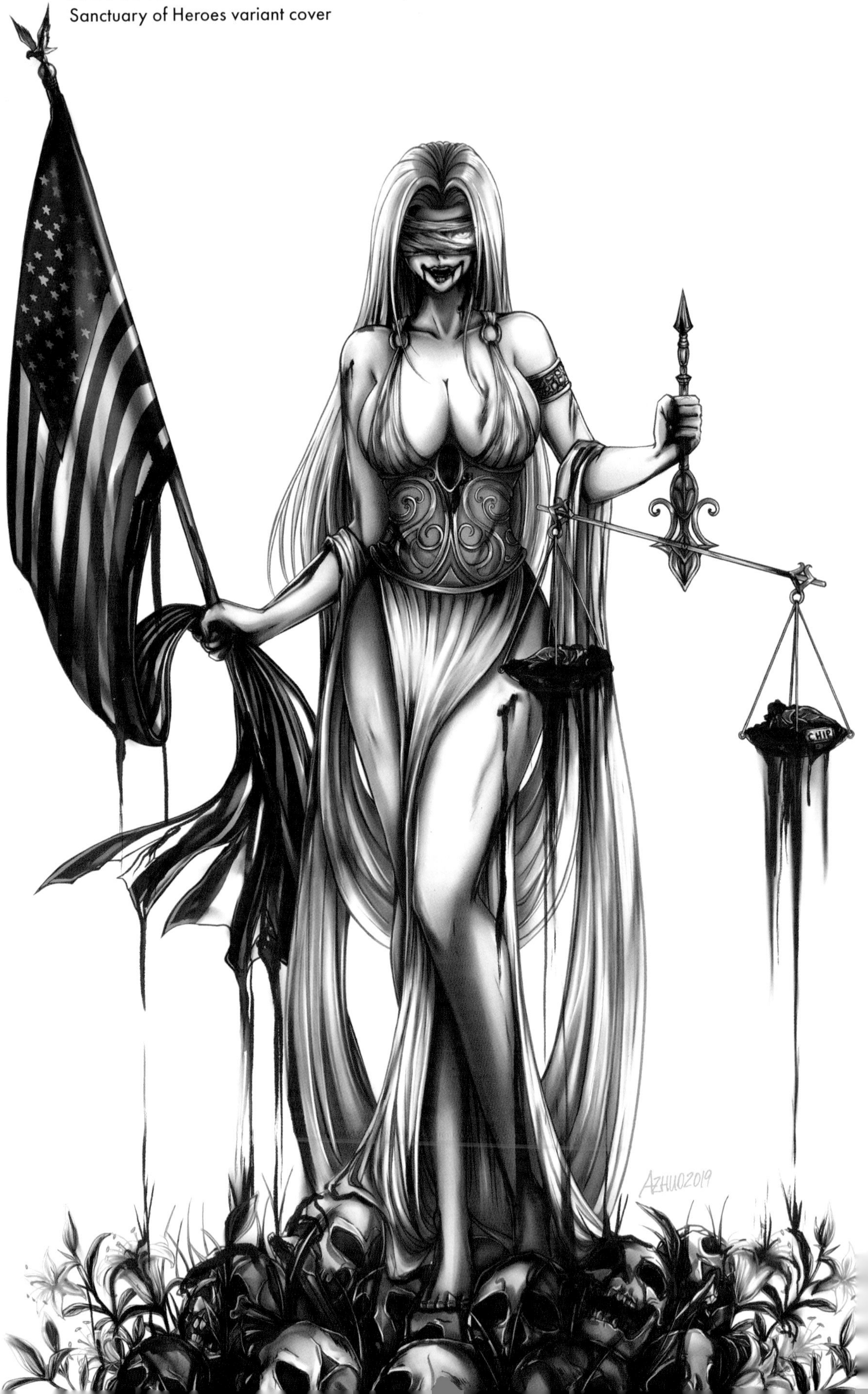
CHIP
AZHUO2019

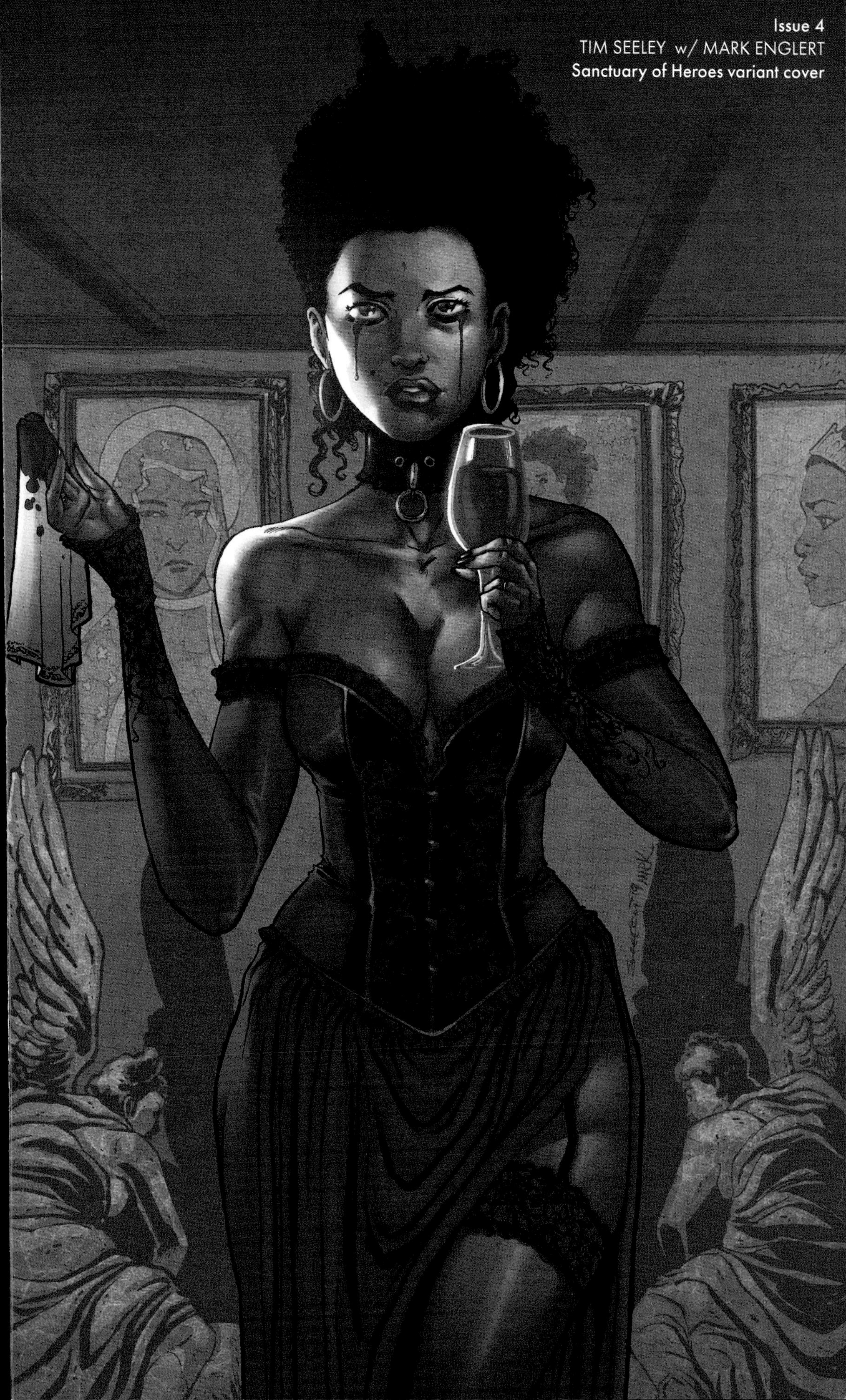

Issue 4
TIM SEELEY w/ MARK ENGLERT
Sanctuary of Heroes variant cover

DARK RED™

sketchbook

art & words by TIM SEELEY

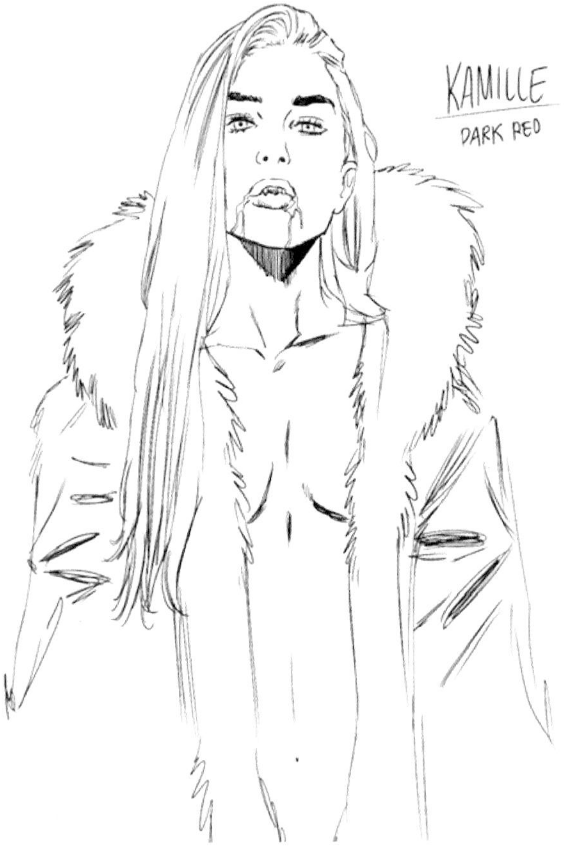
KAMILLE
DARK RED

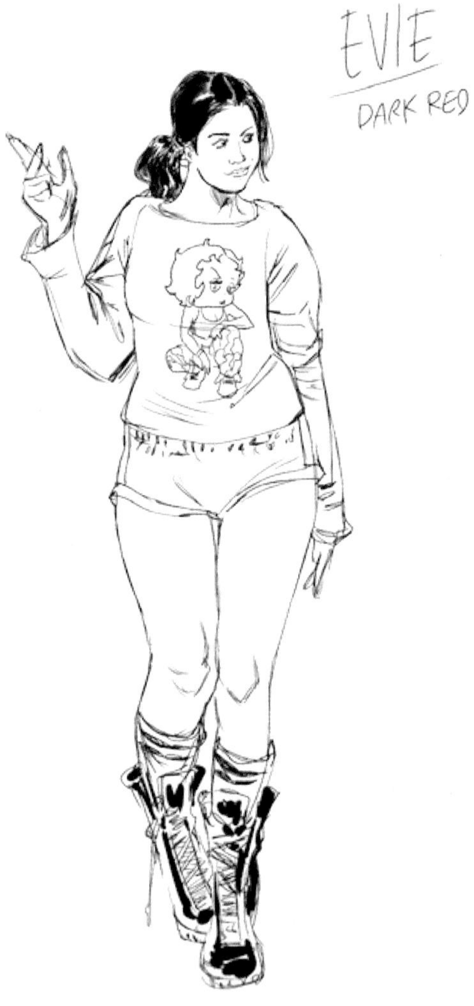
EVIE
DARK RED

Kamille — Member of the Alabaster Bloods. Caucasian. Looks to be in her mid 20s. Really pale. Blond hair. Petite, angular. Comes across initially as a sort of pixie type, but she's the one who pilots the big-ass motor cycle that Victor rides on the back of.

Evie Keen — Half native, half Caucasian. Dark skin, black hair, brown eyes. Late 20s. A little curvy. Charming. Attractive. Flirty, outgoing. Husky smoker's voice. Broke, so she wears a lot of second hand or homemade clothing. Loves 90s hip hop.

STU!

SUPERIOR OIL

CAM

Dirt Spitter

am and Stuart — Two local drunks that
end a lot of time at Dixie's. Caucasian.
am is tall and thin, in his mid-30s. Trucker
p. Flannel shirt. Beard. Stuart is fat, in his
e 20s. Thin mustache. Trucker hat. Bright
ange hunting vest.

HAIR IS SILVER
DESPITE AGE

VICTOR
VARNEY
2.0

DARK RED

APPEARS TO BE
IN LATE 30s

TALL, HANDSOME
BUT APPROACHABLE

LONG OVERCOAT

KNIT PLAID
SCARF (BY HIS
MOTHER!)

SUIT SHIRT
WITH NO
TIE.

BLACK
COAT

BLACK
PANTS

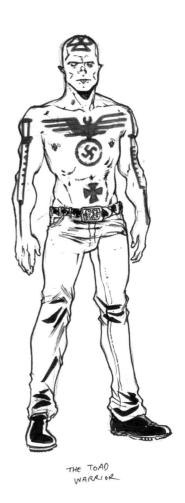

THE TOAD
WARRIOR

The Toad Warrior — White Supremacist
vampire, and member of the Alabaster
Bloods. Idiot. Looks a bit like a Nosferatu-
type vampire. Covered in tattoos.

ctor Varney — The head vampire of the
abaster Blood gang. Caucasian. Looks to
in his early 40s. A button-up-Nazi.

DARK RED™

interview with the vampire (artist)

art by CORIN HOWELL

AFTERSHOCK: How do you approach character design?

CORIN HOWELL: I usually go by the description of the personality first; sometimes there are specific traits we want, like blonde hair or dark skin, but mostly I try to stick to a look that fits the character's personality. Like, if the character is meant to have this suave and seductive personality, you bet they're going to have a classy hairstyle and a smile that makes everyone ooze with pleasure.

AS: How did your background as a manga fan impact your designs? Your storytelling/page layout/acting/etc?

CH: Manga was really all I would read (besides *Transformers* comics—yes, I am a giant transforming robot fan) and I didn't really read any American comics or superhero comics when I was a kid, so everything from my inking style to the extreme close-up and speed lines were all manga-influenced. Now, of course, I have other inspirations in terms of storytelling (French comics, animation, creepy comics, etc.), but the majority of the influence came from manga.

AS: How did other vampires in comics/film/tv impact your approach to vampirism?

Issue #2 layouts pgs.1-4

Issue #2 pencils & inks pg.1

Issue #2 pencils & inks pg.2

CH: The most I've watched of vampire movies include *Blade* and *Blade 2*, *What We Do in the Shadows*, *Dracula*, and *UnderWorld* (don't judge me on that last one), so I tried to take some inspiration from everything I've watched. Especially the costuming: somewhat-Victorian, mixed with new-age goth and techno-punk, or perhaps high fashion with elaborate dresses, etc.

AS: Who is your favorite character in DARK RED? Your favorite design element?

CH: Chip—I just like the fact that I get to draw a main character that is a cute dude. My favorite element to draw of him is his face, especially when he goes all vamp—those fangs are so much fun to draw.

AS: How about your favorite page or story beat in Dark Red?

CH: That's difficult to say! Though if I had to pick one, it would be the last issue where Chip is literally tearing Nazi vampires to pieces. I love me some classic horror gore.

AS: How was it collaborating with Tim on this book?

CH: Working with Tim has been a BLAST, and I really want to continue working with him. He and I share the same love for horror and it's SO WONDERFUL to be working on a book in a genre that I love so much. I want to do more!

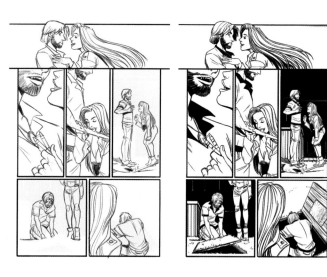

Issue #2 pencils & inks pg.3

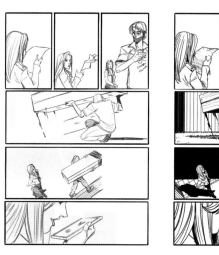

Issue #2 pencils & inks pg.4

Issue #2 pencils & inks pg.20

ABOUT THE CREATORS OF

DARK RED™

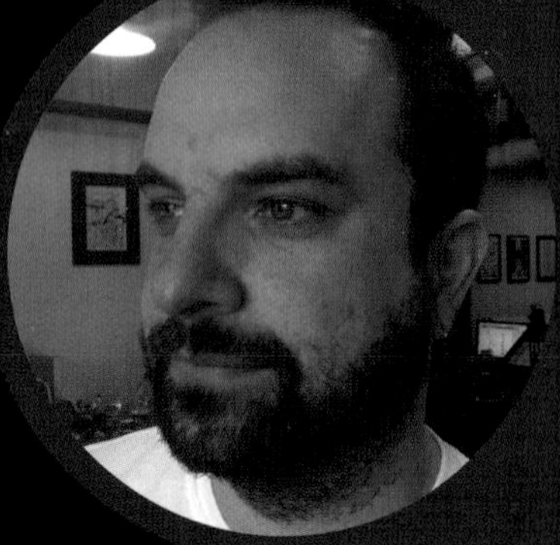

TIM SEELEY writer

@HackinTimSeeley

Tim is one of those "slash" people...a writer-slash-artist. He has drawn a number of different comic book series including *G.I Joe, Halloween, WildC.A.T.S.* and *Exsanguine.* His writing work includes NY Times bestselling *Hack/Slash, Grayson, Batman Eternal* and the critically acclaimed *Revival.* He resides in Chicago, Illinois and works at Four Star Studios where he is never far from his 80s action figure collection.

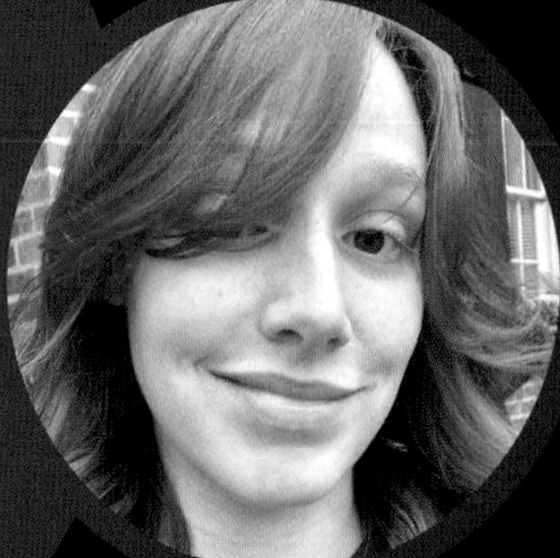

CORIN HOWELL artist

@Rin237

Corin Howell is a comic artist of maidens, monsters and robots. Her titles include *The Girl in the Bay* and *Calamity Kate* with Dark Horse Comics, *Ghostbusters: Answer the Call* and *Transformers Windblade: Combiner Wars* with IDW Publishing, and various other titles. She loves cats, too.

MARK ENGLERT colorist

@markenglert

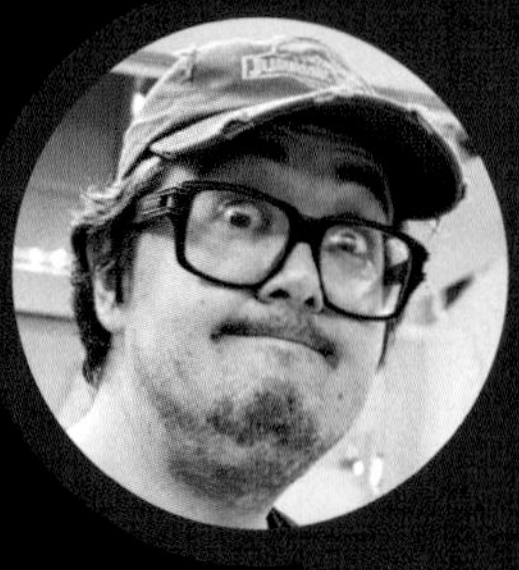

Mark Englert was born in 1979. The first movie he ever saw on opening day was *Star Trek: The Motion Picture* and he slept through the whole thing. Since then, he grew up a little, saw a lot more movies, watched way too much TV, spent countless hours reading comic books when he wasn't busy playing video games. He has been steadily working as an illustrator since 1999, coloring comics, doing concept work at Microsoft and drawing posters for almost every major movie studio. His future plans include continuing to work on comics, illustrating a lot more posters and to one day stay awake for an entire viewing of *Star Trek: The Motion Picture.*

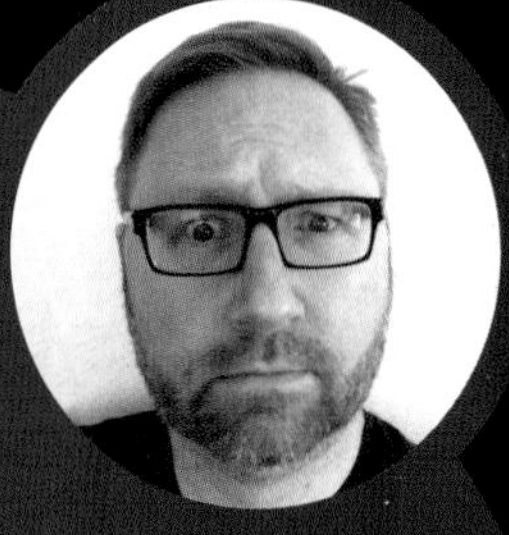

MARSHALL DILLON letterer

@MarshallDillon

A comic book industry veteran, Marshall got his start in 1994, in the midst of the indie comic boom. Over the years, he's been everything from an independent self-published writer to an associate publisher working on properties like *G.I. Joe, Voltron,* and *Street Fighter.* He's done just about everything except draw a comic book, and worked for just about every publisher except the "big two." Primarily a father and letterer these days, he also dabbles in old-school paper and dice RPG game design. You can catch up with Marshall at firstdraftpress.net.